DAMNED to ETERNITY

DAMNED to ETERNITY

The Story of the Man Who They Said Caused the Flood

Adam Pitluk

Da Capo Press
A Member of the Perseus Books Group

Production Services by Lesley Rock for Outbox Creative Partners
Set in 11 point Adobe Garamond by Outbox Creative Partners

Cataloging-in-Publication data for this book is available from the Library of Congress.

First Da Capo Press edition 2007
ISBN-10 0-306-81527-3
ISBN-13 978-0-306-81527-0

Published by Da Capo Press
A Member of the Perseus Books Group
www.dacapopress.com

Da Capo Press books are available at special discounts for bulk purchases in the U.S. by corporations, institutions, and other organizations. For more information, please contact the Special Markets Department at the Perseus Books Group, 2300 Chestnut Street, Suite 200, Philadelphia, PA 19103, or call (800) 255-1514, or e-mail special.markets@perseusbooks.com.

1 2 3 4 5 6 7 8 9

For the 4th Infantry Division of the U.S. Army,
Task Force Bowie of the Texas National Guard,
the Missouri and Illinois National Guard,
the brave men and women who volunteered countless
hours sandbagging in the summer of 1993,
and the numerous victims of those floods.

—◄o►—

CONTENTS

—◄o►—

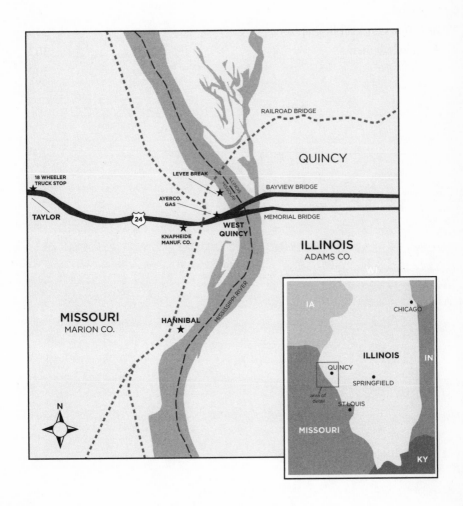

PROLOGUE

◄O►

An eerie calm settled among the volunteers straddling both sides of the Mississippi River. A host of local helpers mingled with more than 1,000 Missouri and Illinois National Guard troops, walking along the shelf of the West Quincy, Missouri, levee. The Guardsmen's energy expended at a higher rate than usual, as the sand they walked on, covered by a gigantic industrial strength plastic tarp and weighted down by sandbags, depressed under their feet with each step.

For two weeks, communities up and down the banks of the Mississippi River, as well as scores of others from the high-ground interior regions of Illinois and Missouri and even thousands more from all over the country, had descended on the West Quincy levee. It was a giant sand structure 20 feet high, with an additional 10 feet of dredged river sand thrown on top to build it up even further.

Across the river was Quincy, Illinois, a quaint, sleepy town of 35,000 residents. The population in Quincy ebbed and flowed over the years, depending on whether a plant or some other large employer was setting up shop or locking its gates. The town exhibited tremendous natural beauty with its ancient oak tree-lined thoroughfares and 19th-century architecture.

Its most picturesque attribute was also its first line of defense: Quincy's jagged limestone bluffs, which jutted out from the base of the river and extended 100 feet above the waterline. It was the bedrock foundation of the town. Residents could take cold comfort in knowing they wouldn't flood, but many of them made their livings across the Bayview Bridge in neighboring Missouri. While there were border skirmishes when it came to athletics, in particular when the University of Missouri Tigers played the University of Illinois Fighting Illini in basketball, the states pulled together in tough times. This was the case in the weeks leading up to the evening of July 16, 1993.

Illinois schools, businesses, churches, and even individual households closed their doors as folks flocked to the Missouri side of the Mississippi River. Biblical rains had pounded the river states relentlessly, from Minnesota to Wisconsin and down to Iowa, Missouri, Illinois, Kentucky, and Arkansas. After three months of prolonged showers, smaller rivers that meandered through the states gradually rose, making usually calm streams surge with sheer volume. Whitecaps were everywhere and banks absorbed each undulating wave as the rivers pushed forward to their emptying point, the aptly nicknamed Father of Waters—the Mississippi River.

It was a furious battle—man versus nature. And for the two weeks leading up to that day, man, or sheer manpower as it were, appeared to be winning. There was a series of close calls, when Old Man River's waters came within centimeters of topping the West Quincy levee. Four days earlier, upriver in Northern Illinois, the Indian Grave levee broke, deluging 9,000 acres and submerging crops and farmhouses. In East Carondelet, Illinois, the Mississippi River came up under the streets, buckling the pavement and blowing out water mains.

But in the evening din, as the relief efforts in West Quincy were shutting down for the night and weary workers were wiping the last of a day's sweat from their brows, all seemed quiet on the Midwestern front. The river was down, filling people with hope that the worst was over.

Three of the thousands of volunteers, Mike Pahos from Santa Fe, New Mexico, and his friends Keith Moser and Pete Fontanella from Santa Cruz, California, left the levee around suppertime. They were just three random guys, indicative of the philanthropic American spirit, who had responded to the Midwest's call for help with the sandbagging effort.

Tired and spent after a long day's work, the men returned to their Illinois motel and plopped down on their beds. They left the levee that evening utterly exhausted, but thinking they'd won the fight.

As they relaxed in their stale air-conditioned quarters, a commotion erupted in the hallway. Someone was proclaiming the unthinkable: The levee had broken.

They ran down an exterior staircase, piled back into their car and white-knuckled it over the Bayview Bridge to West Quincy. Pahos parked in an open lot and led the charge as the men clawed their way atop the dike. To their chagrin, the rumor was true. A huge hole had opened in the levee a few meters upstream and the swirling waters of the Mississippi were surging through it, rapidly filling the adjacent farmland.

They stood with their hands in their jeans pockets for a couple minutes, watching three barges moored to large cottonwood, oak, and sweet gum trees violently rock as the current sucked their bows toward the levee breach. In a matter of seconds, Pahos observed one of the 200-foot-long barges break loose from its harness and float through the gaping hole. The monstrous green boat, bulky, clumsy, and capable of carrying over 1,500 tons of cargo, cruised right through the opening, snapping century-old timber like tooth-picks as it made its way into the open field.

The three men were immediately panic-stricken. Their car was parked half a click downriver in an area that wasn't under water yet but surely would be in a matter of minutes. They frantically made their way down the levee's steep slope. When Pahos turned his head to take one last glimpse at the mammoth breach, he saw another giant barge making its way off the Mississippi and into the new makeshift farm-reservoir. The trees it took out were even larger, and the unmistakable sound of splintering tree trunks echoed off the levee walls.

"Let's get the hell outta here!" he shouted to his companions. Moser and Fontanella didn't need to be told twice: they were already sprinting toward their car. No sooner had Pahos started the ignition, then they were back across the Bayview Bridge to the safety of Quincy. Parked on dry Illinois land, they watched as the Mississippi River consumed everything in its path with a furious gulp.

Keith Moser and Pete Fontanella were silent. They solemnly observed their hard work wash away like sand at high tide. Mike stood snapping some pictures. The only audible sounds on the tiny stretch of land the men occupied were the camera shutter and the rolling Mississippi current, now flowing in an east-west direction instead of its usual north-south.

On the other side of the river, they noticed a man speaking to a reporter. Moser thought to himself that they had better take their interview over the bridge, and right quick. The Caucasian male, medium height, medium build with long, dark blond hair spoke to a lovely female reporter without fear of the rushing water. Moser couldn't make out any details, other than their physiques and some animated hand gestures.

Pahos continued snapping pictures of the disappearing farmland flanked by a setting Midwestern summer sun when a brilliant red light suddenly illuminated his camera's viewfinder. The sound of an explosion almost instantaneously caught up with the preceding flash. The blast pierced the night and shook already jittery nerves to the point of paranoia. Even though dusk was settling on the horizon, a giant fireball quickly brought furious daylight to an area west of West Quincy. The inferno ascended into the twilight, followed by a billowing black plume of smoke. As it disappeared into the sky, flames began to spread across the open field. But the flames weren't spreading naturally. They weren't concentrated in any one particular area. Rather, they were rolling along the farmland as though they were riding together in a drifting boat. It took Pahos a couple of long seconds to focus and realize that the Mississippi River's waters were on fire and spreading further into the interior.

It took him another few seconds to realize that the spot where they had parked their car earlier, the Ayerco gas station, was now smoldering and emitting a pungent odor. Pahos leaned on a rail running along the Illinois side of the Bayview Bridge and observed the peculiar visual of water on fire. Before the shock subsided and he had a chance to ask himself how water could erupt into flames, Pahos watched as the Mississippi River, now surrounding the Ayerco station, fanned out. The gas flames were lighting the path of a V-shaped wake, and Pahos watched as the faint silhouette of a 200-foot unmanned barge sailed over land into the sunset.

PART ONE

Troubled Waters

CHAPTER ONE

—◄○►—

James Scott's back ached. He struggled to work through the pain, but each time his feet hit the loose earth, steady vibrations coursed up his shins and shook his body to the core. He stopped his stride every so often, balled his hands up into fists, and pushed them into his lower back. Then he pulled his chin skyward and stretched the throbbing muscles all along his spine.

It was July 9, 1993, his first full day working on the West Quincy, Missouri levee, along with hundreds of other volunteers from his hometown of Quincy, Illinois. He was one of thousands working along a 50-mile stretch of river from West Quincy to Keokuk, Iowa, a tiny industrial river town at the junction of Iowa, Missouri, and Illinois. The call to the river had been wide-reaching and pervasive. For weeks, as heavy rains pounded Middle America, newspapers and newscasts beseeched all able bodies to report to any number of staging areas along the Mississippi River. Residents were essentially begged to join in the fight of their lives: A fight to save their town.

It was a frightening and desperate call to arms, though more surprising than the call's urgency were the people who answered. They came from all over—as far east as Massachusetts and as far west as the Washington coast. And while Americans from east to west descended in droves upon the dikes along the Mississippi River, the most suspect volunteers came right out of the local taverns and backwater hangouts. Men like James Scott, who, as far as Quincy and the surrounding communities were concerned, wouldn't lift a civic finger to scratch a mosquito bite.

Yet there he was, with sore hands and open blisters; jeans wet from the hem to his knees and an aching back from lifting 50 pound sandbags.

Jimmy Scott had indeed heard the cry go out for help, though it wasn't until he was prompted by Janet Maglioshetti, his best friend's mother—a lady who tired of watching her son and his buddies waste away their summer days frequenting bars and barbecues—that Jimmy donned his soiled blues, laced up his boots, and drove his rusty maroon Chevy Monte Carlo over the Bayview Bridge and into neighboring West Quincy to help. He was reluctant at first. After all, a community effort this big meant that local businesses were shutting down. It meant that he didn't have to punch in at his job at the Burger King off Broadway and clean grease traps. It meant he could sit on somebody's porch all day long and drink Budweisers. And it also meant that come nightfall, he and his buddies—or maybe even his wife, Suzie—could head over to Villa Kathrine Castle on Front Street in the early evening and booze it up while somebody else toiled away in the humid, heavy Midwestern air.

Summer months in towns along the banks of the Mississippi River were always lazy and slow, especially for people like Jimmy—people who spent the workweek at mundane jobs and lived paycheck to paycheck. The temperature was oppressively hot and they endured day after day of wrenching humidity. But at least there wasn't any snow or a biting winter wind blowing off the river, so spirits were high.

Unlike most Midwestern towns that saw their populations grow in the summer and shrink in the winter, Quincy was the opposite. Most of the 1,300 students at Quincy University pulled up stakes in late May and went home. The university, founded by Franciscan friars in 1860, supplemented the town's nightlife during the academic calendar. Although small by college standards, Quincy University was composed of a rather affluent student body. Tuition alone was over $15,000 a year, and many who could afford to attend also had play money, compliments of their affluent parents. The school was religious, but college is college, and students like barhopping to blow off steam.

The local residents who couldn't find the money for college, as well as those who didn't have the motivation for higher education, found comfort in mingling at the bars with the college kids. Once the bar was open and the Budweiser—brewed fresh only two and a half hours away in St. Louis—started flowing from the gleaming taps, the tavern became a grand leveler. Locals and students alike shared jokes and drank either to enjoy themselves or to forget their respective troubles. Either way, September through May was a time for homebodies to ignore their plight and indulge in college life, without the burden of classes, tuition, or grades.

However, when the students fled, they took with them their sheltered, hopeful worlds. They returned home or went off to pursue summer jobs and internships, leaving in their wake some of the shadowy locals, people who would be there long after the students' four-year tenures were up. It made a resident's predicament seem that much more hopeless and permanent.

The river didn't help either. Every day of the year, there it was, 100 feet below the bluffs, rolling along. Barges and other commercial freight traffic would often amble by, carrying their cargo from far away places like Monticello or Minneiska, Minnesota, destined for farther away exotic places like New Roads or New Orleans, Louisiana. They were places that the locals had heard about from the Quincy University students; places where the trees were the kind that only grew in tropical climates and where leisure was as much a part of the local custom as a nine-to-five. Places that were hell-bent on the succession and the eventual destruction of their very state less than 130 years earlier during the Civil War. The river flowed to those mysterious locales, south past their town, then down below the Mason-Dixon Line. Quincy folks who were short on money but big on imagination conjured up substantial back stories about southern backwaters. The people sounded so different from them, yet they shared one causal connection with their northern brethren—the Mississippi River.

Hannibal, Missouri, Tom Sawyer's boyhood home, was right across the way, drawing in tourists year-round. Jimmy and his buddies may not have been college men, but they made it far enough through high school to read Mark Twain and his tales of a simpler time on the mighty Mississippi. Tom Sawyer and Huckleberry Finn would get into all sorts of trouble only to find their way out. The stories always had a happy ending. That's what Jimmy Scott was looking for when he made the choice to help out on the levee. He was trying to revise history—his history. By helping the relief effort and by holding back the river that he envied all his life, Jimmy was in the midst of developing Phase One of a plan to endear himself to his community: to live happily ever after.

Jimmy was a hood, a local bad boy who Quincy residents thought could do no good. He always seemed to be in trouble with the law. There were thefts and petty vandalism, as well as vagrancy, public intoxication, and truancy. After boyhood, when he'd gone to church three times a week for services or youth group meetings, Jimmy shirked his church-going ways and eventually quit going altogether. Pastor Woodrow McCaleb at the Calvary Baptist Church on State Street had tried to teach Jimmy the path of righteousness ever since he was a 3-year-old going to Approved Workmen Are Not Ashamed (AWANA) bible-study meetings. The pastor thought the boy had a bright future, but Jimmy had other ideas. Megadeath's *Tornado of Souls* replaced Thomas Ken's *Awake, My Soul,* and he traded his cross earring for a pentagram. Jimmy went from seeking the light to wallowing in the darkness, and it all came to a head one day in 1982.

When Jimmy was 12 years old, he chose to join his brothers Mike and Jeff in what would become known as the Webster Elementary School incident. Their actions took only a few minutes but would make the Scott boys household names around town. The aftermath would follow him and his brothers around Quincy closer than their own shadows.

By sandbagging, doing whatever the National Guard needed, or just by being there on the floodplain, he thought that the locals might reconsider their opinions of James Scott a tad bit.

"I'll show 'em," he thought as he and buddy Troy Lyons, Janet Maglioshetti's son, made the casual drive across the Bayview Bridge. "They'll see me down there and then they'll say to themselves, 'Jimmy's not that bad. Jimmy's a good kid. Jimmy can do good.'"

His thought process was that simple. Jimmy's mind worked the way Huckleberry Finn's did 35 miles due south a century earlier. Though on any given day, Jimmy, unlike Huck, was more apt to be hung over from Midwestern moonshine.

The eastbound Memorial Bridge had been closed after breakfast on July 2, when the Mississippi River on the Missouri side essentially swallowed it, and Jimmy wasn't used to sharing the Bayview Bridge—the westbound route from Illinois into Missouri—with oncoming traffic. He had to concentrate and place both hands on the wheel to keep his Monte Carlo hewing the white line. Troy sat shotgun surveying the setting. He, too, marveled at the sight of the adjacent Memorial Bridge sitting idle and taking on water.

"Man, if that levee goes, the whole place goes with it," he mused to Jimmy. "We'd have an ocean right here in Quincy!"

He was half-right. Indeed they would have an ocean, but Quincy's bluffs would save her. West Quincy, on the other hand, would be transformed from an agrarian community to a Midwestern ocean, one that God never intended to create and one that cartographers never planned to plot. In 1973, that is exactly what happened as Quincy and West Quincy residents built up the levee another 13 feet with sandbags, only to eventually lose their fight. West Quincy flooded. City officials vowed never to let the Mississippi's waters overrun their banks again. And if the current status of the river was any sort of indicator, they were making good on their promise.

Jimmy and Troy arrived at a staging site near the Knapheide Manufacturing Company, an industry that built fleet truck bodies. There was an irony to a preventative effort taking shape in front of Knapheide: The company had been deluged with 14 feet of Mississippi River water 20 years earlier. Eighty percent of their total manufacturing space had been ruined and employees weren't able to return to work for over three months.

Even though he'd driven down to the relief effort in the early days of July, the scene was that of a pickup game rather than an organized endeavor. Not until July 9 did Jimmy actually do any work. On that day, he carried sandbags and was ordered to stack them atop the black plastic tarp that draped over the levee. The night before workers had filled the burlap sacks outside of Quincy Stadium and trucked them over to West Quincy and Knapheide.

The bags were crude but effective, weighing more than 50 pounds each and solid to the touch. Carrying and placing them was a job reserved for the stronger men and women, as the effort was at critical mass and organizers didn't want to worry themselves with strained backs and hiatal hernias in the midst of stemming the tide.

The West Quincy levee wasn't a continuous wall of sandbags. Certainly, there were spots along the dike of nothing more than stacked sandbags, but in some areas along the river, they were sporadically placed every 50 feet or so and used more to weight down the 100-foot sheets of industrial-strength plastic tarp and keep them from blowing around. Missouri National

Guardsmen and volunteers, like Jimmy and Troy, carried and placed those sandbag paperweights along the top of the levee.

Jimmy started working around eight o'clock the morning of July 9. The air was so muggy on the floodplain that sweat began pouring down his face even before he lifted a finger. The burlap sacks were damp since various people who had carried them from the Knapheide staging area to the levee needed to set them down from time to time to rest. The ground was also wet in certain parts from the previous day's rains and the already-coarse fabric became downright abrasive when it took in water. As Jimmy carried sandbags up and then along the levee, his softened hands abraded along the burlap, and the damp individual threads bore into his forearms, his palms, and his inner-knuckles.

The pain was even more unbearable when Jimmy set the sandbags down to wipe sweat from his brow. The diminutive punctures in his hands became pockets for the saltwater pouring from his forehead, as the solutes teased his nerve endings and caused a stinging sensation.

He trudged on, though. Part of him wanted to quit because the strain of the weight and the heaviness of the day's heat combined to cause greater discomfort than he was used to, but another part of him wanted to stay. There were too many other volunteers who had endured even more hardship and toiled even harder in the midmorning sun than he did. Jimmy was making a statement with his actions and his presence that morning. He also felt a sense of belonging, like he, too, was a military man, a member of a select society.

As the minutes ticked by and the sandbags' weight became burdensome, Jimmy gazed into the calm waters of the Mississippi River. In all 23 years of his life in Quincy, he never remembered the river being that still. There were no freighters or even skiffs moving downstream. Several barges were moored to trees, but their engines were off, and the gentle sound of water lapping against their steel hulls seemed somewhat pleasant. There was hardly any traffic moving along the Bayview Bridge, which was odd not only because it was a busy thoroughfare, but because the Memorial Bridge was closed and the Bayview assumed its sister's traffic. As more time passed, Jimmy noticed something else: For the first time in his life, he didn't hear a single train rumbling down the tracks that paralleled Front Street on the Illinois side.

Although the city of Quincy was protected from the river by natural 100-foot limestone bluffs, the Burlington Northern train tracks were not protected by any levee. The train had ceased operations a week earlier, and the tracks had taken on water. Only the occasional railroad tie was visible from the West Quincy side of the river, and that margin of sight seemed to decrease as the day passed.

Jimmy followed the tracks south with his eyes as they maneuvered under the Bayview Bridge to Clat Adams Bicentennial Park, a two-acre plot of land off of Front Street. There were no Sunday drivers cruising along the scenic roadway, nor were there any families picnicking on the sprawling lawns. In fact, the place was deserted. Just then, the impending Midwestern floods hit home for Jimmy. He thought back to weekend afternoons as a youth spent in that park, playing soccer with his brothers and barbecuing with his buddy's parents. But on that July day, Clat Adams seemed to be sinking. The white gazebo with its blue roof looked like a sinking ship. Barely any grass was visible. Reflecting on his past, Scott mused over the landmarks he associated with his childhood as they took on water.

He momentarily forgot about his aching back and his stinging hands as his adrenaline surged. Jimmy lifted a sandbag, made a gradual ascent up one of the levee's makeshift walkways, and deposited it on the levee's shelf. Then he walked back down, grabbed another, and repeated his motions. The stillness made his ears hone in on the voices of his peers. There seemed to be some chatter that made people uneasy. He approached a knot of uniformed soldiers speaking amongst themselves and eavesdropped. Alexandria, Missouri, a similar river town 45 miles north of West Quincy and situated at the confluence of the Des Moines River coming out of Iowa and the Mississippi running south, had waged a fierce battle for the past week.

The soldiers spoke of their colleagues' heroic efforts, how they stemmed the tide of the rising rivers. But just as the words left their lips, word came down that the battle was lost and the river had blasted through the levee's barrier. Alexandria was under water. The merging waterways combined to pack a furious punch, unlike anything seen in decades, if ever. And a similar fate might be in store for West Quincy. Whether or not it would, the soldiers said, depended on whether the West Quincy levee was raised and strengthened by the time the high watermark made its 45-mile trek. The soldiers reviewed their numbers and were cautiously optimistic: They thought they were ready. At the same time, though, cities straddling both sides of the river—all the way to Minnesota—were being evacuated, with the National Guard playing a role in crowd control. Presumably more troops would be called up, and the already-large preventative effort would grow exponentially. The levee of West Quincy would soon become the Heliopolis of the Mississippi River, and every worker was as important as the next. All available manpower from anywhere was both welcomed and needed.

Jimmy took his newfound information and started passing it along to his coworkers on the levee. They received the incredulous news with widened eyes. It was a horrible report for all involved, as it meant that West Quincy might be doomed. Nevertheless, their reactions made Jimmy feel good. He was the bearer of the bulletin—despite its somber tone—and he was the one they were listening to. The volunteers' concern and undivided attention fortified his own resolve, and for the first time that summer, Jimmy felt like part of a community. For the first time in his life, Jimmy felt important.

CHAPTER TWO

◄○►

Fowler, Illinois, a quaint burg off U.S. 24, is just a stone's throw from Quincy. Still in Adams County, it is the sleepy sister city of its sibling to the west. Many of the residents of Fowler are farmers, and those who do live in subdivisions live either just above, on, or below the poverty line.

One such resident was Dan Leake, a blue-collar guy who spent his days working at Furrows, a hardware store, and his nights throwing loud parties where everyone was welcome and the beer flowed continuously like the waters of the fabled river 12 miles away.

He wasn't the most upstanding citizen. Dan had been arrested for domestic battery, and the police were often called to his house by incensed neighbors complaining of the loud heavy metal music emanating from his house.

Dan threw a beer-buster the evening of July 9, as was his custom during the summer months, and the usual crew consisting of local roughnecks and lawbreaking minors attended, as was their usual custom.

At 35, Dan was significantly older than many of his guests; the elder statesman of the party crowd and an enabling example to the younger sect.

Dan was also Jimmy Scott's half-brother, the son of his mother, Sharon, by another man. Jimmy was a frequent fixture at Dan's house. Because he was a decade older than Jimmy, the two hadn't been close growing up, but that changed when Jimmy became a teenager. They grew closer when Jimmy began attending Dan's parties and mixing with all the jocular people who would come, consume mass quantities of alcohol, and have a wild time.

Jimmy was exhausted on the evening of July 9th, but he attended the party nonetheless. He sought out the few other partygoers who had been on the levee earlier that day and spoke about his own detail lifting sandbags. He also made mention of the news of the levee break in Alexandria and of the angst expressed by the National Guardsmen. The party people who had not been at the levee hung on Jimmy's every word, all but tuning out Metallica's . . . *And Justice for All*, which was blaring in the background. Once again, Jimmy had a rapt audience.

He fed off the attention while he drank and talked well into the morning of July 10. His wife, Suzie, left the party when most others did, around two o'clock in the morning. Jimmy spent the night on Dan's couch. He figured he'd return to the levee and work some more, but his hangover got the best of him and he slept it off at his half-brother's until late in the afternoon.

When he emerged in the kitchen from the den of the modest one-story modular home, Dan was reading the local newspaper, *Quincy Herald-Whig*, which he rarely did—other than the want ads. The pages were chock full of flood coverage, detailing the state of the West Quincy levee by quoting officials from the Fabius River Drainage District (the constituency who oversaw the West Quincy levee). There were stories of other floods in and around the bordering states, too.

"Jimmy, here's your Alexandria flood," Dan said, drinking from a Big Gulp he'd bought at the 7-Eleven while Jimmy was sleeping. "That town got killed last night. And folks are talking about how we might be next."

Jimmy thought about what his half-brother said for a moment. A grin pursed his lips as he took in Dan's words. What Jimmy talked about the previous night was right there in the newspaper. He had affirmation: He spoke the truth.

"Yeah, I told you," was his reply. "Figure I'll go back later today or maybe later tonight and help out."

Dan didn't think twice about his half-brother's comments. The kid seemed motivated, which was more than Dan could say for himself. He continued reading the paper while Jimmy slipped out the front door, hollering "see you tonight" as the screen door squeaked on its hinges behind him.

He walked home to his own modest one-story, two-bedroom prefab home on Dawn Avenue and peeled off his soiled clothes. The grit from his previous day's work on the levee mixed with the sweat and alcohol seeping out of his skin and made his jeans and T-shirt stick to his body.

He turned on his 12-inch TV to the mid-afternoon news and adjusted the rabbit ears. A report announced that some Quincy businesses were giving people a choice: They could come punch in, or they could aid with the sandbagging effort and still make their daily wage. Jimmy put a cursory call into Burger King, where he worked, and asked the employee who answered the phone whether the fast food joint was honoring the bargain he'd heard on the news. The employee answered that they were, so long as the worker called in early enough and didn't hamstring management with a skeletal staff. He told the employee to relay to management that he wouldn't be in for his next two shifts because he was going to West Quincy again. But if he was needed, a manager should call and leave a message on his answering machine.

Jimmy jumped in the shower and then donned a pair of shorts and a T-shirt. He walked outside toward his 1981 Monte Carlo parked on the gravel driveway and prepared to drive back over to West Quincy when the warm summer sun halted him in his tracks. Although it had rained for most of the last month, July 10 was a beautiful summer day. Inland in Fowler, the heat wasn't overly oppressive, and a light breeze caressed his clean-shaven cheeks. His head was still pounding from the exploits of the previous day and night, and the sun was high in the west. Jimmy made an about-face, headed back inside, and grabbed a beer. He was still committed to helping the effort that day—the kudos he had received were still very much on his mind. But he decided to wait out the afternoon until Suzie returned home at 6 p.m. from her job at 18 Wheeler. His wife was an attendant at the truck stop in Taylor, Missouri, about six miles from the sandbagging in West Quincy. He took his beer outside and sat in a lawn chair.

Jimmy was of medium build. Standing approximately 5 feet 10 inches tall, he had broad shoulders and thick ankles and calves. His arms were skinny, which made the sleeveless muscle shirt he wore a joke on his puny body. His sandy blond hair was worn short on the top and long in the back—a classic mullet—and he smiled a lot. Whether out of sheer joy or nervous habit, Jimmy always seemed to sport the proverbial shit-eating grin.

As he passed the time, he thought ahead to Dan Leake's house and another July party. That was what he looked forward to in those days, a chance to get drunk and tell tales.

By the time his wife arrived home from Taylor, Jimmy was buzzed. One beer had turned into five. Suzie changed her clothes and joined her husband for a beer. That, too, turned from just one to many quite quickly. Rather than drive back to West Quincy, they decided to check in at Quincy Stadium, where volunteers had been filling sandbags for four days.

"Q-Stadium," as it is affectionately called, is home of the Quincy Gems, a member of the Central Illinois Collegiate League. Built of stone from local quarries in 1938, Quincy University bought Q-Stadium from the city in 1984 for the heady price of $1. The 6,000-seat structure also hosts Quincy University Hawk baseball games.

Jimmy was no stranger to the Q. A real sports nut, he and his brothers or some buddies would often spring for the $5 tickets. They'd drink in the parking lot before game time, sneak flasks into the bleachers, or both and pass the time watching some solid college baseball. Late at night, they'd head over to the high school's baseball fields and if the lights were on, they'd scale the fence and play an impromptu game themselves.

But on July 10, the Gems' home game had been canceled, and Q-Stadium's infield had become a giant sandbox. Massive sand mounds towering as high as 10 feet commanded attention as volunteers grabbed burlap sacks, pulled them open at the mouth, and shoveled in sand.

Jimmy and Suzie arrived there at around 9:30 p.m. to an empty parking lot. The effort had shut down for the night.

Because it was too late to shovel sand, the couple figured that work on the levee was also over for the night. So they decided to swing by a convenience store, where they picked up a case of Bud, and then head over to Dan's house.

As Jimmy and Suzie popped their cans in Illinois, Missouri National Guardsmen, joined by administrators and volunteers from the Fabius River

Drainage District, paced anxiously at the base and on the shelf of the West Quincy levee. They had a clear night to strategize about how to coordinate tomorrow's activities, but the problem was that the forecast called for rain two out of the next four days.

CHAPTER THREE

◄O►

All of the men down on the levee seemed edgy, especially because of the Alexandria levee breach up north. One man in particular stood out from the others. He wore a look of consternation on his face as he maneuvered among the troops and engineers, listening as they spoke and chiming in with questions of his own from time to time. He was 6 feet tall and muscular, with broad shoulders shaped from three decades of farming. His coarse brown hair, usually parted to the left, was a bit disheveled from the long hours and the humidity. He spoke with command, the words always drawing the attention of others. His half-moon eyes were squinting more than usual that day from prolonged exposure to all 16 hours of daylight in the days leading up to July 11, 1993.

Norman Haerr was the man in charge, the presiding commissioner and president of the Fabius River Drainage District, which was the governing body that oversaw the West Quincy levee. He was the point man for all levee action, lending his ear to National Guard brass, Army Corps of Engineers brass, and on-the-spot district workers.

He held a walkie-talkie in each hand on July 11 and they squawked nonstop. Haerr had just been informed that the weather was about to take a turn for the worse. He was awaiting confirmation from the National Guard and from Missouri Governor Mel Carnahan—who had been declaring several counties a day disaster areas for the last week—that more soldiers were on the way.

The U.S. Army Corps of Engineers is charged with maintaining levees up and down the Mississippi River, as well as other major waterways across the country. Indeed, the Corps has historically built earthen and cement dams to shore up rivers around big cities like St. Louis, Memphis, and New Orleans, but a misconception is that the Corps single-handedly built the American levee system.

In fact, local interests in the late 1800s and early 1900s originally constructed most levees along the Mississippi River. Initially, farmers teamed up and hauled wheelbarrows of clay and compacted sand along the banks of the river to secure their land and crops from an otherwise surging offshoot. Over time, the Corps has made minor improvements on these levees, but they have never dug up the original, tenuous foundations. In this region of the country, the Mississippi Valley Division of the Corps was the overseeing body for dam improvements. But they weren't always the first to know of trouble spots. For that, they relied on the local overseers, like Norman Haerr.

Because of the Corps' role as a maintenance entity, communication between the federal government and local drainage districts has historically been on an as-needed basis. That was the principle upon which Haerr and his staff of the Fabius River Drainage District operated.

And that's why on July 11, 1993, the scene was a bit chaotic along the river. Haerr toiled perhaps the longest number of hours and spearheaded one of the greatest sandbagging efforts in Missouri/Illinois history. His labors were both extraordinary and consequential. He acted as the man-on-the-ground for all intervening agencies. As such, Haerr was also the contact for whom all media inquiries ultimately fell.

The most proactive of the drainage district's five commissioners, Haerr was satisfied with the job his crew was doing. They were working long hours for little if any money, and the tremendous stress placed on them by the task at hand and by the community—looking to them to save their town— weighed heavily on their collective conscience. Norman Haerr was proud of them, of their work, and their spirited resolve. But the news of levee failures upriver had Haerr concerned on July 11. His trepidations were not reserved only for the levee, but to the safety and wellbeing of his men. Haerr needed more help. His office relayed the commissioner's concerns to Governor Mel Carnahan's office, the National Guard, and the Corps.

Volunteers continued to work the levee that day, many sweating profusely though granted a measure of minimal relief from overcast skies.

Quincy Mayor Chuck Scholz reiterated his call to Illinois residents to go help their Missouri counterparts. Already, more than 10,000 volunteers from across the region were contributing whenever they could, and by July 11, more than 3.5 million sandbags had been filled. More were on the way, and more volunteers were needed to carry the bags up the levee and place them on the large black tarps.

Over 2,000 Illinois National Guardsmen were working a 20-mile stretch of levee, and 200 more were called up that evening. Additionally, there were over 1,500 Missouri National Guardsmen on site and another 500 on standby in St. Louis.

Many of the guardsmen who were called to West Quincy had been battling the river in other parts of Illinois and Missouri. Lt. Rick Gengenbacher had been 20 miles north in Meyer, Illinois, with his unit trying to save that town. The troops acted determinedly and managed to stave off floods for more than a week, but just three days earlier, the rain-soaked levee caved and Mississippi River waters inundated 1,000 acres of prime farmland.

It was a distressing defeat for the guardsmen. It hit Lt. Gengenbacher particularly hard because the officer was from Quincy. He knew his region was next, and he mustered up every ounce of strength and every word of motivation to pump up his men. They needed to get Meyer out of their minds and concentrate on West Quincy.

But as soon as relief came in one form, new problems arose. The increased number of National Guard choppers, which were patrolling the levee from the air and transporting scores of sandbags, used all the gas in the area. Employees from the Heetco Jet Center in Quincy literally worked around the clock to keep the birds fueled and flying. Men were divided into two 12-hour shifts and essentially camped out at Baldwin Field in Quincy— the staging area for the helicopters—even when they weren't working: just in case. Normally, Heetco pumped around 700 gallons of fuel a day. That fuel usually went into single engine Cessnas or double-engine turbo props, both of which were relatively fuel-efficient. On July 11, the fuel was destined for Huey and Chinook helicopter tanks. The Chinooks alone gulped between 700 and 900 gallons per fueling, and the Huey's another 100. Heetco was pumping more than 3,000 gallons per day and the reserve tanks were running dangerously low.

With so much going on in such a triangulated area, residents experienced a wide emotional range. The vast majority expressed tremendous optimism that the levee would hold, especially because there was so much help on the scene. "There are always going to be glitches here and there, but no one had to go out to work without the proper equipment," Spec. Jeff Sullivan of the Illinois National Guard said. "Things are a bit chaotic, but it's amazing what's been accomplished in a short amount of time."

Some residents and volunteers, however, were glum in the face of a probable impending tragedy. Editors at the *Quincy Herald-Whig* picked up their sentiments. To rally the pessimists, the OpEd page ran a story along the lines of you're-not-to-blame. The editorial was meant to buck up the volunteers' spirits should their efforts ultimately be for naught. On Sunday, July 11, 1993, the paper ran the following story on the Opinion page:

GREAT FLOOD OF '93

Mother Nature served notice last week that human beings may try to control her rivers and streams, but she will have the final word.

The Mississippi River rises despite record levels already recorded the length of the river basin.

The tragedy of flooding has reached into many nearby communities. Some, such as Alexandria, Mo., were forced to surrender all to the muddy, swirling river waters. The Lima Lake district [the district that oversaw Meyer, Illinois], after Friday night's break, was becoming a lake again. Rains fell again to the north, threatening to engulf more already weakened levees and swell the river to even higher levels.

The battle to contain the river and the Great Flood of '93 is one of epic proportion. It will continue for weeks to come—as long as river levels remain high and the threat of additional rain continues. Mother Nature can be a relentless opponent.

Human anguish abounds. The cost of this flood in both emotional and economic terms is incalculable. Many have lost all they have worked for over a lifetime.

Frustration can lead to a desire to blame someone or some thing for what happens. There are those who may wish to blame federal policy that, over the years, has changed a wild, open river into a predictably navigable

*canal by the addition of locks and dams, and extensive levee systems
designed to hold the river within appointed boundaries during normal sea-
sonal fluctuations.*

*Such blame would be misplaced. The upper Mississippi Valley levees,
most of them, were not designed to contain the onslaught of 1993. With or
without the levee system, it is clear the situation now faced was not pre-
ventable. Either way, there would be devastation and suffering as a result
of this flood. The key now is to do all possible to hold losses to a minimum.*

*This will be done through the heroic efforts of selfless volunteers;
National Guard troops, Corps of Engineers experts, and so many others
working around the clock—by those who fill and deliver sandbags, those
who direct the lines of defense along levees, those who feed and give shelter
to people driven from their homes.*

*The race against disaster changed from a sprint to a marathon, and it
is a credit to the foresight and courage of so many that the toll has not been
far greater.*

While the community newspaper tried to discourage community blame,
Norman Haerr, the go-to media source, was himself succumbing to doubt.
He told the *Herald-Whig* that he'd been on the levee and that: "I was concerned." There was some good news coming in from the north. The levee
break in Meyer actually helped—albeit briefly—the West Quincy levee. It
emptied about 2 feet of water from the Mississippi River, and a late-night
rain compacted the sand volunteers had piled atop the dam. It was a quick
fix, Haerr knew, because more rain was expected, and the river hadn't crested
yet. Still, he adamantly tried to remain strong for the people. "We'll keep
[the river] back," he said. "God willing."

◄o►

The rains held up on July 11, and despite the forecast calling for scattered
showers throughout the day, July 12 began with a brilliant sun warming the
waters and earth below.

Jimmy was called into work at Burger King the previous day, so he
couldn't volunteer his time in West Quincy. On July 12, he awoke with a

renewed vigor. He was needed on the floodplain. Jimmy was anxious to get back down to the levee and help out: Perhaps he'd win over a few more allies with his presence this time around. And perhaps, Jimmy thought, he might actually be able to do some good.

He drove his car westbound on U.S. 24 toward the Bayview Bridge. As soon as he was halfway across the Mississippi River, Jimmy was stunned at what he saw. The labor force from two days ago had grown immeasurably. There were hordes of camouflaged trucks and camouflaged soldiers. The volunteer pool had more than doubled, and the river was alive with more nautical activity. The barges were still moored to trees, but some Coast Guard plastic boats were now in the river, patrolling the levee a few feet from shore.

He parked his Monte Carlo alongside the dozens of other civilian vehicles at the Ayerco gas station. From there, he started walking toward Knapheide to see what needed doing.

The scene at Knapheide was frenzied. National Guardsmen moved between giant bails of straw and stacks of sandbags. They clamored away on their walkie-talkies, describing the actions of hundreds of people who were checking into the manufacturing plant and awaiting instructions. Voices on the other end of the radio gave orders and informed the Guardsmen of helicopters in the area as well as incoming reports of river and levee conditions from Burlington, Iowa, all the way down to East St. Louis. Military operations were now coordinating out of the Quincy National Guard Armory, home of the 126th Ordinance Company. Major General Donald Lynn had moved his headquarters to Quincy because it was centrally located amidst all the action, and because the West Quincy levee seemed to be in dire straits.

Every element of command, from fuel requests to food to sandbags and even additional troops, passed through the new command center, and Maj. Gen. Lynn ran his hub and his men as though the looming floods were an ambushing enemy unit.

Word came over the radio at Knapheide from command HQ that some brave, burly men were needed to patrol the levee and place sandbags over trouble spots. The Fabius River Drainage District was, after all, in charge of roughly 10 miles of levee along the Mississippi River. The National Guard could not realistically monitor every one of those miles at all times, so HQ told the officers to find some men, give them a crash-course on levee maintenance and send them along all points of the levee.

Jimmy was within earshot of a Missouri National Guardsman, who asked if he was ready to help.

"Sure am," he replied anxiously. "What you need me to do?"

The soldier explained that Jimmy would be walking along the top of the levee and looking for seepage, overtopping, boils, or any other glaring irregularities that needed attention. "It'll be tricky for you, since you're not familiar with how levees work," the soldier explained. "You may see a lot of black plastic tarps and in the areas where we haven't laid the tarps yet, you may see a lot of straw placed atop the sand. And it may be wet. We do that to keep the levee from eroding. If the straw is damp, that's okay. It means it's doing its job. But if you see water streaming at a fast pace through that straw, or if you see water coming through the tarp and bubbling up the plastic, or if you see the river running over the top of the levee, find one of us ASAP. In the meantime, throw some sandbags overtop the trouble spot to shore up the leak."

Jimmy concentrated on the soldier's words. It was a tall order, especially because he'd never been on any kind of patrol before. Moreover, it seemed like a lot of information to take in, but the twinge of responsibility he felt in his chest also served to stoke his self-esteem.

He patrolled a part of the levee north of the Bayview Bridge though south of the railroad bridge for over three hours until he became exhausted. Jimmy hadn't noticed any trouble spots—none of consequence, anyway. He grabbed a sandbag every now and then and placed it atop some of the wet straw, but the river seemed to be staying put. When he felt overheated and worn out, he made his way back to the Ayerco station and his car and left the scene.

Jimmy decided to head back over to Illinois and swing by Dan's house to see whether anyone was around. Some of the neighborhood kids were shooting baskets in Dan's driveway, so Jimmy joined them.

He was the oldest guy out there, playing with 16-year-olds Eric Epping, Cory Anderson, and Eric Wagy. Jimmy was a sage role model for the youths. They were from the same neighborhood and poor background as Jimmy, who was one of the "cool guys" who partied at Dan's. As they shot baskets, Jimmy talked about how he'd been tapped by the National Guard to find trouble spots along the levee earlier that day. The boys listened with rapt interest, impressed that a friendly was doing such a consequential job in West Quincy. One of the boys asked Jimmy if he was scared because the levee could give way at any moment. Jimmy grinned and quipped that he was a strong swimmer. "Besides," Jimmy said, "if the levee breaks, then we'll have good catfishing in West Quincy." It was an unfortunate display of chutzpah, but nobody thought much of the remark at the time. Everyone laughed and the pickup game ensued.

Jimmy shot hoops long into the evening. The four guys laughed it up in the remaining daylight as dark, menacing clouds began to gather above. Cory Anderson remarked that it looked like rain, but they continued playing ball.

-◄o►-

Down on the levee, Norman Haerr looked up at the same sky and marveled at just how quickly a sunny day was turning overcast. Despite the fact that levee breaks upriver from the damming effort in West Quincy had lowered the Mississippi River, the gauge from the Quincy Filter Plant indicated on July 12 that the river was rising once again. Coupled with the foreboding heavy black clouds, Norman Haerr privately sulked that this could be the Fabius River Drainage District's last stand.

The West Quincy levee was originally 17 feet tall at the turn of the 20th century, and it remained that way through 1917, when the Fabius River Drainage District was formed. In 1936, Congress passed the Flood Control Act, which put levees under the supervision of the Army Corps of Engineers: They could effectively be called upon to help make improvements in some of the more rural areas of American ecosystems. Between 1960 and 1963, the Fabius district, along with the Army Corps of Engineers and $1.61 million of federal money, commissioned hydraulic pumps to siphon sand from the river and deposit it alongside the West Quincy levee. The dam was thus built up. By July 1993, it stood approximately 24 feet high, and that 24 feet of earthen clay and sand was all that separated the Mississippi River from more than 14,000 acres of farmland in the Fabius River Drainage District. During the floods of 1973, the Mississippi crested at 26 feet and overtopped the levee, which resulted in the destruction of thousands of acres of farmland and some businesses, like the Knapheide Manufacturing Company.

Earlier in July 1993, Haerr was informed by the Corps that this time around, the Mississippi River might rise all the way up to 30 feet of water. The Fabius district was not necessarily up the creek: They could build their levee up to 30 feet, but in so doing, they'd neglect a free board. The Corps highly recommends in their maintenance handbook that levees have a two-foot buffer zone, or free board, between the top of the river and the top of a levee. This safety zone allows a little leverage if the river rises higher than originally calculated, and it also contributes to the structural integrity of the dike. So Haerr and fellow farmer Bob Hoffmeister called in the bulldozers.

A fleet of bulldozers maneuvered to the back of the levee—the side furthest from the river—and actually pushed sand from the base of the levee up the side and toward the top. It worked. The more the bulldozers pushed, the more the levee grew from the ground.

Just as the 30-foot target was being met, the Corps came back to Haerr and gave him the one piece of news he absolutely dreaded. They said that the rains up north in Iowa were heavier and more virulent than once expected. As such, Haerr and company could expect 32.5 feet of water.

Haerr received the news with suppressed panic. He wanted to ask the engineer if this was some kind of joke, but the messenger's face was expressionless—as expressionless as the shocked face that looked back. There was nothing Haerr could do except continue to bulldoze the levee even higher. The machines pushed and pushed, and an industrial black tarp was thrown over the sheer-faced gigantic mound to keep the sand from eroding. In the areas that didn't have enough sand at the top, Haerr had volunteers stack sandbags.

Haerr's strained eyes and clinched fists eased a bit come the morning of July 13, when the river seemed to be holding steady at 29 feet while the levee stood just over 30 feet in the air. The bulldozers continued to push.

Simultaneously, as the levee rose, the skies darkened once again and the air began to smell like rain. It was coming; there was no denying it, and when the skies opened, the river would rise. Just how much precipitation lay ahead and just how high the Mississippi would swell was difficult to determine, but Haerr braced himself for the worst.

He got on his walkie-talkie and warned the other four commissioners of the Fabius River Drainage District to mobilize their workers. This was it: The battle they'd been preparing for was slowly rolling in from the northwest. Haerr asked for all available men to work as long as they could. He planned to station personnel every 100 yards along the levee, and some additional men five miles north of Knapheide at Durgin's Creek. That area, Haerr said, was the glaring red flag. If the rains were strong enough to whip the Mississippi River into a furious eddy, the dam at Durgin's Creek was the one to watch. Up there, two different levees converged, and although both were strong, Haerr was uncertain if the levee's joint was firm.

The National Guard was by and large standing down until later that night. They'd been working multiple shifts and they would need to patrol the levee throughout the night, keeping a keen eye peeled for trouble spots and trouble makers. After all, with such a razor thin margin separating millions of gallons of rushing water from the Missouri interior, a suicidal man or a terrorist could presumably wreak havoc on the Midwest with a stick of dynamite or a hard ram of his car. Or boat.

The drainage district workers positioned themselves and donned their ponchos. Norman Haerr was frantically trying to coordinate the bulldozers, tarp-layers, sandbaggers, and patrols. The skies looked foreboding as word came down that the levee had been erected to 32.5 feet.

They had done it. Haerr questioned the engineers on the scene whether the levee was structurally sound, because although the bulldozers managed to raise the height, they also thinned out the sand walls. Haerr was assured that the reams of black polyurethane would help prevent erosion. Additionally, an enterprising young local farmer devised a way to keep the water from oozing through the seams in the plastic and wearing gulleys into the levee. He rigged the tarp so that the plastic took on water and moved it sideways—rather than front-to-back—and displaced it down the land side of the levee. Haerr liked that ingenuity. He needed fast minds and hands in this situation.

After he barked out his last instruction, Norman Haerr took a moment for himself and inhaled deeply. Just as he exhaled, a raindrop hit his forehead and exploded into miniature streams of water tracing their way into the crow's feet around his eyes. A second drop deposited in the corner of his mouth, followed by another. These were not piercing drops, but rather huge, plump ones. Haerr stood in the rain and pulled the hood from his poncho. He tried to eyeball the river and gauge whether it was rising as the skies opened up with unbridled aggression. He thought he saw the waterline climb, though he couldn't be sure.

◄o►

Dan Leake's party raged late into the night on July 13. Because the weather was so awful and uncooperative, all the bodies that were usually scattered throughout Dan's yard were forced to cram into his modular home. More than 20 people sat inside drinking all sorts of alcohol. They also bantered back and forth about who was the better baseball club, the St. Louis Cardinals or the Chicago Cubs, as Quincy's location forced resident sports fans to choose their allegiance between the two National League teams that divided Illinois. St. Louis was 100 miles closer to Quincy than Chicago was, but Quincy was in Illinois, after all.

Besides the bizarre weather, two other peculiarities played out at the party. For one, Chicago Cubs and St. Louis Cardinals fans started getting along after the music stopped. Secondly, the music stopped! Dan Leake's parties were notorious for ear-splitting music, but on July 13, the 19-inch television was the only noise blaring above the voices of the patrons. The MLB All-Star game was being played in Baltimore, and all National Leaguers were cheering for a common team. Jimmy piped up about a story he'd seen on TV regarding the Cardinals catcher Tom Pagnozzi. Pags told the national news media that he would be spending the All-Star break filling sandbags. He lived in South St. Louis County, about five miles from the Mississippi River and less than one mile from the raging Meramec River, which empties into the Mississippi.

Few paid much attention to Jimmy as he spoke; they were much more interested in what was on the television. One partygoer did hear Jimmy, and he responded with a comment about how the major league player had something in common with the wild bunch in Dan Leake's house: They all were at the mercy of the river.

He was Joe Flachs, a 16-year-old troubled youth from Fowler. Joe's mother, Kathy Flachs, didn't pay much attention to his comings and goings, so Joe came and went as he pleased. That's how he ended up at Dan Leake's house on a Tuesday evening. His mother also hadn't bothered to explain the perils of underage drinking, so Joe did that, too.

He was pretty sauced by the sixth inning, right about the time announcers were prognosticating a six-year sweep for the American League. Jimmy pulled up a chair next to Joe, and they started some drunken banter. They joked around for about an hour, which bored Suzie. After a while, she left Jimmy at the party and went home. When she was gone, Jimmy started ogling the other women at Dan's—and so did Joe.

"Man, if that levee breaks, I hope it strands Suzie over in Taylor so I can party here without her," Jimmy remarked to Joe.

"Shit," Joe replied. "There's plenty of other people I'd rather see stranded over there. Too bad you can't choose who's where when the time comes."

Almost as if on cue, someone at the party put in a tape of Led Zeppelin's anthem "When the Levee Breaks." Jimmy and Joe both looked around to see who the jokester was, and then they turned to each other and let out drunken belly laughs.

The wind whipped up something fierce and blew the falling water around. Fat drops seemed to be running sideways as drainage district volunteers scrunched their shoulders and marched into the weather. Norman Haerr's suspicions were right: The river was rising. According to the gauge at the Quincy Filter Plant, the waterline was teetering between 32 feet and 32.19 feet. That left less than one-third of an inch of free board, or breathing room. Haerr stood where the levee met the Bayview Bridge and leaned into the wind. He pondered the situation: Just a third of an inch kept the Father of

Waters from overtopping his efforts and flooding 14,000 acres of farmland. He forgot his duties as a drainage district commissioner for a moment and thought about his family. He'd talked to his son earlier and learned that the Haerrs were safe, awaiting his arrival at Fellowship Hall in neighboring Taylor, Missouri.

The drops fell so hard and fast—and they were so big—that from time to time, Haerr couldn't tell where the rain ended and the river began. Just one-third of an inch. The walls of the levee were holding, he was confident, as his radio hadn't chirped with news of a trouble spot. Even the boys up at Durgin's Creek were quiet. Haerr told everyone to keep the channels clear and only radio in problems. The Guard was patrolling. Everyone was doing his or her job, but that third of an inch was gnawing at Norman.

He had a personal connection to the farmland next to the river. More than 1,400 acres of it was his, and his soybean and corn crops were coming along nicely thanks to all the sun and rain. But because of the monsoon-like conditions on the evening of July 13, Haerr was on the verge of succumbing to the powers of God and nature.

He surveyed the scene with his limited vision and saw one farmer laying facedown on the ground, the rain assaulting his prone body with reckless abandon while he clung to the base of the levee, arms outstretched. Then the lightning flashed with a prolonged stay of silvery brilliance and the thunder cracked like a derailed freight train crashing into a mountain. The farmer at the base of the levee let out a faint scream. He was scared—and so was Haerr. With all that water in the river, on the ground, and coming from all sides, it was hard to tell where the lighting struck. Lightening seeks water, and in those conditions, the patrollers might as well have painted targets on their chests. The electricity in the air raised the hackles on the back of Haerr's neck, and yet he didn't budge. Norman Haerr didn't let out a sound.

He tried to push out of his mind the thought of 10 feet of the Mississippi River deluging his life's work. Despite his best efforts, he couldn't cast the gloomy, melancholic doomsday scenarios out of his head.

Long into the night of July 13 he prayed to God to hold back the rains, and hedged his bet by praying that one-third of an inch of sand would save his and others' farmland.

CHAPTER FOUR

◄○►

Daybreak came like a surreal reverie. The sky was a scintillating blue in the early morning hours of July 14, and the air was already steamy from the mix of excess rain and a scorching sun. Birds chirped from the trees along West Quincy's levee while mosquitoes and dragonflies collected along the river banks.

Norman Haerr drove his pickup truck to Knapheide and parked alongside the various camouflage Hummers. National Guardsmen were scattered about the manufacturing company. Those who had pulled the previous evening's shift slept deeply in their cots while others smoked cigarettes and roamed the floodplain.

They had survived a deluge of wind and rain and this beautiful rain-free day was their reward. The Mississippi River meandered along, lightly lapping against the raised levee. Water levels were still dangerously high— 32.05 feet to be exact—but despite nature's onslaught, the levee hadn't breached.

Norman Haerr allowed himself a relieved smile. The forecast called for sunny weather for the next three days, and the Fabius River Drainage District president naturally felt that he'd dodged a very deadly bullet. There were still some trouble spots to the north at Durgin's Creek, and a few more sprouted up south of the Bayview Bridge, but the West Quincy levee was holding. Haerr reflected that if that levee could withstand 32.19 feet of water, coupled with a nasty wind and incessant rain, then the worst was already behind him. Still, the rain had saturated the levee. Many areas along the top were too soft to patrol with four-wheelers. "It's seeping though so bad that you can step on it and your feet sink . . . it can go up to your knees," Knapheide maintenance manager Jon Wren told the *Quincy Herald-Whig.* "It's extremely saturated."

Even though Norman Haerr felt cautiously optimistic, he didn't like that there wasn't a free board. The water was still quite high, so the bulldozers turned their engines over again and pushed the levee even higher.

The story became much more than a regional one after the rain of July 13. Americans had been inundated for weeks with dour flood coverage of levees blowing out all along the Mississippi River. Rising from those all-too-real stories told up and down the river was the West Quincy levee: Here was the story of a town that had managed to win a fight against the mighty Mississippi.

While the drainage district employees combed the levee for leaks and the bulldozers revved their engines, a mobilization of another sort was underway. For the first time in weeks, Quincy's Baldwin Field welcomed private planes once again. The airport-turned-military base allowed corporate and civilian jets to land on its lone runway. Lt. Gen. John Conaway, chief of the National Guard Bureau, arrived from Washington, D.C., and boarded a Chinook helicopter. He was flown up and down the river in order to witness firsthand his Illinois and Missouri National Guardsmen—and the volunteers—diligently going about their work.

One of those camouflaged dots 300 feet below rotor-tip was Tech Sgt. Duke Kelley of the Missouri Air National Guard. His unit had been mobilized three days earlier from their base at St. Louis' Lambert Field, the international airport and midwestern hub of TWA. His unit, the 131st Civil Engineers, was part of Gov. Mel Carnahan's mass call-up, and they'd been patrolling the levee around the clock. On July 14, Sgt. Kelly didn't bask in the glow of certain victory. He was a seasoned guardsman, on emergency leave from his day job at the Pepsi Cola bottling plant in Florissant, Missouri. Sgt. Kelly didn't share the collective euphoria of his boss and the drainage district employees because he was charged with overseeing 100 men, and notwithstanding the day's serenity, he was still concerned with their safety.

Lt. Gen. Conaway spent about 45 minutes in the air, marveling at the efficiency of the relief effort. When the Chinook touched back down at

Baldwin, Lt. Gen. Conaway did a couple of interviews and boarded a private jet destined for the nation's capital.

Within minutes of takeoff, as the general's plane ascended to its 35,000-foot cruising altitude, a private helicopter snaked its way through the skies over the Mississippi River and touched down on a helipad in La Grange, Missouri, seven miles north of West Quincy. This bird carried two New York TV celebrities: *CBS Evening News* anchorman Dan Rather, who had broadcasted from Des Moines, Iowa, for the past two days, and *CBS This Morning* co-host Harry Smith. Rather had personally requested the unscheduled pit stop in West Quincy when news of their Custer-esque last stand had filtered back to Des Moines. Like Custer, Rather observed, the men and women working on West Quincy's floodplain were severely out-matched by a formidable and powerful foe. Unlike Custer, they were winning.

Rather was given a walking tour of La Grange, much of which was filled with water from the flooding of the Union Drainage District. He waded through 4 feet of water in La Grange Mayor Harold Ludwig's home as he was briefed on the heroics in West Quincy the night before.

"What we've seen is horror meets heroism and hope," the anchorman said. "I can't say enough about the people . . . the optimism and sense of humor, under these circumstances, is one of the more impressive things I've seen in recent years."

Rather left the area shortly after and returned to New York, but Harry Smith stayed and set up shop in Quincy for a live broadcast. The military personnel and volunteers, Smith announced, were examples of "Pioneer spirit at its best."

Other news agencies, ever-eager to scoop their eponymous counterparts, started looking for other story angles. The heroism for heroism's sake sto-ryline seemed tapped out, so many concentrated their stories around the Bayview Bridge.

The Mark Twain Bridge connecting Missouri and Illinois in Hannibal had been closed on July 2 because of high water. With the closing of Quincy's Memorial Bridge earlier in the month, the Bayview Bridge remained the only east-west viaduct between St. Louis and Keokuk, Iowa, connecting Missouri, Iowa, and Illinois. Should the Bayview Bridge cease operation, no one would be able to drive from one state into the other for a 200-mile stretch. The Bayview Bridge thus became the rallying cry for national media outlets. It was an important-enough reason to mobilize once again, so volunteers continued to descend upon the floodplain and awaited instructions from the National Guard and Norman Haerr's drainage district.

By now, though, Haerr didn't relish anymore do-gooders. He was happy with the professional and military staff on hand. Too many bodies, too many pounding feet, and too little levee knowledge could combine to create an even greater element of chaos. Haerr was grateful for the volunteers' past efforts: He couldn't have held back the Mississippi this long without them. But as the river seemed to stabilize and there were no rain clouds in the sky, it was time to leave the maintenance work to the professionals.

James Scott's head hurt. Bad. Even for a boozer, he had drunk a ridiculous amount of liquor the night before. Background noise, not his own internal clock, roused him from his deep slumber. He realized that he'd passed out with a beer in his hand. It was spilled on Dan's carpet when he finally awoke and lifted his head from the brown couch cushion.

He sat up and smacked his lips together. A pasty white glob of spit clung between his teeth and gums. His tongue tasted like an ashtray. His eyes burned as he looked over and saw his half-brother.

Dan Leake was sitting in a faded blue recliner watching *CBS This Morning*. Co-host Harry Smith stood atop Quincy's limestone bluff, which shocked Dan at first. It wasn't often that a national celebrity came to town. The camera was angled in such a way that Smith's backdrop was the Mississippi River and the volunteers on the Missouri banks. Harry Smith did not, however, celebrate the battle between man and river from the previous night while talking to co-host Paula Zahn and the viewers.

"The floodwaters of the Mississippi continue to rise," Smith cautioned only 12 miles from where Dan sat in his recliner. "One of the two bridges at Quincy is underwater right now. . . . We'll talk about a couple of levees that have gone down just in the last 12 hours. The situation's not good."

"Shit," Dan muttered under his breath, a look of concern on his face as *CBS This Morning* went to commercial. He paid no attention to Jimmy, who sat looking at the TV.

"Hey, who won the game last night?" Jimmy asked. He thought he knew, but he wasn't sure. Things had become something of a blur by the ninth inning.

"American League," Dan said without turning his head.

"Shit," Jimmy declared in the same level tone. "We just can't beat those guys."

They sat silently, waiting for *CBS This Morning* to recommence. Harry Smith's face filled the screen:

"They're still sandbagging 'round the clock around here, Paula. They're working as hard as they can and they're doing their best to win this—win every battle they can. But the war, it looks like, is going to be won by the river."

"Aw, shit!" Dan said again, this time louder.

Jimmy stared past the television and through the house's front window. He observed a beautiful summer day in Fowler. His head throbbed and he smacked his gums together.

"Did Gregg Jefferies get any hits?" Jimmy queried.

"Huh?"

"Jefferies. What he do last night?"

"Struck out on a ball in the dirt in the ninth," Dan said while intently watching the commercials between flood coverage.

"Aw, shit," Jimmy replied.

◄o►

Knapheide Manufacturing Company was humming as it had been in the dire days prior to July 14. Owner Harold Knapheide III had given all 200 of his employees' time off at full pay seven days earlier, though he "encouraged" all of them to help sandbag. When the boss "encourages" you to do something, you would be smart to do it.

Deep puddles surrounded Knapheide Manufacturing on all four sides, but the heavy wind and rain did not harm the structure itself. While the levee workers continued their efforts, some Knapheide employees were tasked with battening down the hatches of the company. It seemed somewhat absurd to take all these preparations *after* the crazy weather last night, but orders were given. The company's communication center was raised 16 feet into the air, a safe height, Harold thought. Most of the equipment was put on Knapheide trucks and hauled to Quincy's high ground. The operation was whittled down to the bare basics: A couple of generators, radios, and some machines that were bolted to the ground.

Harold Knapheide III was still concerned with the condition of the levee. His home was safe from the river should she burst through the dike, but his company would be doomed.

Harold was more than just a well-heeled businessman. He was also a commissioner of the Fabius River Drainage District. He went on patrols over the years with Norman Haerr and the Army Corps of Engineers. And Harold knew that although the levee had survived the rains on July 13, it was a saturated, soggy mess on July 14. He wondered what would happen if the levee broke that day, in the sunshine with the eye of the nation broadcasting from the river's banks. What would happen to those volunteers? They continued to come to the levee even though Haerr didn't need them all. Or did he? Harold looked up and saw a single black cloud blowing in from the west.

The forecast called for clear skies for the next few days, but that one ominous black cloud preceded a squadron of others on the horizon. Midwestern weather changes on a whim, and levee volunteers were more chagrined than surprised when they witnessed an oncoming storm.

◄○►

Jimmy lounged around Dan Leake's house for most of the afternoon. He went outside for a time and shot baskets. When he got tired, he retreated back into the cool confines of Dan's den. Some clouds eclipsed the bright sunshine in the late afternoon, and a few raindrops thudded against Dan's prefabricated roof. Jimmy grabbed a beer and returned to the couch.

◄O►

JULY 15, 1993:

HARRY SMITH: You are looking live at the Mississippi River rising again near Quincy, Illinois. The bridge you see is out. They hope they can save the one behind me and that the levees hold. Welcome to *CBS This Morning*. I'm Harry Smith.

PAULA ZAHN: Good morning, Harry. And good morning to you, everybody. I'm Paula Zahn reporting in New York this morning.

SMITH: Guess what, Paula? More bad news. Steady rain here. They don't have anything less than a 50-percent chance of rain in the foreseeable forecast.

ZAHN: How much rain did you get overnight?

SMITH: I—I don't have a clue.

ZAHN: A lot, though.

SMITH: It's been raining on and off. And there's a pretty good cell over us right now. And it's just the last thing they need. The battle continues along the Mississippi and its tributaries. They're sandbagging like crazy, trying to save these levees, trying to protect precious farmland and business. This is the scene at West Quincy right across the river from us. If they can keep the levee they're working on intact, they'll save 10,000 acres of farmland and they'll keep a major bridge open. That's a big lifeline economically and a major transportation system between here, Muscatine, Iowa, and St. Louis down the river from us. It's a big, big job. The folks here are quite hopeful.

President Clinton, meanwhile, got to the Midwest finally yesterday. You're looking at pictures of him taking an aerial tour. He said he's seen floods before in Arkansas, but nothing like the floods that are damaging the Midwest right now. The president talked with some of the workers, some of the folks filling sandbags near Des Moines. They're still trying hard to keep the Raccoon River out of downtown Des Moines. And he did his best to comfort some of the victims of the flood. ...

PAULA ZAHN: Harry, you finally gave in. It's the first time you've used an umbrella all this morning. I was wondering when you were going to succumb.

SMITH: The rain wasn't so bad before, but it's such a downpour now. I can't—I can't see 'cause it's—just—even with my glasses off I can't see, so I thought I'd better use an umbrella, at least for a couple minutes. I'll tell you . . .

ZAHN: It just—you hear what they're dealing with and then sending up help to Des Moines, it's just unbelievable!

SMITH: Aren't these people something? Gosh, I just can't get over it. I want to give you a little illustration. The mayor was talking about how hard it rained here. I got a couple hours sleep last night, so I'm bright-eyed and bushy tailed. I didn't know it rained that hard here, unfortunately, last night that it was blowing the manhole covers off. Take a look at this picture. It's just down the block from us. See that gurgle, gurgle, splublub-lub-lub? ... That's a manhole cover. It rained so hard, the storm sewers are so full, it's even rattling. It almost sounds like a pot of boiling carrots on the stove. Listen to this.

ZAHN: Wow!

SMITH: Can you hear it?

ZAHN: Oh, absolutely. ... So what—how much rainfall has there been overnight? Can—can anybody get an accurate stati . . .

SMITH: You know what? I don't think . . .

ZAHN: Is it inches?

SMITH: I don't think anybody's had—anybody's had a chance to find out. And I'll tell you what, as hard as it's raining over here—the mayor had a—had the best description because these levees are like jelly and it just—water's just slickering over the—over the top. And it's hard to work out there now; it's hard to move around. It's—it makes it extra dangerous. We—we need this rain to go away. . . .

ZAHN: Harry Smith, are you ever going to come home? I'm sure your wife and son would love to see you.

SMITH: They would. And, you know what, Paula? The more we stay on this river, this story isn't going away, it's not going anyplace, it keeps going. I don't know when I'm coming home, quite frankly.

ZAHN: All right.

SMITH: But I'd like to get dry.

ZAHN: Yeah, I bet.

CHAPTER FIVE

—◄o►—

Jimmy slept at his own house on July 15. Suzie was there, and the couple lay low for the night. As heavy rains battered their roof for hours and halted activity outside, Jimmy and Suzie shared a quiet evening—the first in weeks—as the Illinois storms lulled them in their prefab ranch.

As far as Jimmy knew, Dan didn't have people over either. The locals were recovering from a three day bender and the summer squall was a good excuse to stay in and watch flood coverage. Suzie retired early for the evening because she had to be at the 18 Wheeler truck stop in Taylor by 8:30 a.m. for first shift. Her husband stayed up until midnight—early for him—and then joined Suzie in their cramped bedroom.

He awoke at seven o'clock on July 16 to the sound of Suzie's hairdryer coming from the bathroom around the corner and the television in the living room blaring *CBS This Morning*. Harry Smith was broadcasting live from Quincy, and Suzie peeked her head out from the bathroom to catch glimpses of the scene on the river. The hairdryer drowned out the sound of Smith's doomsday transmission: The water, he said, was cresting after the river rose several millimeters from the previous night's rains. In addition, even though the river was cresting, Smith spoke of the tremendous pressure butting up against the levee walls. Suzie turned off her hairdryer just in time to hear him say that folks shouldn't expect the danger to subside for at least another 20, maybe even 30 days as the water slowly receded. Jimmy heard a bunch of garbled sounds coming from the house's interior, and then he fell back to sleep.

Suzie buttoned her 18 Wheeler shirt, turned off the TV, and hollered from the hallway that she'd speak to her husband later. Jimmy grunted from beneath the covers while Suzie closed the door and started off on the 20-minute drive that would take her across the Bayview Bridge and past the relief effort.

Jimmy finally dragged himself out of bed around 10:30 a.m. He switched on the television, which was now the local broadcast repeating the same story he'd heard for weeks. The only difference this time was that the reporters said the river was done rising.

Temperatures were rising themselves in the late morning hours as the mercury topped out around 92 degrees. Jimmy really didn't want to punch in at Burger King, not when he had an excuse to avoid the joint.

He called Troy Lyons to see what his buddy was up to. Troy was also enjoying a hiatus from the party scene and was lazing around his mother's house. He had no plans. Jimmy suggested heading over to the levee and helping out. The public calls for volunteers had significantly diminished, but West Quincy was still the place to be. They grabbed some Taco Bell around noon and set out over the Bayview Bridge. Jimmy parked his Monte Carlo on the shoulder of the bridge in Missouri, where a knot of soldiers stood milling around.

The two walked to Knapheide, where the usual array of National Guardsmen, Fabius River Drainage District employees, and community do-gooders mingled and awaited instructions. Jimmy and Troy checked in with a Guardsman, and Jimmy explained that he'd received a crash course in locating trouble spots earlier that week. The soldier responded that the mission that day, July 16, was to save the Bayview Bridge. The levee, he said, was holding and the river was cooperating so far.

"It's a matter of spotting trouble spots and responding on the double-quick," he explained. Jimmy nodded and the soldier instructed him to patrol a mile-long portion of levee north of the Bayview Bridge but south of the railroad bridge. He told Jimmy that if he found something worrisome to grab a Guardsman immediately. Jimmy agreed. Troy was needed for some muscle work, as he didn't have his buddy's impromptu levee knowledge. The two parted company and Jimmy joined another man who introduced himself as Rudy and who also had remedial levee knowledge. They started up the land side of the West Quincy levee toward the top.

◄○►

Norman Haerr walked the floodplain with a renewed confidence. The pounding wind and rain did not cause the Mississippi River to breach his levee, and so far, Haerr was batting .1000 on his watch. His radio continued to chirp with news of possible trouble spots up by Durgin's Creek, but the walls were holding and the river was stable. Despite earlier reports from the Quincy Filter Plant that the river was rising, by midday reports were that the Mississippi was tapering off at 32 feet, and falling. Haerr was confident that the worst was behind him, that his district was about to become a nexus of teamwork personified.

While Norman Haerr disseminated information to response parties, Sgt. Duke Kelly of the Missouri Air National Guard had already been at work for the last seven hours. His unit had punched in around 6:30 a.m., just as it had for the past week. The hot, humid air was making the work much more oppressive than it had been. They were patrolling an area of the levee south of the Bayview Bridge, and seemingly every time Kelly looked north, he saw truckloads of sandbags and straw arriving from Quincy. Around 1:30 p.m., word filtered down the levee that food and water were about to arrive at the base of the bridge. Kelly told his men that if they were hungry, they should start heading north—about three-quarters of a mile from where they threw sandbags and laid straw. As he delivered the message, his own stomach started grumbling, and he began to feel dehydrated. The sun was directly overhead and his leg muscles were sore from patrolling the saturated levee. Sgt. Kelly decided to get some grub. He turned north and walked along the shelf of the dam with his men.

◄○►

Jimmy and Rudy combed the dike, making sure to pay particular attention to the seams in the plastic tarp as they searched for boils. There was hardly anyone else on their mile-long stretch of ridge. Although they'd been instructed to walk the area between the Bayview and the railroad bridges, Norman Haerr hadn't considered those areas a problem. Coast Guard boats were patrolling the dam from the river, but very few personnel concentrated on that one-mile stretch. Because the Memorial Bridge was already under water—and the Memorial lay south of the Bayview and way south of the railroad bridge—Fabius River Drainage District employees figured that the fight to save the Bayview would come from the south.

At times throughout the day, as Jimmy looked south and saw the commotion happening more than a mile from where he walked, he was convinced that he was wasting time. Clearly all the action was on the other side of the bridge. He and Rudy discussed whether they should leave their post and head south, but Rudy remained steadfast. "We have a job to do," he reminded Jimmy. "Let's just do what they told us and then we'll go grab some food. I heard the guys in the boats saying it was on its way."

The two men slowly walked north when Jimmy heard the ground splash under his feet. He stopped cold in his tracks to realize that he was standing in a puddle of water. It wasn't a huge crater by any means, but nonetheless, it was a body of standing water on a part of levee that had no sandbags on it: just plastic tarp. Jimmy thought back to the crash course on levees he'd received six days earlier and recognized that he'd actually come across a trouble spot: standing water on plastic meant either seepage or overtopping. The levee was taking on more water than it was designed to in that location. He looked toward the Mississippi River for a Coast Guard boat, but a smattering of skinny cottonwood trees blocked his view.

"Rudy," Jimmy shouted to his partner who had walked another 15 feet. Rudy turned around and saw Jimmy just standing there, pointing down. Jimmy had that trademark grin on his face. "Come look at this."

Rudy walked to where Jimmy stood and looked down at his partner's work boots. Then he looked up and met Jimmy's gaze. "Man, I walked right by it and didn't even notice. Think it's a trouble spot?" Rudy asked. Jimmy was quick with an answer, as he once again felt empowered by someone looking to him for information.

"Yep, sure is," he replied. "This is what the Guard told me about."

"Well, we've got to find an officer," Rudy declared, "though I don't see any around. Heck, I don't see anyone around at all."

"Yeah, guess we were in the right spot after all. Tell you what: You walk north over to the railroad bridge and find someone. I'll walk south to the Bayview. We'll both find officers and bring them here."

"Okay. Grab me a sandwich while you're down there."

"Will do."

They left as abruptly as they'd met. Jimmy was fatigued, but he walked as fast as the soft, sandy levee would allow. He had three-quarters of a mile to go until he'd reach the bridge, and he was anxious to tell someone about his find. The white T-shirt clung to his chest and upper back, and his blue jeans, also wet from perspiration, chaffed his thighs as he moved. He panted softly at first, and then gasped a little as he walked: All those years of smoking cigarettes were taking their toll. He finally approached the Bayview and saw a bunch of uniformed men checking in with one man in particular: He wore the same camouflage as the others, but this man clearly was in charge—of something. Jimmy made a beeline for the authority figure who stood at the base of the Bayview Bridge, munching on a sandwich.

Jimmy approached the man he'd spotted half a click upriver as he was biting into his lunch. The officer responded when Jimmy pardoned himself by covering his mouth and muttering, "Yeah?"

"I've been patrolling just north of here and I've found what I think is a trouble spot. Could you come look at it?"

Sgt. Duke Kelly looked around and saw that his men were finishing their sandwiches and getting ready to head back to where they'd been working all day. It was close to two o'clock, and the area this sweaty man spoke of wasn't part of his sector. Still, if the guy was right, it was worth checking out.

Sgt. Kelly finished the last bites of his sandwich and instructed Jimmy to lead him to the spot.

They made their way up the levee and walked at a labored pace in the direction of where Jimmy had noticed the standing water. Duke had a full belly and trudged along the shelf. Jimmy was so spent from the walk to the Bayview Bridge that he didn't mind the casual ambling. He had forgotten Rudy's sandwich, though.

They walked about half a mile when Sgt. Kelly finally spoke up.

"How much farther is this spot?" he asked his guide.

"About another quarter or half mile," Jimmy replied, still keeping in step.

Sgt. Kelly stopped walking and looked north along the levee. He saw yard upon yard of black tarp. In the areas where the plastic hadn't been laid, he noticed that the sand-based levee was packed from the previous day's rain. Sgt. Kelly followed the landslide of the dam with his eyes and saw no water seeping down the built-up wall. None at the base, either. "You know, my concern is with my men south of the Bayview. I really don't have time to walk all the way up there. Keep an eye on it and if it gets worse, let somebody know."

With that, Sgt. Kelly pivoted and started walking back toward his troops. Jimmy was left standing on the levee by himself. He recommenced his walk back to the trouble spot, all the while keeping an eye out for any other officers—for any Guardsmen whatsoever. There were none.

When he returned, Rudy was nowhere to be found. But the trouble spot was still there. In fact, it was spreading and there was some more volume to the puddle. Jimmy knelt down low and inspected the area at eye level. He saw the faint traces of moving water. It was slowly coming over the top of the levee and collecting in a widening pool. He stood abruptly.

"Holy shit!" he said aloud, though no one was nearby to hear him. He looked around in all directions for another minute to see if a Coast Guard boat was patrolling or a soldier was perhaps walking along the levee's base. The area was devoid of people, just some sandbags stacked every few yards to hold down the plastic tarp. After a minute, Jimmy realized that he was all alone. Rudy wasn't coming back, and because this section of the levee wasn't a major concern, neither was anyone else. He grabbed some nearby sandbags that were being used to hold down the tarp and threw them on top of the puddle.

◄o►

Dusk slowly crept onto the floodplain. Sticky, humid air stirred up by multiple bodies moving through lingering moisture finally cooled as the sun sank behind the western cornstalks. Volunteers' efforts slowly ground to a halt. The river had crested: 31.67 feet was the high watermark and it was holding steady.

Just before eight o'clock, the area was still bathed in the few remaining remnants of natural light. A Quincy teen named Brian was stacking the last of the day's sandbags 200 yards north of the Bayview Bridge with three other 18-year-olds.

The men had sweat clear through their T-shirts and blue jeans. A fiery sun had roasted their exposed skin throughout the day, and the burlap sacks rubbed their hands and forearms raw. Now that the sun was disappearing, their bodies emanated their own dry heat, like bricks that smolder for hours after baking in a kiln. To the south, National Guardsmen prepared for their evening foot patrols. The Coast Guard's plastic boats had cut their engines and gently drifted where they were moored, and the massive barges silently sat in their adoptive, makeshift docks, still tied to a cluster of trees.

Brian ran his dirty fingers through his greasy hair and plopped down on some sandbags. He wiped the front and back of his hands on his soiled blue jeans and grabbed a mini cooler of water. He swigged hard on the bottle, paying no mind to the excess liquid that missed his mouth and cascaded down his face and chin. The cool water stamped out a roasting in his chest and he gulped as fast as his throat would allow.

Just as Brian took a mouthful of water into his stomach, he heard a loud popping sound in perfect timing with his swallowing. He quickly pulled the bottle from his lips and addressed his buddies.

"Did you hear that?" Brian asked the other teens.

"Yeah," one responded. "What the hell was it?"

Brian looked around guardedly. It sounded like a cross between a champagne bottle uncorking and a gunshot.

"Look, the trees are moving!" announced one of the guys. About a half-mile north of where they sat, the cottonwood trees that flanked the Mississippi River began to sway violently. They stood out from the other vegetation on the levee because they were rocking back and forth and yet there was no wind.

Somewhere off in the distance—Brian couldn't determine where—he heard a frightened and bewildered voice.

"The levee broke!" it announced in a high-pitched scream. The sound waves reverberated off the earthen dam, bounced off the limestone bluffs across the river and seemed to crescendo into the lone sound on the floodplain. Brian and his coworkers held each others' stares for only a moment. Instinctively, they all made a dash down the levee's wall to a pickup truck sitting at the base of the barrier.

Brian jumped in the driver's seat and turned the engine over. He twisted in his seat and looked out the back window before leaving the scene. As if in a movie, a huge wall of water was surging toward his truck. He swung back around as though his head were on a swivel, shifted into drive, and stomped on the gas pedal with such force that his arms locked at the elbows and his back dug into the vinyl upholstery. The head of the water wall came within inches of his tires when he floored the truck and sped to the Bayview Bridge. The teen gunned the accelerator of the aging vehicle and crossed over the Mississippi River as one of the passengers noticed a peculiar eddy of water churning in the middle of the river. A vortex opened in the levee and the river seemed to be flowing upstream and then out into the distance, west of the trees.

Brian made it across the bridge and parked on the Quincy side of the river at the intersection of Third and Broadway. The teens filed out and gazed over the river from atop the bluffs. It was the most surreal sight their young eyes had ever seen.

Norman Haerr stood in the threshold of the Knapheide Manufacturing Company and spoke on the radio with his son, who was monitoring the trouble spot up at Durgin's Creek. The levee was holding strong, Haerr was informed, but there was still a tremendous amount of pressure on its walls. Haerr advised his son to stay on it and radio in if the problem worsened.

He put down the walkie-talkie and leaned against the doorframe. Haerr saw Guardsmen beginning to depart for their 8 p.m. patrols, and he heard the sound of choppers not far overhead. It wasn't an unusual sound, as both the military and the news helicopters continued to traverse the floodplain each evening until about 9 p.m., when the natural light had virtually vanished. Just then, a Knapheide employee approached him from behind.

"Sir, you're wanted on the phone."

Norman Haerr turned and asked the worker who it was, as official chatter was conducted over the two-way.

"It's the National Guard. We have a reported levee break in your district. Do you know of it?" the man asked pointedly.

Haerr had but a moment to process this information. He was looking out over the river and everything seemed to be fine. As he began to speak, a helicopter's rotor caused the air around him to echo and he felt wind pressure engulfing his body. A military chopper was landing on a designated helipad near Knapheide. Haerr didn't have a chance to answer his employee because the roaring rotor drowned out all other sound. Just then, another Knapheide employee trotted up to Norman and got in his ear.

"Sir, they want you to go up with the helicopter and confirm a break."

The commissioner was shocked to the point of speechlessness. It couldn't have broken, he reasoned, not if it didn't during that monsoon a couple nights earlier. Haerr needed confirmation with his own eyes, so he hurriedly boarded the Huey and was instantly whisked away a mile north of Knapheide.

Norman Haerr had seen some unusual occurrences in his 30-plus years of working on the Mississippi River system at West Quincy, occurrences such as entire crops being washed out by heavy rains. But what was 100 feet below wingtip was the damnedest of them all. The Mississippi River was streaming into the countryside at a furious pace. A huge 100-foot hole was blown out of the levee, and gushing water was consuming his own field. Most unreal was a giant derrick barge—bulky, long, and impressive—floating over his soybeans. It was a farmer's worst nightmare, worse than a scorching drought or a swarming horde of insects. Yet at the moment, he didn't have time to mourn the loss of his autumn crop: His first concern was for his son up at Durgin's Creek. He got on the radio and shouted over the noise of the helicopter.

"We have a break!" Haerr hollered. He tried to describe the location, but the rotors made too much noise and caused too much static in the background. "It's time to move out!" he screamed before pulling the radio back down. The commissioner didn't know if his transmission was received.

The chopper patrolled for a while longer with Haerr sitting silently by the open side door. He could see both people and cars heading toward Fellowship Hall five miles inland in Taylor, Missouri, and he had a bird's-eye view of the river gaining ground on the floodplain. The Bayview Bridge was taking on water to the south, and Haerr's doomsday scenario of what would happen should the bridge flood was unfolding before his eyes.

There was no longer any way to get from Missouri to Illinois without taking a five-hour diversion through Iowa. He thought about all the families that were being split in half because of the flood: A Quincy relief worker who lived five miles from home would now have to drive 350 miles to see his wife and children. Haerr barely had time to wrap his head around this when he saw an actual house—a white, one-story farmhouse—floating down the Mississippi. He sighed and closed his eyes, praying that nobody was in that home and that the owners had somehow made it off the river bottom and inland to safety.

After 30 minutes in the air, the chopper maneuvered west toward Taylor to drop off its stunned passenger. As it hovered over a landing spot, Haerr heard a giant explosion in the distance. It was so potent and piercing that the blast was clearly audible over the thundering rotors.

Throughout the evening, people gathered en masse at the 18 Wheeler truck stop in Taylor. It was about six miles into the Missouri interior and essentially safe ground. Suzie Scott had been there well past her six o'clock "punch out" time, but her services were still needed because of the steady influx of customers. At around 8:20 p.m., the first of the volunteers arrived reporting the break. They said that the Bayview Bridge, as far as they knew, was still open, but that it was beginning to flood in its own right. It was only a matter of time before the National Guard would shut it down, they reported.

Suzie immediately ran to the phone to call her husband: They hadn't spoken since she'd left early that morning, and they'd barely spoken then. There was no answer. Then she called her parents in neighboring Palmyra,

Missouri, to tell them she'd be staying there for the night, if not for the fore-seeable future.

◄o►

James Scott walked along the levee by the Bayview Bridge when word filtered down that the walls had been breached. He was shocked like everyone else. There were no apparent warning signs because the breach seemed to come out of nowhere.

His initial reaction was to jump in his car and hightail it home. As he descended from the levee, Michelle McCormack, a reporter with WGEM-TV in Quincy who was looking for an interview with an on-the-scene source, approached him. She asked Jimmy if he'd mind doing a brief on-camera segment for the evening news. The Bayview Bridge was still open, and the water hadn't reached the point where he stood, so he figured he had time.

For the TV people, Jimmy looked the part of a guy who'd been working on a levee, though he wasn't covered from head-to-toe with sand and dirt. His T-shirt hung loosely off his shoulders. His blue jeans were also relatively clean, but his arms were grimy and his baseball cap dirty, and taken together, he had an appearance that was good for television. For his part, Jimmy couldn't help but think that all of Quincy would see his image on their screens—that he was about to be the face of the flood.

Michelle McCormack asked rudimentary questions along the lines of "what was your job detail?" and "what went through your mind when you learned the levee broke?" Jimmy stood there awkwardly, hands in his pockets as he fielded the questions. He spoke directly to Michelle about how he'd been out patrolling the levee earlier that day. Then he mentioned that he'd seen a trouble spot.

A seasoned reporter, McCormack probed that response. She asked him what he did to shore up the problem, and that's when a nervous James Scott turned into a boastful James Scott. He bragged about pulling sandbags from one area of the levee and stacking them atop a leaky area. Then his face tightened up and contorted as he fought back surging emotion. He spoke of helplessness, of all the long hours and days of work washed away like so much sediment. Jimmy's demeanor and his sputtering explanations moved Michelle. He was clearly rattled. She placed her other hand—the one that wasn't holding a microphone—on Jimmy's shoulder. The cameras stopped rolling and Michelle thanked him for his time and for his heroic effort. Jimmy nodded and thanked her, too.

He felt proud, as if the Lions Club had just honored him. No longer was Jimmy thinking of returning home. Now he wanted to help the drainage district, the troops, or anyone who was willing to let him pitch in.

Down by the Bayview Bridge, where his car was parked, Jimmy noticed some people from the Coast Guard loading boats off a truck and into the river. He asked if he could help and they told him to grab the side of a boat and start pushing it off the truck ramp and into the water. It took about an hour to unload all the vessels, and Jimmy's back, which was already sore from lifting sandbags, was on the verge of giving out.

A Coast Guardsman asked him if he could swim and when he answered that he could, Jimmy was told to get in the boat and help patrol the levee and keep his eyes peeled for other breaks. He boarded the 22-footer, but the motor wouldn't start. The Guard messed with the outboard for 20 minutes before he ordered Jimmy out of the boat and went looking for his superior officer.

It was dark and the only illuminations were truck lights and the lights of Quincy at a safe distance 100 feet above and across the river. Jimmy started making his way back to his Monte Carlo when Michelle McCormack reappeared with her cameraman. She asked if Jimmy would do another interview, this time for WGEM's live 10 o'clock feed. Jimmy readily agreed: He liked being a TV star. The cameraman got in position while Michelle held her earpiece in place and awaited instructions from her producer across the river. Jimmy stood there silently, waiting for his next 15 minutes of fame.

◄o►

Detective Neal Baker of the Quincy Police Department was at home unpacking his suitcase. He'd returned that afternoon from Advanced

Hostage Negotiation training at the FBI's headquarters in Quantico, Virginia. It was getting late and he was getting tired, so he plopped down on his couch just in time to catch the 10 o'clock local news. His brother, Det. Bruce Baker, had called him earlier that evening to tell him of the levee break, and Neal wanted to see what sort of updates were coming in.

Although he'd been gone for the past five days, the Quincy Police Department had been running on all cylinders in his absence. With the thousands of volunteers in the area came a need for stepped up patrols. Most people who descended on Quincy were goodhearted, so the cops weren't as worried about their activities. They were more concerned with a wave of break-ins and robberies that might come with such a population influx, and they were also consciously aware of increased noise disturbances. Tellingly, Det. Neal Baker was in for a long shift the following day. He turned to the news both to unwind as well as to see what sort of catastrophe he'd be walking into tomorrow.

Before Det. Baker had a chance to ease into a comfortable position— and even before the TV's picture came into focus—he heard a familiar voice coming from the tube. He couldn't place it at first, but there was something about the low, slow Midwestern drawl that he recognized. Cops, especially in medium-sized towns like Quincy, seldom forget a face or a voice of a perpetrator. And Neal Baker knew right away that this voice had crossed his path in the past.

As the picture filled his screen and the audio filled his den, the detective was floored by what he saw. There on the Bayview Bridge, right next to the levee, stood James Scott, telling a reporter on live TV that he'd been working in West Quincy all day long, out of his love for mankind and a desire to save the community.

Neal Baker stared at the TV with a perplexed gaze, his forehead rumpled and his mouth slightly agape. Everything James Scott was saying went against what the seasoned cop knew of the guy. He thought Jimmy was having a hard time answering the reporter's softball questions. He was looking around skittishly as he spoke, and as far as the detective was concerned, this guy looked far too clean to have worked on a levee all day long. He started to notice some other subtle peculiarities: Jimmy wasn't wearing a lifejacket, he had sand and dirt up his arms, and he didn't have anyone with him. Neal Baker knew that volunteers were always supposed to be in pairs.

The off-duty cop shifted into detective mode. He thought for a moment about calling the TV station and speaking with the news director. Instead, he picked up the phone when Michelle McCormack's report concluded and called his brother.

PART TWO

Fear and Loathing in Quincy

CHAPTER SIX

◄○►

The Pepsi Cola Bottling Company on 12th and Locust Street was a big employer in Quincy. That's where Robert Scott, Jimmy's father, spent his working days. Robert prided himself on being a tradesman. There was honor in that. Sharon, Jimmy's mother, worked as a caretaker for the town elderly, spending her days and many nights in the homes of indigents who could barely communicate their needs.

Their children were a clan. Each one born a year apart from the other, Mike, Jimmy, and Jeff roved in a pack throughout childhood. Mike was the oldest and led by example, though he often took his cues from older half brother Dan Leake, who was out of the house by the time the boys were old enough to stay home alone.

They were close in age, but Mike was usually left in charge because he had a year on Jimmy and two years on Jeff. Nonetheless, sibling rivalries between the eldest and the middle child often ensued, especially over control of the television dial and over who wore what. The boys shared everything—including clothes—and Mike usually got first dibs.

Robert and Sharon were concerned parents at heart despite not always being around. Having three mouths to feed meant that work came before family outings, so the boys were often deposited at Calvary Baptist Church. Calvary had youth programs on Sunday, Monday, and Wednesday, and Mike, Jimmy, and Jeff participated in Pastor Woodrow McCaleb's AWANA program. For Robert and Sharon, AWANA was as much cheap babysitting as it was a religious revival. The boys knew it, too.

They were good Christians and athletes. They played every sport the church offered, excelling at baseball and soccer, and they learned scripture. It wasn't until they were old enough to watch Dan Leake and his buddies drinking and smoking out behind the garage that church attendance became a chore. When they were 12, 11, and 10 in 1981, they were more fascinated with the music Dan played and the language he and his buddies used than they were in the church's hymnals and Pastor McCaleb's sermons.

The Scott boys were three crew-cuts who began exploring as much of Quincy as daylight would allow. Come night time, when they became too nervous to venture out on some of the main streets for fear of the city's 10 p.m. curfew for children under 17, they'd bike up and down Elm Street, where Robert and Sharon's modest three-bedroom ranch sat among the other cookie-cutter 1950s houses. Even with their limited ramblings, the boys got into plenty of mischief.

They'd steal decorative statues and wind chimes off front porches. When one of the three was able to snatch a pack of smokes and a lighter off of a friend's parents' kitchen table, they'd lurk in the shadows of the giant elm trees on Elm Street while Mike and Jimmy puffed as many cigarettes as their young lungs could take. They wouldn't let Jeff smoke because he was "too young."

Mike called the shots and mapped out their clandestine missions, but Jimmy constantly engaged in a game of one-upmanship with his big brother. Mike would pull up some flowers, and Jimmy would snap off a car's hood ornament. Mike would let air out of a tire, and Jimmy would slash it with his Swiss Army knife. Mike would ring a doorbell late at night and take off down Elm as fast as he could when the slumbering resident woke to see who was calling on him, and Jimmy would do the same, though he'd retreat behind a nearby car or tree in order to capture the expression on the home-owner's face. Little Jeff, for his part, never said much; the older brothers liked having him along as a sidekick.

They got away with their petty vandalism and they were never picked up for curfew violation. As the months ticked by and the winter doldrums gave way to springtime regeneration, the Scott boys' mischief grew, and the stealth missions became more frequent.

Jimmy liked being the center of attention at the schoolyard and he often boasted of his late-night undertakings to anyone who would listen. He had the collective ear of the other children when he did speak because they were too afraid of parental repercussions to do what he did. Their attention emboldened his behavior and prompted Jimmy to sculpt his "bad boy" image. He started smoking cigarettes regularly by age 12 and he was careful to be within view of a fellow student, so they would tell others. That, Jimmy thought, made him cool.

Kids, like their parents, were fond of rumor, and Jimmy quickly distinguished himself in adolescent circles as the boy who feared nothing. While smoking one day, he decided to light some dead leaves on fire. Such a perilous act—playing with fire—gave him a rush. Blooms were bursting forth slowly as the warm temperatures brought more pleasant weather. The nights remained brisk, and the 50-plus degree chill heightened the scent of burning foliage.

At first, Jimmy and Mike, who had also developed a taste for fire, would round up all the roughage they could scavenge behind neighborhood homes. They'd set these little blazes and admire their handiwork. Crisp, burning leaves have an aromatic smell, and no one in the neighborhood ever seemed to mind. The Scott boys couldn't differentiate whether bystanders were ignorant of their activities, or whether the locals simply turned a blind eye. Either way, they were getting away with it.

In April 1982, when the Quincy school year was in its homestretch, Robert and Sharon Scott were working twice as many hours. They wanted to send their boys to camp that summer, so they worked incessantly for their children's benefit. Loving and dutiful, they had even less time though to keep tabs on their sons' comings and goings. Jimmy became acutely aware of other Quincy families traveling together for spring break or picnicking at South Park, and he and Mike often biked to the park on weekends and glommed on to schoolmates' parents. They'd kick the soccer ball around, hooting and hollering in the grasslands not far from the banks of the Mississippi River. Mike and Jimmy watched as other adults joyfully played with their children. The parents were encouraging—they prodded their children to try new games and enjoy the day. Sharon and Robert Scott wanted their children to have the same luxuries and sense of family as the other parents, but their relentless work schedules precluded their spending more time with the boys.

One sunny Saturday, Mike and Jimmy, along with tag-along Jeff, rode their BMX bikes to South Park and joined a baseball game. Scores of families gathered around the diamond and shouted for their boys when they stepped up to the plate. Some parents cheered for the Scotts, though they were mostly there to root for their own children.

The game lasted well into the afternoon, and Mike, Jimmy, and even 11-year-old Jeff focused on nothing more than playing ball. For them, the afternoon of April 24, 1982, was as it should be for boys their age. School was still a day and a half away and the air was warm enough that they could wear T-shirts and sweatpants. Jimmy swung his bat with the force of a high school athlete, and the 12-year-old rounded the bases and headed for home while the Mississippi River—the river he was raised on—ambled by in the distance. He couldn't see it from the park, but the sound of barge horns resonated throughout the town. Jimmy loved to hear the noises that came off the river. They served to ground him and they made him feel as though he was living in a consequential part of the country. He hadn't been to St. Louis, but he knew the river was going there. Distant places: That's what the Mississippi meant. And the clattering voices of his friends and the ding of a metal bat hitting a baseball made the day nearly perfect. It was, to be sure, springtime in Quincy.

At around five o'clock, the various families started pulling their boys out of the game and headed home for supper. The lads protested and begged to stay for just one more inning, and some parents conceded, but as the sun sank into the Mississippi River, one by one the ballplayers bid farewell to their friends and walked off.

Come half-past five, Mike, Jimmy, and Jeff were the only boys left on the field. They'd been merry and carefree moments earlier. Now all the satisfaction was drained from their systems. They said nothing to each other because no one wanted to admit loneliness.

They were in no hurry to get home because it was likely empty. Jimmy had some cigarettes in his backpack, so he and Mike decided to ride around town and do a little smoking.

The three boys peddled north along 12th Street, past the century-old homes with manicured lawns and expensive cars parked out front. When they got to State Street, Mike, Jimmy, and Jeff cast their gaze on the giant mansions. They were well-kept and striking, with shiny, freshly-painted turrets and wraparound porches. In front of one of them, a husband and wife were sitting on a blanket with their toddler and rolling a ball to him. The child kicked at it, barely making contact, and yet his parents applauded and cheered as if he were Pelé.

It was a depressing visual for the boys. They felt low enough being the only ones at the park without parents on hand, and now they were observing a couple decidedly younger than their parents living in lavish surroundings and idly lounging with their child. Each of the Scott boys grimaced as he rode past the mansion on State and 12th, but no one said a word. They shared an understood, acquiescent silence.

As they continued north along 12th Street, the town's staging began to change. Lavish houses became much more basic. Lawns were patchy from a long, cold winter, and in lieu of turrets, most homes had leaky roofs and damp basements. The Scott boys were peddling back to blue-collar Quincy, leaving behind well-appointed, upper-class neighborhoods. Mike was in the lead. He squeezed his right handbrake and skidded out his back tire at the corner of 13th and Maine with Jimmy and Jeff in tow.

Mike straddled the center bar of his BMX and walked the bike up to the ionic columns of Webster Elementary School. As it was Saturday, not a single light was on in the building. Jimmy and Jeff dismounted their bicycles and walked them up to Mike.

"Let me have one of them smokes, Jim," Mike said. Jimmy removed his backpack and fiddled in the big compartment for the soft pack of Camel Lights and the red Bic lighter. He handed a cigarette to his brother and then lit one up himself. Jeff asked if he could have one, too.

"No, boy," Jimmy replied as he lit his Camel and took a labored drag. "You're too young."

Mike got off his bike and started walking around the aged brick school. He stopped every few feet for a drag on his cigarette. Jimmy stood at the front door with Jeff at his side. They watched Mike walk away while Jimmy smoked and wheezed. A minute later, Mike called out from the distance. Dusk was settling in, and Jimmy could faintly make out his brother's silhouette.

"Jimmy, come over here," Mike belted out in a loud whisper. Jimmy turned to Jeff and shushed him, even though the boy hadn't said a word since he'd asked for a cigarette. Perhaps Mike had found something worth stealing, Jimmy thought. He didn't call back, as he knew—even at the tender age of 12—that sneakiness was a craft.

Jimmy stamped out his Camel, which he smoked to the filter, and he and Jeff walked their bikes along the length of Webster Elementary. Mike motioned for them to follow him around the corner. He laid his bike behind an adjacent oak tree and encouraged them to do the same. Then Mike walked another 10 yards to a rusty, unstable-looking metal staircase that traversed its way up the side of the three-story building.

He regarded his brother with a mischievous gaze. Jimmy looked back wide-eyed, studying his brother's face for a game plan. Silently, Mike started climbing the fire escape. When he got to the third step, he turned his head. With a quick flick of his neck, Mike motioned for his brothers to follow.

◄O►

Webster Elementary School was an aging hulk. Red bricks, indigenous to the Midwest and built to withstand inclement Mississippi River weather, managed to stave off the ice in winter. Although the bricks baked in the summer, they had shielded the thousands of students who had passed through Webster's threshold ever since the doors first opened in 1904.

The school was preceded by the original Webster Elementary, constructed in 1855, on the same location at the intersection of 13th and Maine Streets. Back then, Webster Elementary—only the third school to be erected in Quincy—was a three-story brick structure that severely lacked creature comforts. Built for the shockingly low price of $5,000, each room had a wood-burning fireplace, though its single-paned windows still allowed brisk winds to whistle through its seams in winter.

Quincy became a more affluent port town in the 1870s, which enabled an 1873 remodeling of the classrooms. The remodeling of Webster's interior transformed it into a bastion of academic excellence for years to come, until a fire ravaged the wooden innards in 1881. New floors were put in, desks and blackboards were replaced, and the brick exterior was given a facelift the next year. But contractors neglected to attend to the joists in the basement, and they failed to recognize that the fire's incessant heat, which had burned for quite some time because the fire department was negligently under-staffed, bent most of the braces installed to bolster the weight of hardwood floors. Come 1902, although the brick shell maintained its structural integrity, children were complaining to their parents that the building shud-dered when winds whipped in off the plains.

The city council decided something needed to be done. Webster Elementary—the old Webster Elementary—was demolished in the summer of 1902, and the new Webster Elementary—the one that would be equipped with all the latest turn-of-the-century technology, opened its doors to Quincy youths in 1904. Thousands of students learned their reading, writing, and arithmetic there, including the three Scott brothers in the late 1970s and early 1980s. They'd catch the Webster school bus on the corner of 11th and Elm five days a week.

Webster Elementary School was now home to the Head Start program, classes for pregnant high school girls, and vocational training for plumbers, as a new elementary school had recently opened.

Mike Scott slowly ascended the rusty fire escape while Quincy was bathed in an orange twilight. Jimmy and little Jeff carefully followed behind. The stairs gently rocked in perfect timing with the boys' steps. They were careful not to stampede up the flights and attract attention. A delicate ping sound rever-berated with each soft footfall, and Mike's sneakers caused flecks of oxidized metal to fall from their source and pepper Jimmy and Jeff down below.

When he got to the second story landing, Mike stopped and sized up the double-hung window. The thick white frame was large and heavy. It had numerous coats of industrial strength paint, and the panes were specked with dirt and grime.

Mike put his hand under his T-shirt and pressed the fabric against the glass. He put a little pressure behind it as he tried to rub away the years of soot. Mike wanted to catch a glimpse of his third grade classroom, down the hall and to the left. Elementary school was somewhat of a fond memory for him. He wasn't a standout, but he wasn't the class stooge either. There were the occasional reprimands for talking out of turn and he sometimes bullied the weaker kids, but the teachers liked his tenaciousness.

Mike put his face up to the streaked transparency and cupped his hands on the sides of his eyes to block out the glare. The faint light shining from the outside enabled him to see down the darkened hallway. The school was eerily still. Mike had never been to the building when it wasn't bustling. He and his brothers had been redistricted to Lincoln Elementary when Webster was phased out, and they hadn't returned since it closed its doors.

Jimmy climbed to where Mike stood and muscled himself into a nook below his brother. He too peered inside. Just an empty school, he observed, yet there was something alluring about the prospect of having free reign of their old haunts.

"Are you thinking what I'm thinking, Mikey?" Jimmy queried his brother.

Mike didn't respond. Instead, he pulled his face off the glass, grabbed the window at its base, and heaved. The thing wouldn't budge.

"Gimme a hand with this, Jimmy," he said. His brother pushed against the glass with both hands. The window remained in place while the boys grunted and Jimmy's sweaty hands screeched on the surface. Jeff stood on the landing behind the two boys and looked around nervously.

"Aw, it's locked," proclaimed Jimmy.

"Stand back," replied Mike. Jimmy grabbed Jeff by the shoulders and pulled him against the hand rail on the second story fire escape. Mike plopped down on his butt and raised his sneakers. "Keep an eye out for cops, Jim," he said while his back remained turned. Jimmy nodded in agreement, even though Mike couldn't see his affirmative response.

The 13-year-old gave a light mule-kick to the glass, but nothing happened. He tried a second time with a little more force, and again, nothing happened. On the third kick, Mike put some heft behind the thrust and the windowpane shattered inward, splaying several large pieces of glass and thousands of miniscule shards all over the frame and the inside floor. A few tiny pieces could be heard bouncing off the fire escape as they fell to the ground.

"Get down!" Mike shouted in a loud whisper. All three boys fell to their bellies and put their foreheads into their forearms, hiding their eyes. They listened for a moment to see if they stirred any commotion, though they kept their eyes buried, as if somehow they couldn't be seen because they too couldn't see.

A minute passed before Mike slowly raised his head and peered over his shoulder. Jimmy and Jeff were still prone and looking down. Mike got on his knees and gently tapped the other two boys on the back. They looked up and saw Mike slowly easing himself into the school. He ducked his head down low to avoid the broken glass fragments still stuck in the upper portion of the frame. Jimmy and Jeff followed close behind.

The middle child honed in on the glass crunching beneath his feet as he illegally entered the school. He'd been a party to petty vandalism before, but this seemed a lot more consequential. The thought of serious punishment if discovered heightened his senses like never before. Jimmy felt as though he could hear the sound of rubber on pavement streaming through the empty windowpane. He thought he could see around corners with a preternatural sixth sense. Adrenalin pulsed through his veins and made his heart thump heavily against his chest. Jimmy smirked as the three boys—with Mike in the lead—wandered down the vacant hallways.

They peeked into random classrooms, looking for something to swipe. Rows of desks sat empty. Mike found an old grade book in a teacher's desk and grabbed it—for nostalgia's sake. Jimmy lifted up desktops and peered inside. He found a few abandoned pencils and one petrified eraser. Jeff occupied himself by spinning a globe as fast as he could.

"Let's see what else is around here," Mike said, a little frustrated. The initial rush he got from breaking and entering was wearing off. With such a vast expanse at his disposal, he wanted to ratchet the action up another notch.

They began roaming the halls and headed deeper into the heart of Webster Elementary. Mike pulled open the door to the school's auditorium, where as first graders they performed school plays. From time to time, their parents had showed up. Mostly, though, they didn't have the time.

He fumbled in the dark for a light switch and flicked the first one he could find. It was the toggle for the stage's overhead lights. The wooden platform was instantly illuminated with soft, white light. Dust particles, coupled with asbestos from the ceiling, fluttered in the rafters, adding to the dramatic affect of a lit stage.

Jimmy jumped on stage and peered out over the rows of empty seats. He felt animated as his eyes wandered from atop the wooden platform. Jimmy was never much of a thespian. He was more of an athlete. Yet on that stage, he pictured for a moment being a Hollywood actor, powerful enough to do what he wanted when he wanted, and wealthy enough that his father would never again have to man the industrial bottle washing machine at the Pepsi factory. His mother would have babysat her last ailing elder.

Mike took a seat toward the rear of the auditorium and yelled to Jimmy for another cigarette. He was bored. The three brothers proved they could break into school and run rampant without fear of discovery, but there wasn't any real value in the building, other than the building itself.

Jimmy came down from the stage and plopped down beside his brother in the dank auditorium. He stared up at the stage, taking in the enormous curtain—drawn open—that stretched from the stage floor up into the rafters. The heavy black velvet hung there like a shroud, the individual folds overlapping each other. From the back row of seats, looking over the gray metal frames of the chairs that were barely visible in the dimness, the auditorium's curtain stood out as the only aesthetically noninstitutional element. Jeff took exaggerated strides to come from the front of the auditorium and then sat one row in front of his brothers.

"You gonna smoke in here?" Jimmy asked as Mike took the lighter and flicked it with his thumb. The flint hit the steel and a small flame sprung to life.

"I will if I want to," Mike replied. He kept his eyes fixed on the lighter and then on the flame.

"Then I'll have one, too. I'm not afraid to smoke in school."

"Maybe I don't want to smoke right now."

"Well maybe I do!" Jimmy stated emphatically. He was usually the aggressor.

"Can I have one, too?" Jeff queried from his row.

"No!" Mike and Jimmy shouted in unison.

"Then can I see the lighter?"

Mike and Jimmy looked at each other and shrugged. "Yeah, I guess," Mike said. He passed the red Bic to Jeff, who received it with two hands as though it were a delicate crystal. He wrapped his left hand around the base. The lighter was as long as his palm. Then he put the tip of his right thumb on the circular steel wheel and pushed down. It barely moved.

"You gotta push harder," Jimmy advised. Jeff put the fleshy bulb of his thumb back on the wheel and pulled backward, generating a spark, but no flame. "After you push down, you need to put your thumb on that red thing. That releases the fire."

Jeff tried several more times until he finally got the wheel to strike the flint in perfect timing with his thumb hitting the butane release valve. A yellow flame shot up from the plastic and metal lighter. Jeff's eyes widened as he marveled at what he'd produced. Mike and Jimmy giggled. Their brother was just like them. The Scott boys had a penchant for fire, and now with Jeff's first taste of ignition, they had a common bond.

"Hey Jeff," Jimmy said with a devious sneer. "I dare you to light the curtain on fire." Mike let out a snigger. He figured Jimmy wasn't serious—it was just 12-year-old bravado.

"I can do it," Jeff replied.

"Prove it."

Jeff rose from his seat and walked to the foot of the stage. He got in position and looked at his brothers for affirmation. They were out of their seats now too, walking to the front of the auditorium.

"Go on," Jimmy said. "Do it!" Mike smiled. The oldest brother eased his right shoe off with the toe of his left, just in case the kid did light the fabric and he needed to stamp it out real quick.

Jeff grasped the Bic tightly in his left hand and held it underneath the flowing yards of fabric. Then he took his right thumb and pressed the steel wheel. A flame shot out and melded with the base of the curtain. Gradually, a thin white plume of smoke crept from the exchange and the aroma in the air was no longer mere flint and butane. Scorched cloth intermingled with the auditorium's dank, musty scent. Jeff pulled his hand away as a small flame was suspended in the middle of the curtain's bottom.

Jimmy quickly grabbed the lighter out of Jeff's hand and stuffed it in his right front pocket. They watched their fire for a few seconds as it began to eat up more fabric and spread toward the ceiling. Mike took his shoe and pounded on the velvet, which was turning a brilliant yellow and orange before his eyes. The impact forced the curtain to sway in place, but the fire wouldn't extinguish. Rather, glowing embers dashed from the velvet edges and flew back at them. What was more, the air stream generated by Mike's shoe fanned the flame and caused it to spread to one of the curtain's many folds. A second flame flared up in the middle of the cloth.

The distinct odor of charred textiles began wafting from the stage. Jimmy's stare fixed on the spreading conflagration and his ears zeroed in on a crackling noise. He listened to yards of fabric snap in the blaze and heard a faint sound like a gas leak as the fire continued to spread in the clumped up curtain. It was oxygen being sucked into the fire, fueling its fury.

Their prank was spreading out of control. Mike's shoe was helpless against aged, dry cloth. The oldest brother pivoted on his heals and ran toward the other side of the auditorium. He darted in front of the stage and made a beeline to the only other hint of red in the room, the shimmering exit sign.

Jimmy's adrenaline was already running strong, but it surged to new heights when the reality of an uncontrolled fire set in. "Lets go!" he yelled at Jeff and they followed Mike's path through the seats.

The boys made it out into the hallway just as thick black smoke began to crawl over the theater. Jeff was the last one out. Jimmy slammed the door behind his brother.

Mike sprinted toward the broken second-floor window. He briefly paused at the staircase and contemplated descending one flight to exit through the front door. But he figured he'd waste too much time with that route, and the door might be chained, so he stayed on the second floor and raced for the gaping hole in the double-hung window.

"Wait!" Jimmy yelled from 30 paces away. Mike kept running. "HOLD UP!" he howled. Mike made a jump-stop and screeched his sneakers on the linoleum. "You still got that grade book?" Jimmy inquired.

Mike looked at his brother inquisitively. It took a moment for the question to register before he realized that he had evidence on him. He had tucked the grade book from the second-floor classroom into the front of his sweatpants. Mike pulled the book out of his britches and dropped it on the floor.

"No!" Jimmy insisted. "Fingerprints!" The 12-year-old couldn't have known how difficult it is for investigators to pull prints off of paper, especially with the technology of the times, but Mike had seen enough movies to consider his brother's suggestion. Jimmy snatched the book up off the ground and fumbled in his right front pocket for the lighter he'd confiscated from Jeff.

Effortlessly, he lit a corner of the grade book and moved it around until he was sure the entire tome was going to burn up. Then he chucked both the book and the lighter into a nearby classroom, and the three boys tore down the hallway to the open window. Mike exited first and led the race down the school's fire escape.

They grabbed their bikes from behind the oak tree, mounted up and peddled home faster than their metal BMXs had ever moved. Mike and Jimmy traded leads, though they weren't racing. Jeff brought up the rear, panting and slobbering as he tried to keep up.

It was about a quarter to eight in the evening, and the spring equinox kept a dampened light awash over Quincy. Streetlights were on and cars had their lights on as well. Mike, Jimmy, and Jeff stashed their bikes in their front yard and barged into the house gasping for air. Sharon was in the kitchen reheating leftovers and Robert was planted in front of the TV, watching the St. Louis Cardinals battle the Philadelphia Phillies. The Cardinals had been on a roll, winning 11 straight going into the evening game of April 24, 1982. The Scott boys had been following the series, especially Jimmy. He was a big Lonnie Smith fan, and Smith's bat had been hot as of late.

The boys took their places on the carpet in front of their father. St. Louis was locked in a 4–4 tie in the eighth inning, and the boys commenced watching the game as though everything in their world was normal.

They exchanged hellos with their father. He asked what they'd been up to, and Mike replied that they'd been at South Park all day.

"What Lonnie do so far?" Jimmy asked, quickly changing the subject.

"Two hits and a groundout to short," said Robert.

"Okay," Jimmy stated matter-of-factly. At that moment, the Cardinals' Orlando Sanchez, pinch-hitting for St. Louis reliever Doug Bair, drove in a run with a sacrifice grounder down the first-base line. The Scott boys cheered. Then Jimmy's favorite player, Lonnie Smith, stepped up to the plate and hammered a fastball into center field, driving in Ken Oberkfell and Ozzie Smith.

Jimmy jumped to his feet and started hooting. He pumped his fists into the air and roared "yes!" over and over. Robert paid him no mind. Mike and Jeff sat on the floor and gawked at their brother's antics. He was acting like a maniac.

"Move outta the way if you're gonna carry on like that, Jim," Robert demanded of his son. "I can't see the screen." Just then, Mike picked up on what his brother was doing. By acting up, he was actually acting normally. In fact, Mike realized that by *not* carrying on, *he* was the fishy one in the room. He shot to his feet and exchanged hand slaps with Jimmy. Jeff, wanting to be a part of the action, joined in.

For the remaining two innings, Mike, Jimmy, and Jeff exaggerated their enthusiasm every time a Cardinal got a hit. They acted abnormally morose every time a Redbird flied out or struck out. The game concluded at about 8:30 p.m. with a St. Louis victory, when Jimmy informed his parents that the boys were going to their room to play with their Hot Wheels.

If any actions from that night were going to arouse suspicion, Jimmy's statement should have done it. The Scott boys didn't pronounce their comings and goings. They did their own thing. Why, Sharon and Robert might have wondered, did he all of a sudden feel a need to make known his schedule? What was he hiding? Instead, neither parent went so far as to acknowledge that Jimmy had even spoken.

CHAPTER SEVEN

◄○►

Mike, Jimmy, and Jeff pulled the Hot Wheels out from an old wooden footlocker and ran them across the brown carpet with an air of indifference. They grabbed their favorite cars, though for some strange reason, none of them went for the police motorcycle from *CHiPs*.

Mike and Jimmy plotted a strategy of plausible deniability. They discussed how they'd deal with the fire's shakeout, whether they should boast to Dan about it, or if the fire should be their dirty little secret. By nightfall, Mike and Jim decided that without knowing the magnitude of the damage they'd caused, it would be best to keep this news between them. They turned to Jeff, who by now was genuinely interested in playing with Hot Wheels, and barked out orders.

"Jeff, no matter what, you can't say anything about this to anyone," Mike instructed. The boy nodded, continuing to make vrooming noises with his toy Corvette. Jimmy grabbed the car out of his hand and reiterated the point.

"We're serious Jeff," the middle boy said. "If you tell anyone, you'll catch the worst beating you've ever had!" Jeff nodded.

"And we'll all be thrown in jail," Mike chimed in. "And we'll have to live on bread and water for the rest of our lives. You'll have it the worst, because you started the fire. You'll be in the most trouble, so you better keep quiet."

Jeff was on the verge of tears. He hadn't comprehended the severity of what he'd done earlier that evening. As far as the 11-year-old was concerned, he was merely responding to a dare. He had wanted to show his big brothers how brave he was. Now the same brothers he had tried to impress were telling him he could go to jail and he'd never see his parents again.

"But I didn't mean to do anything bad!" Jeff moaned. "What should I do?"

"Just shut up about it," Mike said firmly. "It'll go away soon."

Mike turned the light off in the room and the boys got in their beds, Mike on the bottom bunk, Jimmy on the top, and Jeff on the trundle. As 11 o'clock rolled around, the first and the third brother drifted off into a panicked state of repose, but Jimmy was slow to fall sleep. He couldn't stop thinking about the fire and wondering how big it was right now, or if the fire department had responded quickly and put it out.

Just after 1:30 a.m., the screen door at 2810 Elm Street squeaked on its hinges. Robert and Sharon crept quietly onto their front porch, careful to close the door behind them out of consideration for their sleeping boys. They stood on the concrete slab and peered out to the west of their modest house. The streetlights were on, which constricted Robert and Sharon's vision to the area inside the light, but off in the distance two miles away, an eerie orange glow permeated the dark town.

Robert and Sharon strained to see past the visor of light casting a muted brightness high in the sky. It was the smell that had roused them from bed. Something was burning, and their house was immediately downwind. A smoky haze settled over Elm Street, with amber tints from the streetlights. They guessed at what could be ablaze in that direction, ultimately assuming that it must be Quincy Junior High School.

Sharon and Robert were half right. A school was indeed on fire, but it was the old Webster Elementary School being consumed.

They stayed on their porch for the better part of an hour, whispering to each other about the strange visual. Other families began crowding onto their porches as well. The commotion, however, never got above a dull roar—for the sake of sleeping children. In fact, the only distinctly audible noise was that of fire engine horns and sirens piercing the night as they rushed to the scene.

Inside his house, Jimmy sat up in bed and inhaled deeply. His throat was sore from the cigarettes he'd smoked earlier, the fumes he'd inhaled from the velvet curtains, and his shrieking during the baseball game. His chest constricted as he turned in his bunk and gazed out his bedroom window. The glass pane had been slid open earlier to cool off the stuffy room. Three boys sleeping in close quarters often raised the temperature a few unwanted degrees, and the nippy Midwestern night air usually cleansed the musty aroma. Not on this night, however.

Curiosity consumed Jimmy. He smelled the smoke, just as everyone else west of 13th and Maine did. The difference was that only he and his brothers knew exactly where the smoke was coming from and how the fire had started. He climbed down the frame of his bunk and gently nudged Mike.

"Mikey," he whispered. Mike pretended not to hear his brother. The older boy was wrought with anxiety. He knew the town would surely gossip about this—hell, he could smell the thing from two miles away. Mike's solution was to ignore it.

"Mikey!" Jimmy whispered a little louder. He didn't want to wake Jeff.

"What is it?" Mike replied, keeping his back to his brother.

"Webster's burning. Can you smell it?"

"No. Leave me alone."

Jimmy saw where this was going. He didn't pester his brother. Mike was obviously trying to distance himself from the situation. Without a sound, Jimmy rose from Mike's bedside and slipped his sweatpants over his pajama bottoms. Then he tiptoed over to the window.

The boy thought he'd heard his parents open the front screen door earlier, but they might just be outside talking or rocking on the porch swing. The 12-year-old laid his thumbs against the window screen's frame and gave a quick, hearty push. It popped out of the window with hardly a sound and landed softly on the side lawn. Like a phantom prowler, Jimmy heaved himself onto the sill and then out onto the lawn. He tucked down low while surveying his surroundings, the way he'd seen Martin Sheen do in *Apocalypse Now* when Dan brought him to an R-rated movie. When the coast was clear, he carefully crept around the house to the front yard. Jimmy's parents were on the front porch, and he saw other families on theirs.

Robert and Sharon were looking west, facing the opposite direction of their marauding son. With catlike speed and reflexes, Jimmy duck-walked into the front yard—right under his parents' noses—and grabbed his BMX. He gritted his teeth while he carried the heavy metal bike across two of his neighbor's yards and then onto the sidewalk. Despite the early hour, all the folks who were standing on their porches at two o'clock in the morning seemed oblivious to everything except the fiery orange silhouette two miles to the west.

Jimmy mounted the bike and rode at a leisurely clip into thickening smog. Quincy seemed like a foreign place that Jimmy didn't recognize. He'd ridden the route a thousand times, but the closer he got to the intersection of 13th and Maine, the thicker the smoke became. City streetlights, positioned every 200 feet, cast a light on the nearby burn. Hazy air held the light in timeless arrest and refused to let the beams dissipate into the blackness. Quincy was cloaked in a shroud of unnatural light, which made otherwise familiar structures take on strange shapes.

The closer he got to Webster Elementary School the more frightened he became. The boy knew that he was returning to the scene of a crime, though he was sure no one else knew. He passed some families every few feet strolling toward the commotion, blankly following the herd at that ungodly hour, like moths to a flame. When he was only a few blocks away, Jimmy caught the first glimpse of his handiwork.

Giant, bonfire-like flames shot out of the second-floor windows and streamed 50 to 80 feet into the heavens. Thunderous cracking sounds were audible from hundreds of feet away as wooden desks were swallowed whole by the raging inferno.

"Whoa!" Jimmy said to himself as he got closer to the fire and the flames shot higher in front of him. However, that wasn't the most awe-inspiring sight for the young boy. Before Jimmy could turn his BMX onto Maine Street, he slammed on his breaks and jumped off his bike. Standing in front of him was a wall of more than 4,000 spectators, all of whom watched curiously as a touchstone from their childhoods burned to the ground.

They stood shoulder to shoulder around the entire perimeter of Webster Elementary. The largest group of onlookers crowded the playground, which occupied half a block of land directly south of the school. When that area filled up and people couldn't see the chaos over their neighbors' heads, the throng slowly fanned out in every direction.

Just west of Webster were the large, roomy historic homes on 13th and Maine. As Webster burned, the sprawling lawns of these mansions became a fairground for pedestrians to camp out and watch the show. The fire became hotter and consumed the school foot by foot, making the surrounding areas increasingly dangerous for watchers. Embers shot out of the second story windows and floated down into the crowd.

To the east was Quincy Junior High, separated from the blazing inferno by a thin alley. Flaming debris from Webster flew over to the junior high and settled on the roof, generating a major worry for firefighters, who were mostly concerned for the crowd and then for historic Webster.

Big fires don't occur very often in Quincy, especially ones that consume 100,000-square-foot buildings. Prior to the blaze lighting up the night's sky, Quincy folks hadn't seen a fire this big since First Presbyterian Church burnt down in 1976. That, too, drew townspeople out of their homes. A few people were injured when firebrands from the church roof caught wind and blew across the street, causing another building to catch fire. But that was years ago.

This fire on April 25, 1982, drummed up the largest impromptu crowd Quincy had ever experienced. This many people only turned out for the Fourth of July parade, when the police and fire departments had months to implement a strategy of handling the throng. Indeed, the Quincy Police Department was up against it at 2:15 in the morning, yet they managed to mobilize faster than they ever had before. Earlier at headquarters, the watch commander phoned his superior, who made an emergency plea to the police department for all officers to respond in order to enforce crowd control. At the same time, the chief of police called the civil defense volunteers and even the auxiliary police force to blockade Maine, Jersey, 12th, 13th, and 14th streets. Still, 4,000 people are hard to contain, especially in a relatively small town like Quincy and especially when this was the biggest event in almost a decade. No Fourth of July fireworks display could match the real-life pyrotechnics they were witnessing.

Quincy Fire Chief Jim Doellman had his hands full. He had been at church around 8 p.m. on April 24 when the fire station on Vermont Street paged him. The emergency code entered in his beeper indicated that a fire was burning in town. That's all he had to go on, but as soon as he walked out of church, black smoke billowed into the evening sky. Chief Doellman, a veteran firefighter since 1971, could tell before he even got in his car that this one was going to be a problem. Doellman had been the fire chief for less than a year, since August of 1981, and although he had proved in that short amount of time to be the right man for the job, in this case he was going to have to make split-second decisions with no past leadership experience to draw on.

He had 77 firefighters on the force and he needed every one of them. He told dispatch to round the men up. The orders were to get in gear, get all the trucks, and get over to Webster as fast as they could.

When he arrived at Webster, Doellman's jaw dropped. The fire wasn't leaping out of the windows just yet, as it was still confined to the school's innards, but when he put his hand up to the bricks they were already oven-hot. The chief set up a central command center right in front of the school and instructed the police to give him as wide a berth as possible.

By the time 4,000 people congregated at around two o'clock in the morning, Doellman had determined the situation was at critical mass. Sparks were shooting everywhere. He sent a dozen men onto the roof of the junior high as a defensive measure. The chief instructed them to douse the roof with water and quickly extinguish any flaming debris. He sent another dozen men into the burning elementary school and ordered them to get a central water stream going from the outside fire hydrants.

In so doing, Doellman had 30 percent of his force committed either inside the building or across the street. Should the conflagration spread, he'd need more firefighters. Even if it didn't, he wanted more trucks and more water pumping into the building.

The chief was using every technique he knew to get the inferno under control, but nothing seemed to be working. The fire spread down the staircase to the first floor and climbed the walls and through the ceiling to the third floor. Doellman kept reassuring his men that they were doing a good job; that the fire was slowly subsiding. Their morale ebbed and flowed however as the evening wore on into night and the night into dawn. They tried to ignore all their neighbors and address only the fire. But the bleak situation intensified as the police department took actions that nearly killed several firefighters.

Doellman's predecessor, Chief Lou Berry, had implemented a policy back in the 1970s whereby if a building taller than two stories was on fire, the police department was instructed to shoot out its windows. It was a practice meant to relieve pressure inside the building as well as to open another chasm for water to enter. The Quincy Police Department didn't know that Doellman had sent men inside the school and that they were battling the blaze on the first and second floors. All the police knew was what they saw: The fire streamed out of the second floor windows and it burned on the third floor. Following past protocol, some officers took out their shotguns and fired double-ought buck through the third-story windows. The onlookers oohed and aahed with each blast of the shotgun. Some even applauded—they didn't realize there were men inside. And this show was twice as dramatic as a Fourth of July fireworks display.

For their part, the firefighters inside heard the discharged rounds and the glass break over the hissing flames. They retreated as far into the interior of the school as the flames would allow.

Doellman immediately ran from his post and tried to get the police to stop, but by the time he sprinted the length of the school, the cops had already shot out all of the third-floor windows. His firefighters slowly trickled out of the building. They wore upwards of 100 pounds of gear and oxygen and their exit was gradual. Doellman breathed a sigh of relief when he counted all of his men and saw that they had made it to safe ground. Some were rushed to the hospital and treated for smoke inhalation as a precautionary measure. In addition, the police officers' actions of shooting out the windows had another adverse affect besides just scaring the hell out of a dozen firefighters.

The Quincy Fire Department is trained to combat multistory blazes from above. In a building like Webster, the goal is to cut a four-foot by four-foot hole in the roof before the windows are opened or shot. All the flames and heated gases that are expanding and trying to get out of the building will be drawn to the hole in the roof. Without that hole, shooting out the windows spreads the fire. The gases can't ascend because there's no opening. Instead, they head toward an oxygen source, which in Webster's case were the blasted windows. Essentially, the Quincy Police Department, although trying to help, made the fire worse. The opened windows pulled the fire down the third-floor hallway and fueled it with fresh air.

From there, the fire spread upward. Doellman thought his men stationed atop Quincy Junior High School across the alley could battle a roof fire because they were in a strategically elevated position. They unleashed a torrent of water on Webster's roof, but it was completely ineffective. Unbeknownst to Doellman, when Webster had been shut down a year earlier, the city decided to use its vast attic space as a book depository. Thousands of volumes of old, dry paperbacks and hardcovers were stacked from floor to ceiling. The fire in the attic spread as though it was being accelerated by a flamethrower, and all two-plus acres of space were consumed in a gigantic paper fire.

Doellman realized that he needed help. Webster Elementary was burning out of control. The chief took cold comfort in the fact that it hadn't spread across the alley to Quincy Junior High School, but the thousands upon thousands of stacked books was a variable he hadn't anticipated. Doellman got on the horn and called in four other fire departments from Payson, Liberty, and Ursa, Illinois, as well as one from across the river in Palmyra, Missouri. The reinforcements responded with blaring sirens and flashing lights, all of which added to the circus atmosphere.

Jimmy stood among the buzzing townspeople and clutched his bike tightly to his side. He listened as they concocted wild theories of what had caused the fire. The spectators marveled at the lightshow and quipped that the flames seemed like they were growing by the minute. And they roared at the sound of the shotgun blasts.

The boy was in a state of disbelief. Never before had he seen the town gather like this. The entire fire department was on hand. The entire police department was there keeping the people in line. Many in attendance he knew or recognized, though there were thousands he'd never seen before. Everyone was looking around anxiously and speaking nervously.

Jimmy clenched his molars. He was doe-eyed and shaken by the event he helped cause, and standing there without Mike made him feel small and alone. The 12-year-old tried to convince himself that he was having a nightmare, that this wasn't really happening, and the technique worked for a while until a discharged buckshot jarred his thoughts and brought him back to the all-too-real fire.

He stood there for the better part of an hour, long into the early morning. Fear of repercussions didn't set in for the longest time. Flames were leaping from the windows, but because he couldn't see inside the school, for all he knew, only the area of the building by the windows was on fire. He kept waiting for the flames to subside and the firefighters to walk out, get in their trucks, and head back to the station. It wasn't until the roof caught and erupted into a blistering holocaust that he recognized there'd be no quick fix for this one.

The fear metastasized in his nervous system and numbed the tips of his fingers and toes when he saw a parade of fire trucks from distant departments arriving on the scene. It was then that he realized this fire could not be put out; only contained at best. At 3:30 a.m., just about the time Jimmy was ready to asphyxiate from overwhelming guilt, he turned his BMX around and peddled home in great haste. He gasped for air as he labored to breathe.

Jimmy stopped a block from his street and attempted to collect himself.

"I'm really gonna get it," he thought repeatedly. "I'm really cooked this time." He looked around and saw that everyone who'd been out on porches an hour earlier had returned to bed. He was by himself. Elm Street was back to normal. There wasn't a police car in front of his house, and there were no signs that one had come earlier and picked up Mike and Jeff. They had gotten away with the perfect crime.

Jimmy relaxed and figured he was home free, that everything was going to be alright. He weighed his crime against the fleeting thought of punishment. And he smiled.

CHAPTER EIGHT

◄○►

Jimmy snuck back into a dark house and a silent bedroom. He carefully replaced the screen and then tiptoed to his bunk. Mike heard his brother enter, though he pretended to be asleep. He figured if Jimmy sensed trouble then he'd wake him. He also figured that if the fire was big enough to talk about, Jimmy wouldn't be able to contain himself, but Jimmy said nothing as he effortlessly ascended the frame of his bunk bed.

He lay awake for most of the night, reflecting on the chaos they had caused. Surely the newspapers would cover this story, and probably the television news as well. He was about to be a celebrity in a town that loved to gossip. His only regret at the moment was that he couldn't tell anyone what he'd done.

Morning came on Sunday, April 25, 1982, and the big story around town was that Webster Elementary was not only on fire the previous night, but it was still burning 12 hours later. Quincy's fire department was acting decisively and heroically and the rookie fire chief had made all the right moves. He'd managed to contain the fire on Webster's grounds only, despite free-flying firebrands and the proximity of Quincy Junior High School.

Mike shook Jim's shoulders as soon as he awoke. Trepidation hindered his curiosity in the wee hours, but now that the sun was up and there were no signs of immediate danger, he was eager to learn of Jimmy's clandestine exploits.

Jeff was still asleep and both boys wanted to keep their little brother in the dark as long as possible, so Mike climbed the bunk bed's frame and sat beside his brother. Jimmy positioned himself the way a storyteller might and he built up the suspense by grinning at his brother without saying anything.

"Come on!" Mike demanded. "What happened?"

Jimmy launched into his account, sparing no details. He started by describing the eerie bike ride and the paranormal haze over Quincy. The homes looked like ghost ships, he recounted, and the buildings looked like castles from werewolf movies. Mike listened in amazement. He was dying to hear about the fire—and Jimmy delivered.

"As soon as I pulled up to Maine Street, there was like a million people standing there. And the fire was shooting thousands of feet into the air. People were scared because there were embers shooting everywhere. And the police were getting angry because there were so many people, so they started shooting at the school to scare everyone. But their bullets caused explosions that made the fire worse, so like 50 more fire trucks showed up and there was like a whole bunch of water brought in from the Mississippi River and sprayed on the school."

"Whoa!" Mike said in sheer astonishment. "What then? Did anyone get hurt?"

"Naw, but then all the people got nervous and they started looking around. And they were blaming people and saying, 'I bet I know who started the fire!' And some of them were looking at me, so I started walking away from them and when they weren't watching, I rode home. It was getting pretty late anyway, and I was tired. But man, you shoulda seen all them people!"

"Do you think they're on to us?" Mike asked with a catch in his voice.

"I thought so at first, but before I came back in the house, I waited out behind some trees for a while and watched for CHiPs. None were even out cruising, so we're okay."

"Are you sure?"

"Yeah. They'd have come and talked to us by now. That's how Ponch always does it. As soon as he thinks someone did something, he goes right to their house, even if it's at midnight. Besides, the fire was so big that they'll never figure out how it started. I mean, the whole darn thing was burning!"

Mike felt relieved. He momentarily shared in the jubilation but then he thought about how Webster had been in Quincy forever. His parents had even gone there. He comforted himself with the fact that at least no one had been hurt in the mess.

"Look, Jim," he said, exercising his big-brother status to command the conversation. "We got lucky on this one. We coulda got in a lot of trouble. So let's lay low and not say a word to anyone about this. And don't tell Jeff what you saw. Just play dumb if he asks what happened. This will go away, but it'll be a while."

"Aw, they'll never find out," Jimmy replied. "It coulda been anything that started that fire. Maybe a cook left the stove on in the cafeteria. Who knows?"

"Just the same, let's be quiet. There's probably thousands, or millions, or even hundreds of hundreds of millions of dollars in damage to that school, so they're not just gonna let this thing lie. You hear me?"

Mike didn't like the fact that Jimmy was so cocksure of their escape. Loose lips sink ships, and Jimmy was a braggart. Then again, so was he.

"This'll be our little secret. Mikey and Jimmy fooled the town!" the big brother said.

"Yeah, that's awesome!" Jimmy wasn't intending to tell anyone anyway, but he liked that he had Mike on the defensive.

They sat there a while longer until Sharon came in the room. She was surprised to see them up so early because the Scott boys usually slept in whenever they had the chance. She told the boys to get Jeff up and to get ready for church. Mike and Jimmy shot her a puzzled look. It wasn't Easter. But before they could contemplate why all of a sudden their mother was bringing them to church, Sharon was already in the next room. Mike and Jim followed her orders.

Sharon wasn't so much interested in going to Calvary Baptist to hear a sermon that morning. She wanted to hear the gossip about the Webster fire.

Twenty minutes later, the three Scott brothers and their parents were piled into the family sedan and driving to church. When they crossed Maine Street, all of their eyes were drawn to the scene 11 blocks away. Webster was still burning in parts, though much of it was now smoldering and emitting thick black smoke. "Jesus," their father muttered aloud. Mike and Jimmy stared blankly out the window. Jeff's bottom lip began to tremble.

◄○►

Chief Doellman stayed with his men and the burning building until 4:30 a.m. on Sunday, April 25. He tried to fight back fatigue, but he'd punched in at around 7:30 a.m. the previous morning and was exhausted. He retreated to the Vermont Street station and caught three hours of restless sleep before returning to the fire.

Right around the time the Scott family was heading to church, the Quincy Fire Department was stamping out the last of the flames and dousing the structure with torrents of water.

Webster's roof was gone. It had burned furiously through the night and eventually buckled and caved. Other than some men suffering from smoke inhalation, the Quincy Fire Department managed to escape the biggest fire in almost a decade without injury.

The school was a total loss, though. That much Chief Doellman could tell just by looking at it. Preliminary talk among city officials was that the skeletal structure could be salvaged and rebuilt as an example of community success and teamwork, but Doellman wasn't so sure.

As soon as the flames were extinguished and the fire chief determined that there was no chance for a flare-up, Quincy's arson investigators arrived on the scene.

The chief suspected that the fire had been started intentionally. It was burning hotter in two separate areas of the building than in others, which to him meant two separate fires. By the time Lt. Dale Dietrich arrived, Chief Doellman was prepared to brief the investigator on the particulars of the previous night. He warned Dietrich that the work might be harder than usual because the attic had acted as a giant accelerator and because it had collapsed into the central corridors. Doellman told the arson expert that the police blew out the windows before his men had a chance to cut a hole in the roof. Dietrich understood. He thanked the chief and donned a mask. The investigator and three firefighters entered the charred edifice.

Lt. Dietrich observed the torched interior. The banister that ran along both sides of the staircase was gone and the blue walls of the classrooms were cooked black. Eyewitness accounts said that flames were initially seen on the second floor, so the arson investigator began his examination there.

Dietrich methodically studied each section of the second floor. He was looking for a sign of malfeasance, either an accelerator or some sort of incendiary. Because the auditorium was centrally located, Dietrich commenced his systematic investigation there. Right away, he saw the hoof prints of arsonists.

Snaking along the charred walls near the stage were crisscrossing streaks known as "V-patterns." When a fire burns, it does so up and out from the point of origin, leaving behind these V-shaped telltale signs. The investigator had his source: Somebody had lit the curtain. From there, Dietrich read the markings on the walls as a blind man reads Braille. He touched and prodded certain sections of wall, which led him into the adjacent hallway and then down further toward a corner window.

Many elements can determine which way a fire accelerates. A normal fire will spread in a path of least resistance, making it possible to trace its steps. Just like human nature, a fire will walk right through an open door or head toward an open window.

That's what Dietrich did as he roamed the second floor halls of Webster Elementary. Yesterday, the fire had taken the same path, right to a window whose glass was broken and shattered. The investigator figured that perpetrators, not buckshot, had broken this window because the fire had spread from the auditorium down the hall.

Then he noticed something else. There was discoloration on the walls near one classroom. The left side of the hallway was decidedly blacker and more wilted than the right. Dietrich entered the classroom to his immediate left and noticed some more V-patterns starting in the corner of the classroom near where a teacher's desk might have sat. He squatted to take a closer look, running his fingers along the blackened floor. He couldn't tell if someone had lit the desk or whether a Molotov cocktail had been hurled. His suspicion was the former because there were two foreign objects lying in the vicinity of the V's point: a rounded piece of metal—the kind found on cigarette lighters, blackened from the burn, and an inch from that find was a tiny metal wheel, such as the kind used to strike flint in a cigarette lighter.

There was also a long metal spring. It was elongated, like the kind used to hold a notebook together. Dietrich held the spiral up and studied it: Bingo. The arsonist hadn't been working alone, he deduced, because there were two different points of origin. The first fire had started in the auditorium, and the second fire had started moments later when a second criminal lit a notebook on fire. He burned the lighter too, thinking that he was destroying the evidence. He had forgotten—or just didn't know—that even the smallest piece of metal won't burn.

Dietrich returned to the school the following day, and gave the building another once-over before reporting his findings to both the police and fire departments. Police Chief Charles Gruber asked that neither Dietrich nor Fire Chief Doellman report their findings to the press right away. Gruber needed a day to brief all his officers on the turn of events and get their informants planted in bars and clubs where someone might go and boast. Because the 26th was a Monday, they needed one more day so that teachers could be both briefed and on the lookout for suspicious conduct and chatter in the schools. A task force was assembled, informants were planted, and teachers were educated with the knowledge that young arsonists may be in their midst.

All day long at school, children talked about the town fire. They were embellishing the details, as children are prone to do, and while already devastating, the fire's sheer size seemed to grow exponentially by day's end.

Most of the boys Mike fraternized with in the sixth grade talked about how cool the fire was. Some of them were actually brought to it by their parents. They wished aloud that it was their school that had burned down and not old Webster. Mike chimed in for the sake of acceptance, even though he had to force the words out of his mouth. The teachers discussed the fire in the hallways, talking about the shame of it all and rhetorically asking how something like this could happen.

Jeff was suspiciously quiet. He was usually a social kid who had lots of friends and who participated in class discussions. On April 26, however, he sat in his assigned seat with a forlorn scowl on his face. He was testy when other students tried to talk to him, and two different teachers pulled him aside and asked him if everything was all right at home. Both times he replied with a simple "yes."

Jimmy Scott, on the other hand, listened to his classmates chatter in extremis about the "huge bonfire." He grinned. The children seemed to be in such awe of a burning school. They, too, wished it were theirs. He was desperate to tell them he was there—that little did they know, he could give a precise play-by-play of all the events that transpired.

"I heard that some kid who flunked out started the fire," one boy quipped.

"Well I heard that someone hid some dynamite inside and tried to blow it up, but the dynamite didn't work so the fuse lit the building on fire," added another.

"It wasn't anything like that," Jimmy said at last. He *had* to say something.

"How do you know, Jimmy?" they tested.

"Because I just know, that's all," he replied. His certitude seemed to register heavily with the boys.

"You don't know nothing," said one.

"Okay. Believe what you want. I don't care," was Jimmy's smirking retort.

That evening, families gathered around supper tables throughout Quincy. Parents queried their children about what they learned in school. They talked about math and about baseball with all conversations ultimately steering toward the fire. It was the front page story in the *Herald-Whig* and the lead story on the evening newscasts. Most of all, it was good town gossip and something that could be made into a lesson for children: Fires are bad.

Some parents of fifth graders heard schoolyard gossip that night. It seemed Jimmy Scott had knowledge of the fire but wasn't telling. Most parents dismissed their children's tattling. Jimmy was just trying to be a big shot, they said. But not all of them were so sure.

The next afternoon, the *Herald-Whig* hit stands with breaking news: Webster Elementary was intentionally set on fire. Authorities suspected arson and were in the process of interviewing people of interest. Preliminary estimates projected damages in amounts upward of $4 million. The school was most likely a total loss and city administrators were wrestling with what to do with its remains. The Head Start program and the classes for plumbers and pregnant women were moved to neighboring Lincoln Elementary indefinitely.

The Scott boys didn't get wind of this news until later that night, when Sharon said in passing that Webster was set on fire deliberately. Mike and Jim went blank.

"How do you know?" Mike challenged.

"I saw it in the newspaper," his mother replied.

The oldest brother shot Jim a glance and motioned with his head to the bedroom. Jimmy followed him in. Jeff was close behind.

"Jim," Mike said in a horse rasp. "You didn't say anything to anybody, did you?"

"Not me," Jimmy said. "I haven't said a word."

"I haven't said a word either, Mikey," Jeff volunteered.

"All right. We're still safe then. Just remember to keep quiet! We don't want anyone to think we knew or did anything."

Though they managed to hide their fear of being discovered, the Scott boys were visibly scared now. Jimmy told the truth: He hadn't said anything to anyone. He only corrected his buddies when they speculated about the cause of the fire. He struggled with whether to disclose this tidbit. He figured his comments were benign enough; he was just talking smack at the schoolyard. Still, with a tragedy of this magnitude, Jimmy couldn't help but be a bit paranoid. Perhaps the Scott boys should concoct an alibi if they were questioned. He thought about an excuse only briefly. Jimmy Scott was an accessory to one of the two fires inside the school that the paper reported, and the cause of the other. If he did get picked up, it was because they had him cold. Lying would make the heap of trouble he was in 10 times worse. Jimmy considered what discovery would mean, though he of course thought the worst. For the time being, he pushed thoughts of jail out of his mind. He'd cross that bridge should he come to it.

Right about the time Mike was debriefing his brothers about how to act, the phone started ringing at police headquarters. Folks were calling in tips. A few of these leads were patched directly into Chief Charles Grubner's office.

CHAPTER NINE

◄○►

The Quincy Police Department, Quincy Fire Department, and arson investigator Lt. Dale Dietrich acted swiftly. Several parents told the same story of their sons coming home after school on Monday and reporting that James Scott knew something about the fire, even though he wasn't giving details. Teachers from Jeff's fourth grade class also reported peculiar behavior from the 11-year-old. The alliance of firefighters and law enforcement now had a starting point for their investigation.

Police Chief Gruber went through the proper channels and obtained the requisite paperwork needed to bring the Scott boys in for questioning. He figured that within the first 30 minutes the boys would slip up or out themselves as having been witnesses or actual perpetrators of the fire.

Mike, Jimmy, and Jeff were already known around the fire and police departments. The boys thought they were being stealthy on their clandestine midnight missions. They also thought no one had ever seen them set their leaf and brush fires. But tipsters had actually phoned in to the departments and informed on the kids, and from time to time, Chief Gruber confronted Sharon and Robert Scott about a particular incident. The parents, however, always had alibis for their children's whereabouts. Mike, Jimmy, and Jeff were nuisances, but their fires were more or less confined to their own property—and the tips were never detailed enough to pursue. Webster Elementary School was a step up for the boys. They'd graduated from petty crime to criminal trespass, felony arson, and reckless endangerment.

Shortly after Mike, Jimmy, and Jeff concluded their meeting of the minds—the one where they determined that a low profile would be the best means of avoiding suspicion—Sharon and Robert heard a knock on the front door. Standing at the threshold of the modest house on 2810 Elm Street were two uniformed officers.

Sharon immediately raised her hands to her mouth. "Oh my God!" she gasped. "What happened to Dan?"

Dan Leake had been teetering on the brink of self destruction. He'd been an alcoholic ever since he'd left home a year earlier and he'd been involved in at least two burglaries.

The cops looked surprised. Maybe they had the wrong household. "Ma'am, we need to bring your sons in for questioning." Sharon's paranoia quickly disappeared. She went from fearful to testy almost instantly.

"Why do you want to talk to my boys?" she asked the police officers, a scowl on her face and her hands on her hips.

"They're suspects in the Webster Elementary School fire," one of the officers replied.

"That's impossible. They were home with us all night long."

"Can you account for their whereabouts during the early evening of April 24?"

"Yes," Sharon replied automatically. Then she had to stop and think. A loving mother, she had long been a staunch defender of her sons' actions, first with Dan, and later, when her boys acted out or were accused by neighbors of vandalizing their properties. "They were . . . at . . . the park. All day long. At the park."

"You'll have an opportunity to make that statement, but we have orders to bring them in for questioning. You and your husband can wait at the station if you'd like, but it might take some time."

Sharon asked the officers to wait while she rounded up her sons. Then she ran into the bedroom and briefed Robert. He, too, was taken aback. Mikey and Jimmy couldn't be a part of the disaster—and certainly not little Jeff. Together, Robert and his wife marched into the boys' bedroom, where they were playing with Hot Wheels.

All three looked up and knew just by the presence of both parents in their bedroom that they'd been nailed. It was Sharon who spoke.

"Boys, there are policemen here. They say you did the Webster fire, and they want to take you in for questioning."

"It wasn't us!" declared Mike. "We don't know anything about it."

"You're going to have to go to the station with them. The important thing is that you tell the truth. If you know something, you need to tell them. If you don't, then you tell them that. But you can't fib to the police. We'll be down there. Now it's time to go."

Jimmy was the first to stand up. He was surprised by how quickly the police had pieced the puzzle together—though he still didn't know how. However, he wasn't completely shocked. In fact, he suspected that his passing comment might have given them away.

Mike stood, and then Jeff. They solemnly walked through the house, past the television, which was broadcasting another St. Louis Cardinals baseball game, to the waiting officers. The Scott boys were escorted to the police cruiser and an officer opened the back door and watched as first Jim, then Jeff and then Mike crawled in.

Sharon and Robert Scott retreated back into the house and went straight to the phone. Sharon dialed the police station and asked for an officer to call her when her boys were ready to be picked up.

◄○►

The Quincy squad car pulled into the underground garage of police head-quarters with three scared boys in tow. The building at 507 Vermont Street received its suspects through an underground entrance both for convenience and to maintain the veneer of downtown Quincy as being "perp-free."

The Scott boys tepidly filed out of the cruiser and marched single-file into the station's bowels. Two detectives, one of which was a trained juvenile police officer schooled in dealing exclusively with young offenders, met them.

Mike was first. The detectives explained his rights and then led him into an interrogation room. Jimmy and Jeff were led into a holding room, where they were unknowingly watched and recorded.

The first two detectives cracked Mike within a matter of minutes. They didn't even need to good cop/bad cop him as their questioning was more of a fact-finding fishing expedition. They informed him that they already knew he started the fire in the auditorium. Mike looked up shocked. How did they know it had started in the auditorium?

"I didn't start it," he confirmed. Though by the way he worded it, the police knew instantly that they had the right boys. The detectives leaned on him with more direct questions: Who did start it? Whose idea was it? What did you use to start the fire in the classroom? Mike answered honestly and the seasoned cops could tell, but they still needed to put a little fear into him, not only to make sure he wasn't hiding anything, but they wanted to march him out of the interrogation room in tears. That way, Jimmy and Jeff would know he'd spilled his guts. They'd be wise to do the same.

The first detective warned him that he was only making matters worse for himself. Mike wasn't being truthful, they said, and lying to detectives was a sure way to guarantee the harshest possible punishment. Mike started shaking: He told them everything he could think of, even about Jimmy chucking the lighter into a vacant classroom to destroy the evidence. Pressure kept coming until Mike finally erupted in tears. He didn't know what they wanted, which was chiefly why they started the fire. He kept stressing that he had his shoe in hand to stamp out the flames—that he never meant for it to grow out of control. He was convincing, but Mike Scott had to be broken. And he was.

He marched out of the interview room with swollen, puffy eyes and a runny nose. Mike tried to collect himself as best he could and project a "tough guy" image to save face with the officers in the hallways, as well as his waiting brothers. The detectives, however, didn't give him enough time. Mike didn't know their actions were intentional. He was ashamed and refused to make eye contact with his brothers as they sat in a holding area.

They brought Jeff in next. He started sobbing at the sight of his brother and swallowed hard when the door to the interview room closed behind him. The detectives were more tactful with the 11-year-old. He was shy and scared, quiet but edgy. They felt it wouldn't take long to break him down. The detectives would have to ask more pointed questions to extract information because 11-year-olds tend not to volunteer information unless asked.

The detectives already knew the sequence of events, and they knew Jeff was the fire starter, but they recognized that he was coerced into lighting the curtain. He was the youngest, thus the most susceptible to his brothers' dares. Jeff was needed more to confirm if the Scotts were being abused or neglected at home and to point the finger at which brother was the antagonizer.

Jeff answered each question posed to him with one-word answers. When they asked who told him to start the fire, he simply said "Jimmy." When they asked him whose idea it was, he gave the same answer. He also admitted that his brothers had started other fires around town.

The detectives pressed him about his home life, trying to discern whether the boys were physically abused. Jeff said no, and the cops believed him. The boy didn't resort to any facial tics or body language that would suggest he was lying to protect his family. He also answered each question truthfully about how often mom and dad were around. Jeff managed to paint a perfect picture of negligent parents. They were loving and Jeff loved them: The cops recognized that, but Sharon and Robert worked too hard and too long to be effective role models and caretakers.

Jeff was red-eyed and sniffling at the end of the interview. The detectives didn't need to browbeat the kid because he was so cooperative. Jimmy was the one they prepared to come down on hardest. Both brothers implicated him as the provoker, so he was the real prize of the day.

Jimmy watched Jeff exit the interview room in a similar condition as Mike. He too was whisked away to another part of the station without a word. As he waited for his turn under the lights, Jimmy went over a game plan in his head. He'd tell the truth because the cops clearly knew everything by now, but he'd stress that it was an accident. That would draw some of the heat off him. And he'd try not to cry if for no other reason than to show Mike how resilient he was.

But the cops didn't come. He sat there patiently for an hour, then another, then another. Had they forgotten about him, he wondered? What sort of trick was this? Jimmy started getting paranoid. He worried about his brothers and wondered if they were being roughed up. That's how it happened on television and in the movies. Then he started concocting scenarios in his head: Maybe the police already had what they needed from the Scott boys and he was going to get a jump from the station. After all, his brothers were crying worse than he'd ever seen. He sat silently as his mind constructed doomsday scenarios. Jimmy didn't like the loneliness. He was actually anxious for the detectives to come and get him. There was no clock in the holding room and he had no idea what time it was. It must have been late at night by now because it had already been dark when they picked him up. How much longer would they keep him here? He kept his eyes trained on the door and more specifically, on the doorknob. Each time he heard a noise in the hallway, Jimmy became momentarily excited.

The detectives didn't forget him, and they certainly weren't roughing the other two boys up. Mike and Jeff were together again awaiting the next round of the legal cycle, which would take them to a juvenile detention center and later, a courtroom.

At long last, the detective and the juvenile officer fished Jimmy Scott out of his holding pen and brought him to an interview room for questioning. His face remained stoic when the large oak door opened and the two men—well-dressed in brown suits and wearing aloof facial expressions—asked that the boy follow them. Jimmy leaped from his hard wooden chair and stumbled momentarily because of the hours spent on his tailbone.

He followed the detectives deep into the station's vestibules and none of them uttered a word. Jim prepared for some hard questioning while he waited. He told himself repeatedly as he walked down the corridor to keep his cool. "Don't get excited," he thought. "Tell them it was an accident. Tell them what they want to hear and don't tell them anything more than they need to know."

The detectives were going to ask pointed questions, yes, but they would use a completely different line of questioning for the middle brother. They had what they needed from an arson investigation standpoint: The other two Scott boys had confessed and they were confident that this last one would talk as well. The seasoned officers tried to extract varying information from each brother to paint the broad picture.

Jimmy would fill in the holes. He'd detail how often the boys set these little fires, when they'd steal away into the night. The cops hoped they'd get a definitive answer for that one proverbial question that still eluded them: Why?

The 12-year-old entered the interrogation room and took the lone wooden seat. He put his arms atop the wooden table and stared straight into the muted beige room. One detective shut the door while the juvenile officer explained the boy's rights. Jimmy heard everything the man said though he listened to none of it. He was lost in his own head, still replaying his strategy over and over. When the first question came, he was asked whether he understood what the juvenile officer had just said. Jimmy sheepishly nodded. "Let the questioning begin," he thought.

The detective commenced the examination with an interestingly-phrased inquiry, one that Jimmy hadn't prepared for. "What went through your mind when you lit the grade book on fire?"

It was a loaded question. The detective posed it that way deliberately, and it served its purpose. Jimmy immediately went blank. He scrapped his calculated game plan and answered on the fly.

"I don't know," he started. "I guess I just didn't want to get into trouble."

"So you didn't think what you were doing was wrong?" the other detective chimed in.

"I guess so, but we never meant for it to happen," he replied.

"Come on now, Jim," the first detective said. "You really expect us to believe that lighting a grade book on fire and tossing it in an empty classroom was an accident?"

"No," the boy said. "I just . . . didn't want to get in trouble."

The cat and mouse game went on for over an hour. The detectives managed to get Jimmy to admit lighting little brush fires and he even confessed that he was prone to sneaking out some nights. As far as the detectives were concerned—and based on Jimmy's answers—he was the ringleader of the brothers; in terms of criminal activity, anyway. He was so preoccupied with currying favor with Mike and showing how brave he was that he would always take their misdemeanors to the extreme, blurring the lines as to whether he was just some punk kid or a career criminal-in-training.

"One last question," one of the detectives began: "Are you sorry for what you did, or are you sorry that you got caught?" The officers watched their suspect's body language as the boy lowered his head and his eyes. Jimmy's physical stillness and subdued reaction answered the man before the boy's mouth had a chance to. This kid was not concerned with community or civic pride.

Jimmy tried to think through this question carefully. He was sorry that the school went up in flames, but truth be told, he was even sorrier that the evening was progressing and he was missing the Cardinals game. After a 20-second silence, the boy raised his head to address the detectives. His eyes remained impassive and opened lazily, and his mouth seemed to smile a little. The cops were giving him the perfect opportunity to atone.

"I'm sorry for what I did," he said. "*And* I'm sorry that I got caught."

◄o►

The detectives had their confessions and their collar. They promptly relayed all of their findings to the Adams County prosecutor's office as the boys were remanded to the custody of the state pending formal charges and a hearing.

Meanwhile, the City of Quincy wanted answers. Both the newspaper and the television news had requested statements from the police, the fire department, and the prosecutor's office, but the formal line up to this point was that officials couldn't comment on an ongoing investigation. Now, five days after the fire, Police Captain Donald Capps allowed an interview with a *Quincy Herald-Whig* reporter.

Capps told the journalist that three local youths were being charged with arson. He confirmed that their ages were 11, 12, and 13 and that they were being lodged in the Adams County Youth Home until their court appearance, scheduled for the following day. He couldn't disclose their names to the press per police protocol.

The paper reported that the fire wasn't premeditated. "It was a spontaneous act rather than a planned and motivated act," Capps told the reporter. "There really was no motive." A cigarette lighter had been found in the building's charred edifice.

Adams County State's Attorney Anthony Cameron was assigned the case, and despite public outcry, he decided to keep the case in juvenile court instead of trying the boys as adults.

The Scott brothers stood tall before a juvenile judge on April 30, 1982. Each of them wore sweaters and slacks, and for the first time in years, they washed their faces and combed their hair. Robert and Sharon sat on a wooden bench behind their three sons as a court-appointed defense attorney flanked Mike, Jimmy, and Jeff.

The boys stood there bewildered. State's Attorney Cameron read the charges against the brothers. They turned their heads to watch a stranger address another stranger in their presence, say all these bad things about them, and then act as if they weren't there. Mike started to tremble. Jeff kept glancing back at his mother, searching her face for a comfortable, familiar expression, which she feigned for his benefit. Jimmy, on the other hand, locked his eyes on the attorney. He didn't like the tone in his voice, and he certainly didn't like the words Cameron used to depict his character. As he listened to Cameron methodically walk through the events of April 24, the boy became angry.

The judge read each brother's body language the way Quincy's detectives had in questioning. He saw how panicky Mike was, how disoriented Jeff was, and how cold Jimmy was.

It didn't take long for the judge to realize that these were troubled boys. One of them showed genuine remorse while the middle son showed none. The youngest was just too young to send upstate. The judge spoke directly to the brothers as he read their sentences. Mike wasn't a fire starter, though he was an enabler and in addition to exercising poor judgment, he was negligent in acting as his brother's keeper. Mike would be on probation until he was 18. The judge allowed him to go home with his parents, but they'd have to attend weekly family counseling sessions in Springfield and be evaluated by the state each month.

Jeff's punishment was harsher. Although coerced, he did indeed light the curtain on fire. The judge linked such foolish and reckless behavior to poor parenting. He would be taken from his home and placed in the foster care system. Upon hearing that she was losing her baby boy, Sharon began weeping loudly in open court. Jeff didn't understand what the judge had said, but he started crying right along with his mother.

As for the 12-year-old, he'd receive the harshest sentence, though it wasn't nearly as bad as it could have been. He'd finish out the school year in the Adams County Youth Home after which he'd be sent to Springfield for evaluation at the McFarland Mental Health Center. Once there, if it was determined that he was of sound mind, he'd return home and be subject to the same probation and counseling as Mike. But if it was determined that he had some deep-seated emotional psychosis then the McFarland Mental Health Center might become a more permanent residence.

◄○►

The Adams County Youth Home was a large, menacing institution on the eastern outskirts of Quincy. Like Webster, its dark brick exterior rose three stories in the air and was the tallest building in the area along 52nd Street. It was also at critical mass. After the Webster fire in 1982, there were more than 1,000 "students" within its walls.

Jimmy marched into the county's youth ward in early May 1982, young and quiet, small and scared. A multiracial collection of violent offenders lurked within. Most of the boys were older than he was. They were already developed—or developing—and Jimmy felt as if he was a child among grown men. Although burning down the school was a particularly devastating crime, the fact that no one was injured made his offense seem tame in comparison. Many were in for aggravated armed robberies, sexual assaults, and some even murder.

Jimmy didn't say much to the others for his first week in the joint. Instead, he donned his uniform of blue pants and white T-shirt, crammed into his modest dorm room with another white juvenile offender who was 14, and tried not to engage in conversation. His ghost-like presence worked at the outset; the other boys basically left him alone. But even though residents of the Adams County Youth Home all shared a common criminal bond, special status was given to the most dangerous offenders. Inmates had access to newspapers, and Jimmy's crime didn't go unnoticed for very long.

One of the 17-year-old ringleaders approached Jimmy in the yard two weeks after he'd arrived. The juvenile introduced himself as Trigger, aptly named because he'd been holding people up at gunpoint since he was 14. Trigger was a large, muscular white boy with disheveled brown hair and dark brown eyes. He asked Jimmy if any of the black inmates had messed with him.

"No," Jimmy replied timidly. "Are they going to?"

Trigger explained to him that the two races pretty much kept to themselves. That's how it'd been in the year-and-a-half since Trigger had been there. Jimmy appreciated the olive branch this older kid offered. By the same token, though, he was already developing a criminal awareness and wit. When Trigger asked Jimmy what he was in for, the boy played his story up for safety's sake.

"I did the Webster fire," Jimmy replied proudly.

"No way!" Trigger yelled. "All by yourself?"

"You can say that."

"Anyone get hurt?"

Jimmy flashed his mischievous grin. "Oh yeah, a whole bunch of people. I waited for all the students taking classes to show up and then I did it. A few people might have died by now. I don't know. And I don't much care."

It was a lie, the grandest lie he'd ever told. In all honesty, Jimmy grew nauseous at the thought of hurting people with his fire. The severity of juvenile home *made* him sorry for the fire, and the idea that he might have actually hurt someone made him want to cry. Nevertheless, his grin was genuine, mostly because the young joker was putting one over.

"Whoa, kid. That's mean. Good to know ya. Let me know if you need anything."

With that, Jimmy was accepted. He had a sponsor, someone older in the system to make sure none of the other juveniles—white or black—got to him. He also had some mild celebrity status. Once Trigger spread the news about the new kid, Jimmy received a certain amount of respect. Even his roommate, who had been in the dorm first and who initially tried to mark his territory, backed off and let Jimmy lounge where he wanted, even on his side of the room.

He was doing good time. Adams County Youth Home was regimented like a military school except when classes were over in the morning and at the conclusion of afternoon recess (yard time), the boys were locked in their dorm rooms until evening chow. Then they were locked down again at night.

Jimmy spent six weeks in juvenile hall. In addition to school, he attended counseling meetings with the institution's resident psychiatrist. The doctor introduced himself as a friend—someone he could feel comfortable talking to. What he was really doing was making keen observations and writing up notes that would follow the boy to Springfield for his mental evaluation.

The psychiatrist didn't notice anything completely out of the ordinary in this case. He was clearly troubled, most likely, he noted, because of parental neglect, though based on the boy's comments, mom and dad weren't purposefully negligent. They were the working poor who tried to provide a more comfortable life for their kids. The doc had seen it a hundred times. Because Jimmy was the middle child—essentially being raised by a brother only a year older—he was trying to circumvent the middle-child syndrome and carve out a piece of identity for himself. That, too, the psychiatrist had seen a hundred times.

In late July, a police officer and a juvenile case worker arrived to transport Jimmy to the state hospital in Springfield. The boy bid a brief farewell to his "friends" at the Adams County Youth Home. It was a rather chilly goodbye considering all of these boys had lived in such close quarters for the past two months. And they'd treated Jimmy like their kid brother, which filled a void he so desperately craved. He wanted to keep in touch with Trigger, but the youth didn't volunteer his correspondence. The truth was that although Jimmy was leaving, Adams County long-timers knew far too many fellow prisoners who were taken on the 116 mile drive deep into Illinois' interior for "evaluation," never to return. Trigger and the boys knew—or they believed, anyway—that if the courts figured you needed a mental going-over, then they were already convinced you were a bug. The checkup itself was a formality. A judge ordering a psychological examination was a veiled way of sending the kid to the loony bin.

Jimmy took his seat in the back of an unmarked blue Ford Crown Victoria. He buckled his seatbelt, put his uncuffed hands on his lap, and peered out the window for the next two hours. All three in the car sat in virtual silence. The two officers talked to each other in muffled tones. Neither of them addressed Jimmy. The boy just watched the cornfields whip by. It was beautiful outside—sunny, cloudless skies, and a horizon bathed in green. He didn't think too much of his impending fate in Springfield. Jimmy knew he wasn't crazy, or at least he didn't think he was. Besides, he thought, the worst that could happen to him was that maybe he'd have to spend some time in a hospital.

When they arrived, the state hospital didn't look all that different from Blessing Hospital in Quincy. It was huge and sprawling. Some buildings were larger and taller than others were, some brick and others white concrete. There was a lot of commotion and people wearing hospital scrubs and white coats. Jimmy passively exited the Crown Victoria and followed the two men into the hospital. The place snaked around like a giant maze with people hurriedly moving about. Jimmy and his escorts leisurely meandered through the hallways on several different floors as if time were not an element of their schedule. They eventually came to a halt in the evaluation ward.

◄○►

Jimmy received his own room, which he appreciated after having been crammed into an eight-foot by eleven-foot chamber with a roommate. There was a twin bed with white linens that was rigged to a remote and moved up and down. The room had a sink, toilet, some comic books on a nightstand, and a huge mirror that stretched almost the length of the back wall. There wasn't a TV, which aggravated him somewhat, but at the very least, he had something to read other than school books.

A woman welcomed him and said she'd bring him food in a little while. Jimmy softly thanked her. Then she left and casually closed the door behind her.

He tried the door several times throughout the night; especially when hunger set in and his promised meal didn't arrive. When the heat started rising in the room, he did shout out "hello!" but he never became excessively panicked. He grabbed the "Archie" comic books, got under the white linen sheets, and read. He fell asleep an hour into the comic, awoke, read some more, and went back to sleep.

His second week there, Jimmy was permitted a visit with his parents, who eagerly made the drive from Quincy. Sharon and Robert hadn't seen their son in over a month despite coming to Springfield for Mike's court-ordered therapy. Jimmy's doctors weren't permitting visits while he was under evaluation.

Sharon and Robert were allowed in their son's room for two hours. The two-way mirror and wired audio concealed in the air-conditioning ducts allowed the doctors to monitor their visit.

His parents asked Jimmy how he was holding up and they told him how much he was missed back home. "I'm lonely and I want to come home," he said. "And I think a lot about the fire. I feel so sorry for it. I just feel really bad about what I did. I wish I could go back and make it so I never did it."

Jimmy was passing psych tests and making life easier on himself, though he had no way of knowing it. In fact, most of the doctors and psychiatrists assigned to his case didn't know what sort of sentence the Adams County judge had imposed. The court had ordered them to gauge his mental state, and that's what they were doing.

All things considered, Jimmy was diagnosed with a mild case of depression and another mild case of hyperactive disorder, or attention deficit disorder. His condition wasn't severe enough to deem him a threat to himself or others, but it had the propensity to become so if not treated. The doctors prescribed an antidepressant and a moderate dose of Ritalin, then they recommended to the courts that he receive therapy once a week for at least a year.

Several days later, Jimmy was discharged from the Springfield psychiatric ward and back home in Quincy. He and Mike were reunited, but there was something different about his big brother. Mike had developed vicious mood swings and he no longer said much.

The boys tempered their illegal activities. In part out of regret for the past and out of a desire to stay off the local authority's radar screens, but also because a social worker began visiting the Scott home every couple weeks to observe living conditions.

The house was a little lonely without Mike and Jimmy's resident sidekick. Jeff was in a foster home across town. His involuntary domicile, however, didn't last long. Jeff was distraught. His new family couldn't console the 11-year-old. All day and night he'd weep for his mother. Sharon practiced a similar routine in her Elm Street bedroom.

Life got to be so uncomfortable for Jeff's foster family that they petitioned their case worker to take Jeff back. The boy desperately wanted to return home, and his mother, for her part, made a lot of racket down at the courthouse for custody to be reinstated. Mike, Jimmy, and Jeff ended up spending just over three months apart. By August 1982, the Scott boys were all under the same roof again, playing Hot Wheels and watching Cardinals games as though nothing had ever happened. They committed to each other, their parents, and the Adams County legal system that their rambunctious conduct and misbehaving were behind them. The future would be bright and full of promise for Mike, Jimmy, and Jeff. That was their pledge.

Notwithstanding the boys' best efforts and church-like manners, the town of Quincy decided that it wasn't ready to forget the Webster Elementary School fire. And the townspeople demonstrated through word and deed that they certainly weren't ready to forgive three brothers.

CHAPTER TEN

◄○►

The Scott boys well of friends dried up in a matter of weeks. Parents didn't want their children associating with arsonists, and for their part, they didn't want to associate with the parents of arsonists. Sharon and Robert were similarly shunned. They often heard snickers coming from the church pews, at the grocery store, and at the Pepsi Bottling Plant. Even Sharon's indigent clients had a hard time holding their tongues. They questioned her directly about how she could let her sons go so astray. The solemn, demure woman with the fleshy cheeks, curly brown and gray hair, and wide-rimmed glasses didn't have an answer. She just clasped her hands together tightly and lowered her head.

Mike and Jeff wore their anguish openly while their more aggressive brother, Jimmy, tried to suppress his embarrassment. The eldest let his studies and social skills suffer. He slipped into a pervasive melancholic state that flared up the moment he stepped foot outside his Elm Street house. Mike became particularly preoccupied with what others were saying about him and his parents in hushed corridors. As the senior of the Scott boys, he couldn't help but think that the ire of Quincy was cast upon him: As Robert Scott's eldest son, he should have known better than to let the Webster fire get out of control. Mike voluntarily stepped up his counseling sessions. He had a tutor when school resumed in late August, but that didn't help. By age 14, Mike was diagnosed with a severe learning disability and a mild form of dyslexia. Whether it was a new condition or one that was long-simmering only to surface as a component of his depression was unknown. He transferred midway through the first academic quarter to Quincy's Franklin

School, where Quincy's special education program was housed. Mike Scott, the socially adept brother, was now riding the short bus to school and wallowing in an ever-deepening reservoir of self-loathing.

Little Jeff became a teary, insufferable adolescent. Failed foster care heaped weighty insecurities upon his slim frame and narrow shoulders. The youngest Scott grew completely suspicious of outsiders and strangers. A random knock on the front door by a solicitor became an episodic event for Jeff. He'd freeze up and stare blankly at the house's entry. "They're back!" he thought. "They're taking me for good this time!" He had such a nervous disposition that the boy couldn't even rouse himself from the floor to run and hide in a closet or under his bed. When the knocking finally ceased and the stranger on the stoop left the property, Jeff's deep-seated anxiety crept into his lungs and made him hyperventilate. He'd wheeze and choke as panic attacks seized him and made him cough and cry. He never wanted to leave his mother's side. When he did, Jeff retreated to a place inside his head. He spent his school days in a despondent, almost catatonic state and no longer sought company. Other than his brothers and parents, the boy just wanted to be left alone.

Jimmy meanwhile was absolutely perplexed by the tone of the town. He thought Quincy—especially the boys he'd grown up with his entire life—would get a kick out of the Webster fire. Although a savage act of vandalism, at the very least, it showed a devil-may-care attitude. He'd seen so many times over the years just how jazzed the locals became over a little notoriety. Jimmy's fire made more than four Page One news stories. That must count for something to someone. He also thought the boys would be clamoring to hear about the Adams County Youth Home and of the nuthouse in Springfield. A smattering of junior criminals did, but most Quincy youths were too afraid of him now to be around a known delinquent.

He was a convivial boy who lacked social skills. Jimmy had no problems interacting in a group but he did have a hard time initiating conversations, especially in one-on-one situations. He was shy, and the shyness intensified with the public knowledge that he was a fire-starter.

At the same time, he didn't want the town to know they were getting under his skin. He tried to smile as he walked past people in his neighborhood and in the schoolyard at Quincy Junior High. Jimmy's smile, however, was frequently misinterpreted as being an ominous, shit-eating grin.

◄○►

James Scott robotically trudged his way through Quincy Junior High and then Quincy High School. He was no longer his older brother's wingman, as he'd been throughout elementary school. Mike was in the city's special education program for the rest of his academic career. He began having seizures when he was a teenager and was diagnosed as an epileptic. His manic depression would trigger the dormant condition. Although he'd graduate from Quincy High School, Mike rarely had classes in the same wing of the building as his brother. Other students teased Mike when he walked through the halls, especially after he had a seizure in the middle of the cafeteria. Jimmy became his big brother's protector. He'd confront the bullies with all 170 pounds of his muscular five-foot ten-inch frame. He wasn't a violent person, but he flew into an uncontrollable rage when someone picked on Mikey, who at this point was too troubled to fend for himself.

High school became a chore. Jimmy hated going to classes: His grades dipped dangerously close to failing, although he managed to buckle down mostly at the last minute for exams. Some teachers, like his English teacher, went out of her way to help the troubled teen. She knew the Webster story—she'd even been one of the thousands of residents standing on the street in the middle of the night watching the former school burn. And she witnessed firsthand how cruel students can be.

Jimmy roamed the hallways alone. Come lunchtime, he sat in the cafeteria with a band of fellow miscreants. They were the gear-heads and head-bangers: The ones who wore heavy metal T-shirts and spent considerable time smoking cigarettes in the school parking lot.

As more time passed, Jimmy's isolation morphed into contempt. He internalized his frustration with a town unwilling to forgive his actions as he drifted in and out of periods of depression. When he was 16, Jimmy discovered alcohol. On a Saturday night in Quincy, half brother Dan Leake brought Jimmy to a gathering at Villa Kathrine Castle on Front Street. The party crowd was a regular who's who of high school dropouts, power drinkers, and recreational drug users. They rolled up in their Corvettes, Camaros, Monte Carlos, and modified Skylarks. They blasted Metallica's new tape, *Master of Puppets*, and bellowed along with the angry lyrics.

The Budweiser was pouring long, and the rolling waters of the adjacent Mississippi River lent a picturesque backdrop to the old-fashioned Midwestern beer buster. Dan and his buddies thought it'd be fun to get young Jimmy drunk for the first time. The girls agreed because Jimmy was a cute kid and they thought it'd be entertaining to see him inebriated

He downed his first Bud and let out a burp. Jimmy felt a little light-headed though still in control. His nerve rose a bit: Jimmy didn't feel so intimidated by the older kids. He managed to approach a couple of girls at the party, something he wouldn't have done without the liquid fortification. After the fourth beer, his mind no longer kept his speech in check and Jimmy said exactly what he was thinking, which included telling girls that he thought they were hot. One girl, Tina, was a year-older than him yet a sea-soned partier. The two of them made googly eyes at each other throughout the night, and Tina—realizing that Jimmy was too shy to approach her, despite being tipsy—approached him. They became something of an item that night, leaning against cars, drinking beers, and stealing occasional kisses.

Jimmy stumbled around the parked cars and maundering partygoers. He whooped and hollered along with the rest of the crowd long into the night. For the first time in a long time, he forgot about the fire, the nut-house, and the way the people of Quincy treated him.

Dan noticed the jovial demeanor of his half brother. He liked seeing the kid positive, a rare occurrence over the last few years. Dan encouraged him to stay loose, to drink as much as he wanted. Jimmy didn't hesitate. He boozed himself into a blackout that night.

The next morning, he awoke in his bed but he couldn't remember how he got there. Dan had helped him home while the Scott family slept. Jimmy's head was splitting and his mouth tasted like an ashtray. He stumbled off the top bunk and into the hallway bathroom.

The 16-year-old didn't mind that the Burlington Northern train seemed to run over his head from temple to temple; he was happy. He had sketchy memories from the previous night, and even though he couldn't remember everything in detail, he recalled enough to know he had been content. Alcohol had made him forget. It was a brief holiday from the harsh realities of Quincy life, but it was a holiday nonetheless.

Jimmy started drinking every chance he got. He didn't have a fake ID, but he had the next best thing: An enabler that never seemed to mind saucing his sibling. Dan had moved out of the Elm Street house five years earlier, and now that they had partying in common, Jimmy became a fixture at Dan's ranch house. Jimmy became Dan's sidekick. He spent most of his time after school and all of his weekends hanging around Dan's house, drinking with the hangers-on while neglecting his studies and becoming more and more estranged from his high school chums, with the lone exception being Troy Lyons. Troy liked to hang around Dan's house also, and he too developed a penchant for beer.

The alcohol-fueled days began to run together. The burst of empowerment Jimmy initially felt after his first encounter with cocktails and parties slowly morphed into degradation and despair. Getting drunk no longer meant forgetting. After a while, getting drunk amplified his troubles and brought on new ones. He was a teenage alcoholic and he knew it. What was more, Jimmy's future seemed bleak. College was out of the question; he wasn't sure he had high enough marks to even graduate high school. Life for him consisted of going through the motions at school, then retreating to Dan's or to Villa Kathrine Castle to cut loose.

Despite his slump, Jimmy was scheduled to graduate from Quincy High School in January 1988, without ceremony. There would be no cap and gown, no walking across the stage to receive his diploma, no proud parents in the gallery snapping pictures and embracing each other. Quincy High School would simply drop a diploma in the mail. He had a C-minus average with auto shop helping to pull him through: He just needed to maintain for two and a half more months.

Still, Jimmy would achieve a milestone that few thought he could. Many folks in Quincy figured he'd be in jail by the time he was 17. He looked forward to proving the naysayers wrong. James Scott, the Webster Elementary School fire starter, would be a bona fide high school graduate. In November, he'd turn 18, and Jimmy wanted to travel abroad, meet foreign people, and leave Quincy behind forever.

A recruiter from the U.S. Marine Corps visited Quincy High School that October. He spoke of faraway lands, respect, pride, accomplishment, and community. Of belonging. He spoke eloquently and looked regal in his Marine dress blues with a shiny sword strapped to his side. The recruiter sold Jimmy on a Marine's lifestyle. The teen decided he would enlist that summer. He just needed a little more time to get the partying out of his system.

◄o►

The last few months of high school were like a death march. Autumn transformed Quincy into an array of brilliant colors, and the changing foliage and crisp air made Jimmy restless. Sharon and Robert continued with their busy schedules and weren't around much. Jimmy never went to them with his unease, as they had enough to deal with being the parents of the Webster fire starters. No news was good news as far as Sharon and Robert Scott were concerned, and Jimmy thought better than to burden them with his spiraling downturn anyway.

Mike had a hard time holding onto jobs, so Jimmy didn't want to saddle him with his ills, and Jeff was wrapped up in high school girls and friends. At least, so it seemed. Nevertheless, the middle brother hesitated to complain to the kid who idolized him. Sometimes he'd talk to Tina, but she was more of a drunken fling than a true companion. They also started experimenting with each other sexually. Despite Jim's excessive drinking (and Tina's also, for that matter), he always treated her with respect in the morning. He nursed her when she'd black out. Mostly, he held her head over the toilet when she got sick. It was Jimmy's act of chivalry, a trait he learned from his mother. "You respect women," she'd say to him all throughout high school. "And you respect their emotions." Good advice, he knew, yet self-respect seemed to come harder than respecting the opposite sex.

He felt close to Tina, especially when they'd lie together in Dan's spare bedroom, cuddling close in the small twin bed, forced to hold each other through the night for fear of rolling onto the laminate wooden floor. He liked to kiss her forehead when they finished making love, no matter how stone drunk they were. Jimmy couldn't see her face when he did, but Tina smiled each time and quietly cooed. It wasn't love because behind each other's backs, there were other partners, but it was the closest thing the troubled 18- and 19-year-old Quincy teens could muster. And it was all they knew.

Those were special and sincere moments for Jimmy. They were a quick fix: A Band-Aid on a sucking chest wound because the teen had a broken heart. He didn't pine for a woman, nor was he lovesick for love's sake. James Scott's heart hurt for past transgressions; for shattered childhood dreams, overworked parents, an epileptic brother, a brother he feared would follow in his misguided footsteps, the first Burlington Northern train out of Quincy, and a steerage ticket on that wayward freighter.

Jimmy tried to lose himself in music. Angry lyrics calmed his nerves from time to time. It gave him an emotional outlet, especially Guns N' Roses. The quintet recently exploded on the music scene with *Appetite For Destruction*. Jimmy would put on his Sony Walkman and scream out lyrics in perfect time with lead singer Axl Rose. He requested that Dan play the album at parties, and he would often pop in the cassette tape with "Out Ta Get Me" ready whenever he got in a friend's car. That was his bad-boy anthem.

Yet when he was alone in the Elm Street home, Jimmy would casually slide one of his father's 1970s albums off the den shelf and cue it up. He closed his eyes and lay motionless on the couch as James Taylor crooned from a crackling vinyl LP over tattered speakers. Track One in particular held a special meaning for the troubled young man. The song spoke of a young cowboy who lived on a range, accompanied only by his horse and cattle. He plied his trade from the saddle and he slept in deep canyons as he waited for the coming of summer and any sort of varvel change.

The song always penetrated Jimmy's leathery exterior. It was as though Taylor had been in Jimmy's predicament himself, as though he'd dived into the deep end of the river before ever testing the waters. The singer's mild baritone made Jimmy's skin tingle. His arms grew goose pimples and his lips quivered each time he played that song, especially at the chorus. Taylor bid goodnight to the moonlight ladies, softly drifting off to sleep as he did. Visions of deep greens and blues floated ethereally through his head as he was left alone with his dreams, to rock-a-bye, Sweet Baby James.

Jimmy always surprised himself with just how deeply his emotions ran as the words filled the house. Sometimes, when he knew nobody would be home for hours and he was sure not to be walked in on, he'd play that song repeatedly, cranking the volume up a little louder as he did so as to truly hear the inflections in Taylor's voice. He related to the imagry when the singer spoke of snowcovered turnpikes on the first of December, of algid mountains taking on fairytale shapes on the outskirts of far off wonderlands like Stockbridge and Boston, of mile upon mile of empty roadway in front of him, of endess possibilities and of a past safely behind him in the rearview mirror.

Jimmy felt at peace for the moment, as if he had the ability to read between the lyrics and see music in a more visionary manner than anyone else in town. Then the song would end and Jimmy realized that there were probably kids just like him in towns like Stockbridge and Boston—wherever they were—doing the same thing. Of all the Jimmy's in Quincy, he was the last one the people would readily refer to as Sweet Baby James. That much he knew.

On a gray, crisp Hallows Eve in 1987, 18-year-old Jimmy sat in his parent's house and watched the snowflakes coat Elm Street. The streets had a thin layer of snow and it was mounting steadily, even though winter was still a month away. Plows rumbled through town for the first time all season and he saw some neighborhood children bundled in their winter gear preparing to play in their yards. He momentarily longed for his childhood, to be out there as carefree as they were. He contemplated what it would mean to be 12 again, only without the task of carrying the town's angst around everywhere he went. He smiled as he watched his neighbors enjoy the afternoon. The smile, however, didn't last long.

As the minutes ticked by, Jimmy grew disheartened. If he even approached those children and volunteered his help with a snowman, a parent peering out from the window would surely snatch their kid up and rush him inside. "I want you to stay away from that man," would be the command. "He's no good."

It was a bitter truth that he had to face. Because of the Webster fire, Jimmy wore a scarlet W everywhere he went. Mike wasn't around to shoot the breeze, and Dan was working at the hardware store. Jeff was watching TV. He went into his bedroom, grabbed a pack of Camels, donned his red plaid flannel coat, and casually walked past his brother and out the front door. Jeff didn't ask where he was going, which was good because Jimmy didn't know himself.

He strode into the garage and fumbled behind the garbage cans for his Budweiser stash. The air was as cold inside the carport and he grabbed four frigid bottles and stuck them in his coat pockets. Then he set off down Elm Street, looking for a quiet place to polish off some brews and smoke some cigarettes.

He followed Elm Street west toward the river for more than a mile. When he got to 15th Street, where many of the 50-year-old homes were in a state of disrepair, Jimmy headed north for a block to Lind Street. He made a left and came to a halt in front of a dilapidated one-story house flanked on all sides by trees.

He drew a Camel out of the soft pack and put it between his dry lips. He lit the cigarette, continued walking past some of the older, more decrepit Quincy homes, and then reached the outskirts, where some abandoned structures sat collecting dust and snow.

Jimmy inhaled deeply, feeling the nicotine pierce the back of his tongue as he drew the hot smoke into his frosty lungs. The contrasting sensation melded in his throat and when he exhaled, he wasn't sure if he was blowing smoke or steamy breath. He liked the aroma of burning tobacco in cold dry air, and the cigarette gave him a slight buzz. He pulled a beer out of his flannel pocket and popped the cap off with his teeth: An amusing trick he'd learned while hanging around Dan's crowd. Jimmy took a long swig, letting the liquid sit in his mouth for a moment before he swallowed. It tasted refreshing, like that snowy Midwestern day if he could assign a flavor to Halloween.

He walked toward an abandoned detached garage behind a beat-up house at 1510 Lind. There was a rusty, antique tractor inside that probably hadn't run in over a decade. The carport was slowly crumbling with two-by-six planks separated from the base and slowly being overtopped with falling snow. Jimmy passed under the threshold where a door used to be and leaned up against the tractor. He lit another cigarette, finished his Budweiser, and opened a second one. The young man stood there in the still of the late afternoon. Evening light began to draw out the bite in the air, yet it also managed to stamp out the pervasive white glare of the snow and turned the landscape into a Robert Frost poem.

He drank the second beer quickly and tossed the bottle nonchalantly on the floor of the garage. Wasting no time, he bit the lid off the third.

His long, curly blond hair tussled as a wintry wind whistled through the old planks and lingered in the rickety enclosure. His three-day-old facial hair stood on end and his thin mustache began to freeze from his repetitive lip-licking. Jimmy's lips split from the mixture of below freezing temperatures, dry air and saliva. They ached each time the Budweiser bottle rose to meet them. He lit another cigarette and used the speckled brown filter as makeshift gauze. Jimmy blotted at the festering sore on his bottom lip with the butt, then pulled it back and studied it. Dead skin and faint traces of blood transferred from his mouth to the cig. He really began to feel the effects of three beers consumed in a short period of time, coupled with nicotine. Jimmy was one beer away from officially being loaded. And he wanted to achieve that heightened state on the double-quick despite knowing that his condition to come would be a crap shoot. He'd either feel jovial and happy, or the alcohol would propel him into a gloomy, melancholic place. The garage on a winter's day was a peaceful enough setting to experiment with his emotions, so Jimmy chugged the last half of his third beer and immediately started in on the fourth.

By now, Jimmy was drunk. He mumbled his thoughts out loud and answered himself with giggles. On a dime, however, Jimmy turned surly. He rocked back and forth against the tractor as he polished off the last Budweiser. He heaved the bottle against the wall and it shattered with tremendous velocity. Jimmy struggled to remain upright from the force of the throw. The inebriated teen recoiled piecemeal, like a plastic lure on fishing line.

Jimmy stood there for a moment and looked around aimlessly. He had four cigarettes left in his pack, although his throat was too raw to smoke without having a frosty brew chaser. Jimmy put his hands in his hair and blew the air out of his lungs. Then he closed his eyes and rocked tenderly in place.

"There is a young cowboy he lives on the range," he sang softly. "His horse and his cattle are his only companions. He works in the saddle and he sleeps in the canyons, waiting for summer, his pastures to change."

He strained to get the last words out as a disturbing tempest welled from within. Snow continued to fall and collect around the garage and the alcohol played havoc with Jimmy's head. Webster was back on his brain again. Simply knowing he couldn't walk home without someone saying to himself that there went James Scott the arsonist paralyzed his soul. The Marines couldn't save him fast enough. He didn't want to go home, yet he had no where else to go.

Jimmy pulled the lighter out of his jacket pocket and grabbed another Camel. He lit the cigarette and drew the flame back while keeping his thumb on the butane release. The yellow flare flickered and danced in the crisp October air. Jimmy heard a plank creek from the wind. He stretched his arm and held the flame a few inches from the board. "Burning wood smells good," he thought. "I'll just toast a board and get that aroma in here with me. It'll make me happy. I won't let it catch. Just change the smell up a little."

Jimmy robotically put flame to wood. Wisps of gray smoke immediately emanated from the spark. It did smell good. The aroma was that of a fire-place, like one of those over on 14th and State streets with its giant chimney.

The metal top of his lighter grew hot, but it warmed his thumb, which warmed his whole body. A black tracer crept north along the plank and the flame grew taller as it drew in oxygen and ate away at dry wood. "Deep greens and blues are the colors I choose," Jimmy said aloud as the flame jumped upward to another board. "Won't you let me go down in my dreams, and rock-a-bye Sweet Baby James."

He stayed in the garage as the lighter's flame transformed into a structure fire. The east wall methodically came to light, tempered from the outside by wet, snow-covered wood. Jimmy stood there until the heat from the blaze and its accompanying smoke became the only breathable air in the joint. The light was as intense as the heat. Jimmy lowered his head and ducked underneath a gaping section of the garage. As he exited the structure, his eyes took a few seconds to adjust. Dusk had settled over Quincy. Jimmy wondered how long he'd been in there. He wasn't wearing a watch, but the winter glare and flat light were gone. In fact, the only lights he saw were the faint house lights of the beat-up structure at 1510 Lind Street, which were now directly in front of him. And the yellow corona of light that began to enlarge and crackle behind him as it lit his way back to the sidewalk.

◄○►

The following afternoon, Jimmy nursed his hangover. When he returned home from the Lind Street garage a night earlier, he made a beeline to his parent's garage and polished off the rest of the beers in his stash. After the last one, he laid down for a nap and blacked out, only to awaken at 10 o'clock in the morning.

He moped around the house in a funk waiting for his head to clear. After a while, Jimmy grabbed the *Herald-Whig* from the front porch and perused the day's news. There in the police blotter was his fire. He struggled to remember the details.

The paper spoke of a fire that leveled an old car port and scorched an antique tractor inside. Beer bottles had been left at the scene, and fire officials suspected arson. An investigation was underway.

He finished the story, folded the paper, and took his place on the sofa. Then Jimmy fell back to sleep.

He awoke that evening to the sound of the television. Mike was sitting in the recliner blankly staring at a rerun of the show *Press Your Luck*.

"What's up, Mikey?" Jimmy asked as he sat up and turned his attention to the Whammies dancing across the screen.

"Nothin'," Mike replied. He was wearing soiled blue jeans and a blue button-down short-sleeve uniform atop a long-sleeve cotton undershirt. The older brother had just finished up his shift at Q Car Care Center, a carwash on Broadway. Jimmy sensed he was upset, however he couldn't discern if Mike was troubled from an event at work or if he was in one of his depressions.

"Something happen today?" Jimmy asked in a matter-of-fact tone.

"No," Mike responded curtly.

"You sure?"

"Yeah."

Not until the theme music played over the credits was another word spoken.

"My boss is a jerk," Mike volunteered.

"What he do?"

"He yelled at me and told me to stop acting stupid."

"What did you do?" Jimmy asked, now genuinely intrigued.

"I didn't do nothin'. I just stood there."

"Well screw that guy."

"Yeah, screw him." Mike never broke his stare from the television. He sat in the recliner and gritted his teeth.

"You sure you're okay?"

"I told you I'm fine."

But Jimmy knew he wasn't. Mike returned to work day after day for a week and never seemed to cheer up. It bothered Jimmy that he couldn't raise his brother's spirits. For the last six years, their relationship had been strained, mostly because of Mike's deteriorating emotional and mental state. They couldn't relate to each other on the same level as when they were kids. That's why Jimmy didn't tell Mike about the garage fire. Back in the day, the middle brother would be busting at the seams with his news. These days, he felt too sorry for Mike and his predicament.

◄O►

Friday, December 4, 1987, began normally enough. Flurries fell throughout the day. Jimmy had started working at Kroger's Grocery Store a few days earlier as a bagger. He opted to apply on his own volition as he needed money to support his drinking habit.

The work was tedious but steady, and he felt a sense of self accomplishment when he got his first paycheck that afternoon. It wasn't much: $4.50/hour, but taken together, he had a $100 check, and Kroger allowed store employees to cash in at the end of their shift. Jimmy had five $20s burning a hole in his wallet right before the beginning of the weekend, which meant he had beer, fast food, and cigarette money. It also meant Dan's house would have a good stash of Budweisers, as Jimmy was ever the generous partygoer when he had extra scratch.

He went home to shower and change before the evening rowdydow. Jimmy washed his long hair and even shaved his cheeks. The mustache was growing in nicely, he thought. He put on a holey yet clean pair of jeans—as was the style—and a Guns N' Roses T-shirt. While he readied himself, Mike walked in their room and plopped down on the bottom bunk. He didn't say a word. Jimmy asked him if he was alright, and he gave his stock reply.

"Yeah."

Jimmy thought better than to press the matter. Besides, he was getting thirsty and was burning too much time at home when he had two full cases of Bud sitting in the snow outside, chilling. Tina was on her way to give him a lift and Mike was being a downer.

He turned to exit the room and asked his brother whether he wanted the light on or off. Mike didn't answer. Jimmy flicked the switch off and closed the door behind him. Then he went into the living room and waited. Tina pulled up into the driveway moments later and honked. He started toward the front door when he remembered he forgot his comb on the nightstand. Jimmy double-timed it back toward his room. As he went to turn the knob, he heard whimpering coming from behind the wooden door.

Mike was crying into his pillow. The loud sobs and sniffles saddened Jimmy. He contemplated rushing in there and holding his brother, rubbing his back and telling him everything would be fine. Robert and Sharon were working, and Jeff was somewhere in town with his friends, most likely at Quincy Mall. The thought of Mikey all alone in a darkened room, in a darkened house with no one to confide in made Jimmy want to cry as well. He took a deep breath and pivoted. The middle brother stormed out of the house, slamming the front door out of frustration as he did.

Tina and Jimmy rode in virtual silence over to Dan's. The hair band Poison was playing, and Tina sang along. When "Talk Dirty To Me" came on, she turned to Jim and sang in his direction. He wasn't amused, his mind was on Mike.

They arrived at the party to a scene of people scattered all over Dan's yard. Partygoers packed inside the house as scores more congregated outside and smoked while the flurries streamed down from the sky. Jimmy's favorite band, G N' R, roared from the inside. Ordinarily, the sound of Axl's wailing and Slash's thunderous guitar solos put him in the perfect party mood. On that night, however, he didn't so much as crack a smile, nor did he sport his trademark grin.

Jimmy tore in to his beer, slamming back Buds with reckless abandon. Some people approached him and tried to engage him in conversation. After all, he was usually the life of the party and a drunkard's best friend. But all Jimmy could think about was Mike. "I shouldn't have left him," he thought over and over. "I shouldn't have come here."

The hours ticked by and he wandered in and out of the house. He made excuses to go smoke a cigarette and he purposefully left the beer in Tina's car so he had a reason to be alone. Jimmy drank himself into that familiar haze and by one o'clock was fighting mad. "I should find Mikey's boss and beat the shit out of him," he thought. "I'm not gonna let him do Mikey like that." He surprised himself with the last statement. Jimmy spoke the words out loud. He didn't know who the boss was, and he certainly didn't know where he lived. All he knew was that Mike was at home crying himself to sleep.

The alcohol was running strong in the teen's system and he felt brave. Jimmy stormed back into Dan's house and located Tina with a knot of women standing by the stereo.

"Tina, I need a ride," he interrupted.

"Now?" she asked surprised. "I'll give you one later."

Jimmy firmly grabbed her wrist and looked directly into her bloodshot blue eyes. "Tina. Now." She got the hint. He wanted something, and despite the fun she was having at the party, she knew Jimmy needed her help. They made their way out of the house together without speaking another word.

He swung the passenger door open and dropped hard into the upholstery, instructing her to drop him off at 30th and Broadway. Then he pulled the tab back on another beer, cracked his window, and lit a Camel. Tina turned the ignition and shifted into drive. They drove off as silently as they arrived. Tina didn't query her occupant: He was in way too crabby a mood. She steered her car onto the snow-covered street and carefully monitored her speed.

They arrived at the intersection 10 minutes later and Tina pulled over. Jimmy had to force the door open because the car was butting up against a snowdrift. He tossed his empty beer can into an adjacent parking lot and slammed the car door behind him without saying goodbye. Tina made a U-turn and headed back to the party.

The streets were empty. Inclement weather kept most people inside, and at that hour, all the shops in Quincy's commercial district were closed anyway. Most of their signs were off too, except the yellow sign that burned bright two blocks away: "Q CAR CARE."

He stood in front of the unassuming gray-painted cinderblock building and grew angrier with each ticking second. The edifice didn't seem all that imposing, yet somewhere inside there was the source of his brother's apprehension. Just knowing that made him insane. Jimmy wanted to lash out at all those who picked on Mikey—past, present and future—but no one was around to feel his wrath. A *Herald-Whig* newspaper box stood at the entry of the carwash. The drunken teen saw it as a projectile that would make a nice big hole in the window.

Jimmy looked around to make sure the coast was clear. Then he grabbed it from both sides and heaved with all his might. It didn't budge. Like the other newspaper boxes around town, this one was bolted into the concrete. He looked around for something else he could throw through the glass, but Broadway was like a ghost town.

Jimmy put his hands in his pockets and felt some loose change. He fingered his quarters and bought a newspaper from the box. He wasn't interested in the goings-on around town: Jimmy needed an accelerator. He fished around in his flannel coat for the lighter, the same one, ironically, that he used on Halloween to torch the garage. His hands trembled from the cold, not from what he was about to do, as he flicked the steel wheel and robotically brought the lighter to life. Then he held it under a corner of the dry newsprint.

The paper quickly lit and spread. Jimmy got on his knees and ignored the icy water that penetrated his jeans. The paper was almost completely engulfed in flames when he carefully slid it under the front door of the Q Car Care Center. He gave the paper one last shove as the flames kissed his fingers. Then he quickly rose to his feet.

Jimmy stood outside the carwash and pressed his face against the front door's square window. The newspaper was burning and the flames were merging with the carpeting. They quickly began to spread. He grinned at his reflection in the window just as the first car of the evening made its way down Broadway. Its high beams were on when it approached the intersection of 28th Street and then they quickly dimmed. Jimmy realized that the driver saw him and turned his lights down to avoid blinding the teen. That considerate action immediately snapped Jimmy out of the moment. He turned his back so the driver couldn't make out his features, and the car continued down the road. When it was a block past him, Jimmy broke out into a wind sprint the likes of which he hadn't engaged in since he rode his bike in record time home from the Webster fire. He pumped his frozen legs down 28th Street just as fast as he could. His wet knees were exposed to the elements through his holey jeans, and his bare skin burned from the headwind.

He did the mile run in just over five minutes and arrived at his house openly gasping for air. The cold bit his lungs as he slowly crept around to the side, trying to collect himself. All of Elm Street was still at that hour. The Scott family was sleeping and unaware that Jimmy wasn't home.

To avoid waking his parents, he decided to sneak in through the side bedroom window, something else he hadn't done since he was a kid. Jimmy eased the screen out of place and pushed open the unlocked pane. He crept into the house and carefully slid the wooden frame down.

"Who's there!" Mike gasped, alarmed to hear the bedroom window creak open at such an ungodly hour for the first time in years.

"It's okay, Mikey," Jimmy said softly. "It's just me. Go back to sleep."

Mike didn't respond. He put his head back down on his pillow and immediately slipped back into a peaceful state of repose. Jimmy stood above his brother for a minute and watched as his slumbering body and steady breathing made the heavy blue quilt rise and fall in perfect timing. He smiled at how relaxed his big brother seemed at the moment. Mike didn't look as though he was fettered by life's inequalities and imbalances. He exhaled ever so lightly. The visible tension that usually settled around his eyes and was illustrated through premature wrinkle lines on his forehead were absent.

Jimmy fought for his brother on that night: He made an emphatic, symbolic gesture on the underdog's behalf. The sense of pride and accomplishment was tangible. He was so overcome with unbridled emotion that tears of joy streamed down his frozen cheeks. Then Jimmy surprised himself; he knelt beside his quiescent brother and whispered "I love you" in his ear. The older brother unknowingly beamed. Jimmy leaned over, ran a hand through Mikey's hair, and gently kissed his forehead.

CHAPTER ELEVEN

◄○►

Jimmy rang in 1988 at Dan's house. He had a few cases of beer, which he knew he'd need in order to celebrate New Year's properly. He'd be graduating high school in two weeks, a full semester behind the rest of his classmates, but graduating nonetheless.

The 18-year-old was hanging on Tina that night. They were happy and intoxicated. By 1988, alcohol was such an element of their social life that it was tough to imagine a day that didn't start out with a beer and a smoke. Likewise, it was tough to imagine an evening that didn't conclude with beer, cigarettes, and heavy metal music, either at Dan's or in a smaller, more intimate setting, like Tina's house.

The two used to joke about having a child together. Neither one was ready for the emotional responsibility let alone the financial commitment that comes with a baby. Tina had barely made it through high school herself, and truth be told, she was more interested in landing a husband than getting a degree. Jimmy wasn't interested in making that happen. The last thing on Jimmy's mind was commitment of any kind; which made the idea of having a child together all the more absurd.

After one long, alcohol-soaked February day, Tina and Jimmy retreated to her house and took refuge from the bitter winter bite under her lime green comforter. She cued up Poison's "I Won't Forget You," which always put her in a sexually-charged mood, especially on languid days when a heavy blanket was the only material separating the cold from their naked bodies.

Poison's Bret Michaels brayed in the background: "I should let you fade away, but that just wouldn't be me." Jimmy and Tina lost themselves in each other. Their bodies meshed as they fumbled under the covers for a semblance of love and a feeling of togetherness. A momentary lapse in judgment caught Jimmy off guard. He felt comfortable in Tina's arms as his lithe body relaxed atop hers—and he failed to pull out.

Tina didn't care. She was enthralled with the music and the moment. She focused on their heartbeats while they lay together for an hour before both of them drifted off to sleep.

◄○►

Neal Baker sat behind his desk at the Quincy Police Station and ran a hand over his bald head. He'd been a detective for only a couple months, making the move from patrol in December 1987. While the new rank gave the eight-year veteran a higher stature and a slightly higher pay grade, being a detective wasn't a promotion per se, at least, not in Quincy: It was more of a pit stop on the way to becoming a sergeant, which Baker knew he'd inevitably be. He was, after all, one of Quincy's finest, one of those cops who was constantly on the beat, day and night, out there, and dedicated.

One of the first investigations that crossed his desk was a series of arsons around town. Back in August 1987, someone had set an apartment house on fire. The building—over on North Eighth Street—wasn't a total loss. There had been one person inside but she had escaped unharmed. However there was more than $6,000 in damages. Two months later, on Halloween night, someone torched an old garage over at 1510 Lind Street, and two months after that, the Q Car Care Center on Broadway got hit.

It was a rather daunting assignment for Baker because Quincy wasn't ordinarily a hotbed of criminal activity. Sure, the cops often nailed people for noise violations and the occasional teenager for breaking curfew. Most detective work, however, centered on drugs. Those cases often baffled Baker as well as his kid brother, Bruce, who was still a patrolman at the time. They'd often scratch their heads whenever a big shipment of marijuana made it to town because law enforcement knew no local could move so much volume under their noses.

This case was different, though. Arson was a felony on all fronts, whereas drug possession often fell under a misdemeanor, except for the occasional bust where a large quantity of narcotics was involved.

Baker was perplexed and troubled by the fires. Aside from being law enforcement, he was also a local, born in Quincy and raised most of his life there except for high school, when his folks had moved across the Mississippi River to Palmyra, Missouri. Baker needed to solve this case not only for his own peace of mind, but to keep the locals from exacting revenge on the wrong individual.

He had one lead for the fires, though admittedly, it was a reach. Someone driving down Broadway had seen a man with long hair and holey blue jeans standing outside the Q Car Care Center in the wee hours of a December evening. He didn't provide much of a physical description, short of Caucasian male, medium height, medium build, and long, dark hair.

The detective poured over the various complaints and the reports submitted by the Quincy Fire Department. He was looking for a pattern to the fires. He kicked back in a wooden swivel chair and read.

Baker was a physically imposing officer. He stood about 6 feet tall and weighed a solid 260 pounds, a holdover from his days playing nose tackle on his high school football team and a testament to time served in the weight room. He had a well-kempt mustache and his brown hair—what was left of it—hugged the sides of his shiny bald head. Indeed, Baker had the appearance of the quintessential detective. To top off the look, he wore his brown suits well and made sure his shirts were always neatly pressed and tailor-made.

Baker often marveled at the interesting turns his life took. The path he started off on wasn't one that automatically leads to the local police force. A decade and a half earlier, Baker was a young high school football star who had just enlisted in the Air Force.

In 1972, he wanted to see the world like many high school grads. He figured a career in the armed forces could satisfy that itch. Initially, Neal put in to be a "recreation specialist," which at the time was essentially a glorified gym teacher. He'd be in charge of running the base's fitness program and arranging intramural competitions, but more importantly, his office would be in the weight room. Baker had a 56-inch chest and was bench pressing over 400 pounds, so working in a gym was right up his alley.

Unfortunately, he wasn't the only person jockeying for that position. Baker received his second option, Air Force law enforcement, equivalent to the military police in the Army. He thrived at the job. Baker was tasked with keeping the airmen in line for two and a half years at Whiteman Air Force Base in Missouri, and he did so as much by technique as by his corporeal appearance.

In late 1974, Baker put in for an overseas transfer and ended up at Anderson Air Force Base in Guam, home of the 36th Expeditionary Wing. It was just the sort of life-changing overhaul the 21-year-old was looking for. He met people of different cultures and enjoyed all the benefits befitting an overseas posting. Guam had everything Quincy didn't, right down to the foliage and vegetation. Palms replaced the Midwest's oak trees, orchids replaced daffodils, and Mississippi River sandbars were traded in for the South Pacific's coral reefs. Baker did a 16-month tour in Guam and then just like that, in 1976, his military career was over. He'd done his requisite three years and was ordered to rotate back to the civilian world.

For him, that meant returning to Quincy and to any industry job that was hiring at the time. He found work immediately as a laborer at Electric Wheel, a division of Firestone Tires. Neal approached his entry-level position with an inordinate amount of drive, and he plied his trade with military precision. The people at the plant liked him, as did management. He was promoted to part-time supervisor and would have most likely been promoted to full-time supervisor had an economic recession not hit the country in late 1979. In April of 1980, Electric Wheel shifted into reverse and locked the factory doors.

Baker, through no fault of his own, lost his job. Losing anything however, be it a football game, a chess match, or especially a job, didn't sit well with him. He was a winner who was accustomed to getting what he wanted thanks to a good old-fashioned Puritan work ethic. That's how he'd ascended up the ranks of Electric Wheel so quickly. Now that the plant was gone, Baker was faced with a dilemma. He was ready to work—and work hard—but Pepsi wasn't hiring, and neither were any of the other industries around town. In reality, Baker wasn't qualified to do anything other than physical labor and law enforcement. So he approached the Quincy Police

Department in August of 1980, and he was practically snatched up on the spot. A week later, he was on a shuttle bus with other cadets to Springfield and the Illinois Police Academy.

The Quincy Police Department wasn't always community oriented, not back when Baker became a full-fledged black-and-white in October 1980. A decade earlier, when Neal and kid brother Bruce were growing up in town, the police were more of a good-ol'-boy network of badges who were prone to loitering around town almost as much as the local grifters. It took a series of outreach programs and a revolving door of superior officers before the QPD earned the respect and appreciation of the community. Neal and Bruce, who joined the force four years later, helped to give the department a much-needed makeover.

So it was in February 1988, when Neal Baker, now Detective Baker, sat in his uncomfortable swivel chair and meticulously pored over arson documents. He kept coming back to that one lead—caucasian male, medium height, medium build, and long, dark hair. It was the dark hair description that threw him off.

Baker had been on duty that fateful night in 1982, when Webster Elementary School sent awesome 80-foot flames shooting into the night's sky. He wasn't on the scene, as he and a handful of other officers had been charged with maintaining order over the rest of town. But he knew from the town gossip who was responsible.

The Scott boys were notorious at police headquarters. While he mulled over potential fire starters, Baker dismissed the older brother out of hand because of his physical and mental condition. Besides, Mike Scott had managed to stay out of trouble since that one incident six years earlier. The youngest brother might have done it, as Baker and the other cops knew from reputation that Jeff Scott was teetering on the edge of criminal activity. Yet Baker's suspicions, part detective's intuition and part logical guesswork, centered on the middle Scott, the aggressive one. The thing was Jimmy didn't have dark hair. In 1988, his hair was dirty blond, and distinctively so.

Baker decided to roll the dice and bring him in for an interrogation. He documented that James Scott was a legal burden and he had a prior arson on his resume. The court was satisfied with Baker's conjecture and he was green-lighted to question Jimmy on suspicion of arson.

In late February, Detective Baker bundled up and went looking for the 18-year-old.

—◄o►—

Kroger's was slow during Jimmy's shift. The holiday splurge had ended and the baggers sleepwalked through their day. Jimmy was more exhausted than his fellow bag boys were because he'd been out partying almost every night that month. Dan Leake had the prescription for the winter doldrums—high-octane cocktails, loud music, and a warm place to socialize. For Jimmy, it was the quintessential swan song he longed for before summer and the Marine Corps.

Tina had been acting strangely for the past couple of weeks. She came to the parties, but she wasn't boozing at nearly the frequency Jimmy was used to. That and she was always tired or nauseous, and she spurned his sexual advances.

Still, tonight was another night and things might be different. Five o'clock was nearing and the bagger was counting the minutes until shift's end. He went through the motions of loading bread and eggs into brown sacks. He thanked the customers for shopping at Kroger's. When the clock struck five, Jimmy removed his apron and speed-walked to the Employees Only room to punch out. Then he donned his red flannel coat and headed for the double automatic doors.

Parked right in front of the store was an unmarked blue Crown Victoria. A muscular, mustached man with a wool hat sat in the driver's seat, eyeballing the people as they came out of Kroger's and searched for their cars in the snow-covered parking lot. The driver gave most of the folks the once-over and then forgot about them, as they were women in housecoats doing the day's shopping. Then one long-haired man, who could have easily passed for a woman from behind, drew his attention. He was a Caucasian male, medium height, medium build with long, blond hair.

Neal Baker was laying in wait for his arson suspect. He'd already made a stop at the Elm Street house but no one was home. He questioned some of the neighbors and learned that James Scott was a bagger at the grocery store and that he usually finished up around five o'clock. Baker didn't want to make a scene in the store, especially if his hunch should prove wrong. He sat and waited patiently, like a seasoned police officer. Jimmy didn't notice him or the suspicious car with the long CB antenna as he exited the store and strode into the cold February air. The grocery bagger walked right past Baker's cruiser and out across the parking lot.

The detective shifted into drive and followed close behind as he maneuvered the Crown Vic up a slushy isle and into a clearing. Then he sped up and drove right in front of the line Jimmy walked.

"James Scott?" Baker asked as he emerged from the car. Jimmy didn't recognize the man. He thought hard and tried to place the face, but nothing registered. He hoped that Baker hadn't been someone he mouthed off to while drunk at Dan's house, because this guy was huge and would surely kick the shit out of him.

"Yeah," Jimmy replied reluctantly.

"I'm Detective Baker of the Quincy Police Department," he said, flashing a badge. "I need you to accompany me down to the station for some questioning. Why don't you go ahead and hop in."

Baker was polite and engaging, a far cry from the stories Jimmy heard from friends of their dealings with the QPD. In fact, the cop was so civil that Jimmy didn't even deduce that he was Baker's prime suspect in a string of arsons.

"Okay," was all the 18-year-old said as he eased the passenger door open and took a seat beside the behemoth.

Although a rookie detective, Baker was a seasoned officer. He knew better than to harangue Jimmy from the get go. The "good cop" method was always a more practical trap to spring on people who were inherently leery of law enforcement.

"Cold enough for ya?" Baker quipped as he turned the cruiser onto Broadway and headed west toward the station.

"Yeah," Jimmy replied while keeping his eyes fixed on the road in front of him. The banter served to relax him a bit, though he was still skeptical.

"They say it's gonna get worse here in the next few days," the cop said. Baker shifted his eyes between the slick road and Jim. He was looking for suspicious signs, like what the 18-year-old was doing with his hands. Jimmy wasn't aware of his nervous tell, but he sat there with his hands clasped firmly and his fingers interlocked.

Moments later, they were at the police station. Baker parked the cruiser and asked Jimmy to follow him into the all-too-familiar structure. He was marched through the same door as when he was 12, and then through an underground passage into headquarters and a flurry of activity.

Jimmy's stomach knotted. He suddenly felt like that scared kid who'd burned down Webster Elementary, a feeling that amplified when Baker led him into the same questioning room he'd been in six years earlier. The place was a time capsule: Nothing had changed, from the wooden chairs to the beige walls.

Baker took his place behind one of the chairs and asked Jimmy to have a seat in the remaining one. Then the cop produced a tape recorder from under the table and pressed the record button.

"I want to ask you some questions about the fires," Baker started. He purposefully kept the questions open ended whenever he conducted an interrogation in order to give his suspects an opportunity to implicate them-selves. "Where did you get the gasoline from?"

Baker knew that fuel wasn't used in the fire. His technique, however, was also to feed a suspect misinformation, the goal being that the accused would offhandedly correct the record. Jimmy Scott was a little too seasoned to fall for that right away.

"I'm sorry, sir," he said. "I really don't know what you're talking about."

"Sure you do. The fire you started in the garage on Lind. You doused the place with gasoline, lit a cigarette, and then lit the gas. What I want to know is where did you buy the stuff? Or did you rip it off?"

Jimmy was surprised with the detective's emphatic, cocksure tone. On the one hand, he knew who'd started the fire, but he was wrong about the method. Jimmy stonewalled again.

"Sir, I'd like to help out, but I don't know nothing about no gas."

In that moment, just by Jimmy's slight screw up, Baker knew he had his man. The 18-year-old didn't know about the gas because there wasn't any. He failed to deny the fire the second time. For Baker, this personal technique always led to an admission and later a conviction, refined by years on the beat interviewing suspects. He knew other cops who would use their size and their authority to browbeat information out of people. And Baker had more size than just about everyone else on the force. Yelling and throwing your weight around, he had learned, did one of two things: Either it scared someone so much that they clammed up, or it scared someone so much that they'd give a false confession. Above all, Baker was an ethical cop: He wanted the credit for the collar, but it was the conviction he was after, not the collar for the collar's sake.

Jimmy was caught off guard by Baker's friendly demeanor. He treated the outcast with respect, significantly more than anyone else in town. Jimmy reciprocated in kind. He was waiting for the hammer to drop; for Baker to leap to his feet and stick that huge bald head and push-broom mustache in his face. But it never happened. They sat there in the Vermont Street stationhouse and had a very civil, cordial conversation.

The detective had what he wanted from Jimmy: Baker gave the suspect some rope in those fleeting minutes, and Jimmy went ahead and figuratively hung himself. He decided to let the teen off so he could return to routine daily surveillance. Meanwhile, Baker would write a report of his findings and file a warrant on suspicion of arson. It was a cat-and-mouse game, and like it or not, Jimmy was about to play the mouse.

Baker gave Jimmy a lift home at around eight o'clock. Still early, the free man thought ahead to Dan's house. In the winter months, there were no sports to talk about or to follow. The St. Louis Cardinals football team had finished their 1987 season without glory, and the players, including star quarterback Neil Lomax, were probably at home packing for their move to Phoenix. The baseball Cardinals were months away from spring training, and St. Louis didn't have a basketball team to get behind. They had the Blues, a professional hockey team that was struggling, so no one in Quincy paid much attention to them. Barring a game to watch or a team to talk about, Dan's parties were good old fashioned, late-night throw-downs. The guys hit on the girls, and the girls flirted for a while before giving in to their suitors. Jimmy was hoping that Tina would be there, so he planned to wash and comb his hair when he left Baker's unmarked car and walked in his parent's house.

Sharon and Robert were home. His mother asked in passing where he'd been since he'd punched out. Jimmy said he'd grabbed a bite to eat with a coworker and that he was going over to Dan's. No one pressed the issue.

As he turned to leave, Mike sat watching TV. He didn't acknowledge his brother when Jim walked into the living room, choosing instead to remain in a catatonic-like trance. Jim plopped down beside him for a minute and watched the same program. *Alf* was on, and it didn't take much to elicit a laugh from Jimmy. He loved that ridiculous creature—always running around the Tanner house, trying to eat the family cat. Mike didn't so much as crack a smile.

"See ya later, Mikey," Jimmy said as he rose to leave.

"Bye," Mike replied. He didn't turn his head.

Jimmy had been vague on the evening's activities with his parents, but as soon as he got to Dan's house and in the company of the rowdy guests, he immediately started bragging about his standoff with the Quincy Police Department. The fuzz, he said, questioned him about some fires. Logically, some of the people asked if he was the culprit. "I might know a thing or two about 'em," Jimmy replied. And out came the grin.

He had their undivided attention, which made him feel omnipotent. They marveled at his bravery and attitude, and how he had managed to stave off a monster like Neal Baker. All night long, people came up to hear from the braggart what they'd just heard from friends, and each and every time, Jimmy indulged them with a tale of pyrotechnics like out of a Paramount movie set.

"Aren't you scared about getting caught?" one partygoer asked him with childlike inquisitiveness. "I mean, if they get you, you'll go to prison!"

"Yeah, I suppose I will," the brazen teenager replied. "The thing is, they tried to pop me once and I got away with it. I can outsmart cops."

◄〇►

By mid-March, Detective Neal Baker had his warrant. The courts moved quickly on his request because the town was putting pressure on the authorities to get an arrest. There hadn't been a fire since Q Car Care Center but

Quincy residents didn't want to wait around for another fire before jailing the perpetrator.

Neal brought his brother on for the arrest. Bruce Baker—who was his big brother's spitting image, except he could only bench 425 pounds to Neal's 450—had just made detective and was ready for a weightier assignment than catching drug dealers and the occasional serial burglar. In addition, Neal figured James Scott might not go down quietly. The detective wasn't worried about whether he could handle himself in hand to hand combat should the situation present itself, even though in all of his years of law enforcement, he'd only been involved in two brawls. The first was from his days in the Air Force. A drunken airman started mouthing off to a bunch of people at Whiteman Air Field. Neal showed up to quell the situation when the beer-strong airman took his motorcycle helmet and cracked the lawman upside his head. Baker managed to get a portion of his forearm between the plastic and his dome. The shot was one he'd felt before. Back in his high school football days, Baker sometimes rushed helmetless into the end zone to celebrate with the offense. From time to time, a jubilant running back fresh off a score embraced the nose tackle and knocked his helmeted head against Neal's unhelmeted one. He'd succumb to a monster headache later in the day, but at the moment, epinephrine got the best of him. Same situation in the Air Force. Baker got pumped up by the incident. He drew back and landed a straight right flush against the airman's nose. The blow sent the drunkard stumbling back into some chairs. The guy got up and dusted himself off, but he didn't want to fight anymore. Years later, Neal got out the lead and chased a robber through downtown Quincy. He made a leaping football tackle and pinned the thief down until he relented. The moment Baker let up, he caught a fist to the jaw and a headbutt to the bridge of his nose. The cop responded with a couple of wallops to the man's head, and the robber also lost the will to square-off with Neal Baker.

James Scott didn't seem like the kind of guy who would try to duke it out with the detective. At least, not from their brief encounter. To Neal, Jimmy Scott gave the impression of being more of a crafty behind-your-back type of criminal. Still, Neal didn't want to take chances. He was going to arrest him and charge him with two counts of arson stemming from the garage fire at 1510 Lind, two counts of arson for the Q Car Care Center fire, two more counts from the arson of an apartment building on North Eighth Street, and a disorderly action arising from his conduct after a party at the Castle one night. In all, the city of Quincy would bring seven charges against their least-favorite native son. If convicted on all counts, Jimmy was staring at a possible 50-year prison stint. People facing that much time don't always go quietly.

That's why Neal brought his kid brother onboard. Docile James Scott may have been in the interview room a month ago, but that didn't mean Jimmy would willingly confess.

Neal and Bruce packed into the Crown Vic on a Wednesday evening in mid-March and drove to Kroger's Grocery. Neal parked off to the side of the store's automatic doors and the brothers sat for an hour while Jimmy finished his shift. Neal was inadvertently teaching his kid brother something on that stakeout. The bigger Baker was big on respect. Jimmy treated him with respect the first time around, which is why he didn't want to charge into the store like John Wayne and drag Jimmy out in front of God and everybody.

Just like always, the teenager was lumbering through a shift and looking ahead to an evening drink. Wednesdays weren't pay days, so he could only afford a case of Natural Light beer, which was down a rung from his usual preference. It was a warm pre-spring day and Jimmy wore a long-sleeve T-shirt and a pair of jeans. He started home with his six-pack in hand when a blue unmarked police car darted in front of him and two behemoths with bald heads and mustaches emerged. Jimmy rubbed his eyes as if he were in a cartoon. He wasn't drunk yet, but he was seeing double. They both looked like Detective Neal Baker, which for him meant neither one was a pleasure to look at.

"James Scott?" one of the Neal Bakers said.

"That's right," he answered.

"We have a warrant for your arrest. You have the right to remain silent. Anything you say can and will . . ." As Neal Baker number one read him his Miranda Rights, Neal Baker number two engaged Jimmy with his eyes as he slowly made his way toward the shell-shocked teen and reached for his wrists. The rights-reading continued as one of the Baker brothers cuffed Jimmy's hands behind his back.

"Dammit," he thought as the cold steel wrapped around his joints and cut off the circulation to his hands. "They got me. I don't know how but they got me. Okay. Now here's the real test." His mind started working like a career criminal's. "They have evidence, but I have to somehow counter it. I have to give them nothing. I should probably . . ."

"Mr. Scott, do you understand these rights as I've read them?" a Baker asked.

"Huh?" he stammered. Jimmy hadn't heard a word.

"Do you have any questions for us?"

"Yeah, what are you arresting me for?"

"Six counts of arson and one count of disorderly conduct stemming from an incident at the Villa Kathrine Castle."

"Whoa," Jimmy replied. He was shocked, especially because one of those men had been so nice to him just one month earlier. He tried to lighten the mood. "Sure you got enough charges?" asked Jimmy as he sported his typical grin. The Baker brothers looked at each other and started laughing an identical laugh.

"Come on, Jim," one of them said. "We have a lot to talk about." With that, Bruce Baker helped the handcuffed man into the back seat. Neal took his place behind the steering wheel and turned over the ignition. The door slammed shut and they chauffeured Jimmy to the Vermont Street Police Station for the third time in his young life.

CHAPTER TWELVE

◄○►

Once again, Jimmy followed two men down a narrow hallway at Quincy Police Headquarters. Once again, he took a seat in a beige-painted interview room, and once again, he tried to remain stoic and vague. Neal didn't beat around the bush with open-ended questions because he didn't have to. He began the interview by placing his tape recorder atop the wooden table, pressing "record," and laying out the facts of the fires as he understood them. Of course, he embellished a little, thereby tempting James Scott to correct the record.

"The fire on North Eighth Street last August, the one at the apartment building, you tried to kill that woman inside, didn't you?"

Jimmy pretended not to know what the detective was talking about. He maintained that the August fire wasn't his: He wasn't even in full-blown pyro-mode until October. But the way Neal Baker described it, Jimmy knew who started this fire. He remembered Jeff bragging to some buddies about the North Eighth Street blaze. The kid had graduated to the big boys club, old enough to be tried as an adult and with a prior arson on his record. Jimmy faced a moral conundrum: Taking the fall for Jeff would mean making matters worse for himself. The flipside, however, was even grimmer. He'd have to roll over on his own brother—his friend and sidekick. "Can we come back to that one?" Jimmy asked the detective.

"Sure," he answered, still maintaining a conversational tone. "Do you want to talk about the disorderly conduct charge or would you rather stick with the fires?"

"It's your world," Jimmy quipped. He had a hint of defeat in his voice. The 18-year-old breathed out slowly as he spoke, and he slouched slightly in the stiff wooden chair.

Baker described the disorderly conduct charge. He was outed by a fellow partier one night at the Castle on Front Street for being loud, drunk, and refusing to leave when police arrived on the scene and ordered everyone to cease and desist. Jimmy didn't remember that particular incident. It sounded reasonable. He was, after all, a drunk. Being loud, stubborn, and stupid was just part of an evening's work in his social circle. "I can't say for sure that it was me, but it could have been," Jimmy said. Neal Baker nodded and smiled. Bruce took notes.

"All right, moving right along," the detective continued, "let's talk about the Halloween fire in the old man's garage on 1510 Lind. What did you have against the guy?"

Jimmy paused. He shot a look over to Bruce and then back to Neal, and then he smiled. "Man, how does anyone tell you guys apart?" the suspect asked. Both detectives chuckled.

"I'm the good-looking one," Bruce said, making his presence in the room known vocally for the first time since the interview began. "Yeah, you wish!" Neal jabbed. All three men shared a momentary lighthearted laugh.

"Jimmy," Neal said. "Come on. Let's stay focused here. There are a lot of angry people in town that want your scalp. Right now, you're safer in here with me and skinny over there than you are on the street. So let's get through this and then we can all get on with our lives."

Neal Baker truly was a pro at interrogations. With a detective's acumen and a surgeon's precision, he made Jimmy feel like he was sitting around Dan's living room, shooting the shit with the boys. Jimmy opened up like a lotus, hesitant at first and then bam, all the colors of the spectrum revealed themselves. He explained the fire in the garage in great detail, including a statement about how he felt empowered walking away from the blaze. It reminded him of the Midwestern sunsets he loved so much. He even painted a picture for the Baker brothers: Lately, when he wanted some "alone" time, he'd ride his bike over to Villa Kathrine Castle and sit on the steps as the sun gradually dipped behind the Missouri horizon across the "creek." It was a spectacular vista. Occasionally, some Quincy University girls would be running along Front Street, and Jimmy wouldn't know who to focus his attention on: Mother Nature or some hot chick. Neal got a kick out of that.

Next he moved on to the fire at Q Car Care Center. There was major damage to the interior offices and the waiting room. Luckily for Jim, the owner was insured. Even luckier, the car wash itself and its expensive equipment were cordoned off from the flames by a concrete wall. Jimmy told them everything about that one, too. He said he lit a newspaper and delivered it under the door. He mentioned that Mike worked there, though the one detail he purposefully left out was the retaliatory nature of the arson. Best to keep Mikey out of this, he thought.

This brought them back to the initial fire on North Eighth Street. Baker learned through the course of his investigation that a woman lived there who knew Jimmy. Apparently, she was one of the party people, and Baker heard through the Quincy grapevine that ol' Jim had made a pass at her before. The fire, Baker figured, was payback for rejection. He explained his findings to the teenager, slightly embellishing the details. He said the woman barely escaped with her life. The truth was she got out at the first sign of smoke— the heavy black fumes woke her up. Had she been a sounder sleeper though, Baker's hunch may have been right.

"I'll say this: I know this woman you speak of, but I didn't know she lived there," Jimmy responded. "And because I didn't know she lived there, I had no way of knowing she was home when I set the fire. I was drunk and wasn't thinking."

Jimmy became the fall guy for his younger brother. Now he officially was both of his brothers' keepers: He'd set a blaze to settle a score with Mikey's tormenter and he'd taken an arson rap for little Jeff.

Bruce scribbled furiously. Neal cracked a smile, which made Jimmy's grin emerge. They had a verbal confession. Next came the signed one. Jimmy obliged, signing off on the official documents that pronounced him as the guilty party. Case closed.

"Jim, I like you," Neal said after the dye had been cast and lay drying on the paper. "I mean it. I really do. I want you to know this isn't personal because I think you're a nice guy. The bottom line is that you broke the law, and I can't have you running around town breaking laws. You know what I mean?" Jimmy nodded.

Protocol required that James Scott be booked and remanded to the custody of neighboring Adams County Jail pending trial. He wasn't surprised. The same thing happened six years ago. He went to the police station with two detectives, answered a lot of questions, and then disappeared into the bowels of the police station until he could be transferred to the jail.

Jimmy knew he was in big trouble, though he didn't understand the severity of what he did, at least, not there in the interview room. He felt ashamed more for his family than for himself. Quincy had long since done away with James Scott. Sharon and Robert Scott, on the other hand, were law-abiding Christian citizens. Through no fault of their own, they were bound to get sucked down the drain right along with their middle son. That's just how the town worked. Jimmy couldn't think about anyone or anything other than his mother. He remembered the look on her face when they took Jeff away from her. She expressed a similar look over the years as Mike's health and sanity deteriorated. He took cold-comfort in knowing that at least her baby wouldn't go down for the North Eighth Street fire. Jimmy felt compelled to talk to his mother right then and there. He felt duty-bound as a loving and ashamed young man to break the news. His heart couldn't bear the thought of an indiscriminant police officer knocking at the front door. He knew his mom would automatically think the worst: Jimmy's dead. Her heart would skip a beat. She'd be relieved to hear that he was alive, but then she would be crest-fallen when she learned Jimmy was in trouble again. And what if these two detectives in front of him were the ones chosen to break the news? Their sheer size would make her imagine that her son was bruised and battered in a jail cell, with pitiless guards wantonly neglecting his pleas for a doctor.

As it turned out, the detective was half-right in his prognosis. Jimmy did indeed react like a caged animal, though his knee-jerk reaction wasn't to lash out physically. Rather, he became anxious, and all of a sudden, Jimmy fretted for his mother's mental stability.

The Baker brothers rose from the table and asked Jimmy to rise as well. Bruce opened the door and Neal got behind their man as they escorted him to a waiting cell.

"Detective?" Jimmy spoke. Bruce halted his stride and turned around.

"Yes?" he asked. Jimmy had figured out which Baker was which when they had stood up earlier. He realized the one behind him was slightly bigger. He ignored Bruce and turned to face Neal.

"Would you please let me call my mom?" Jimmy humbly requested.

Neal Baker read the frightened expression on the criminal's face. Ordinarily, that wasn't enough for him to give in; but the kid had been a gentleman throughout the interview. He had also confessed like a man. Neal appreciated the fact that he sat there and took his medicine. The detective wasn't buying, however, the I-was-drunk excuse. A man needs to be disciplined and own up to his actions. Hell, even Detective Neal Baker was prone to fits of anger from time to time. That didn't mean he went and burned down a building. The lawman wrestled with his desire to afford respect while not being too soft.

"I'll give you five minutes."

◄o►

Adams County Jail was ghostly quiet. The concrete floors and painted-blue cinderblock walls cast a dreary spell over the large dorm-like residence area. The vast expanse, which could hold up to 15 men in that particular wing, was cavernous. A payphone hung in the corner where inmates could make collect calls and on any given Friday or Saturday night, a line would form.

On that night, however, only three other men sat on their steel cots and feigned sleep. The florescent lights flickered from above, emitting the only sound on the corridor. Save for the sound of an occasional steel door opening, then slamming shut.

Jimmy used the solitude to reflect on the conversation he had with his father. Sharon was at work so Robert answered the phone when the teen dropped the dime for his five-minute call.

Robert was angry with his son when Jimmy broke the news that he wouldn't be coming home that evening. Not that it really mattered anyway because his arrival would have likely gone unnoticed. His mother would have been at work and his father asleep.

"I warned you that your drinkin' would get you in trouble, didn't I?" Robert said sternly. He had warned Jimmy to stop drinking, only after he quit drinking himself a month earlier. Jimmy had paid him no mind. Yet sitting in the police station, all he could think to say back was, "you were right."

"Dad, tell mom I'm sorry," he beseeched his father. "Tell her I didn't mean to hurt her. Tell her I'll make it up to her. I promise."

Robert changed his tone. "You be careful in there, Jim. I'll be by on my next day off to see you. Take care, son."

As he lay there in jail, Jimmy tried to think ahead to the early morning hour when his mother would return home. She'd be exhausted from a long night of feeding and changing the terminally ill. Dad would most likely wake up to break the news to her. Jimmy just hoped he'd do it gently.

Over the next few weeks, Jimmy was told when to rise, eat, sleep, and shower. Jimmy resorted to the same anonymous tact he took when he had first arrived at the Adams County Youth Home. He stayed off the radar of the other inmates and he said nothing. As a result, he did his time without incident, but he felt utterly alone.

In early April, Jimmy received two visitors on the same day. Much to his delight, the first visitor was Tina. She looked beautiful, he thought. Her long brown hair was cut a little shorter than when he'd been locked up and her brown eyes were accented by eyeliner rather than doused in the stuff, as was her goth tendency. He greeted her with a sly, shy grin, embarrassed by his predicament. She flashed a tiny smile. He went to embrace her in their designated corner of the visiting room. She greeted him with an artificial hug and patted his back the way two distant relatives do.

He felt vexed. This woman who shared her bed with him was acting very strange. He chalked it up to the location and invited her to sit on the plastic chair across the table from him.

"I miss you so much," he started before she had a chance to speak. Tina smiled again and looked down at the table. She ran her fingers along the wooden grooves as she fumbled for the right words. Tina had been dreading this day ever since word of his incarceration made its way around the party people. "Are you okay?" he asked at last. She kept her head down as she spoke.

"No, Jim, I'm not." Her eyes remained at a 40-degree angle. Her fingernails were no longer tracing their way through the seams. She dug them

Fabius River Drainage District President Norman Haerr stands in the threshold of Knapheide Manufacturing Company in West Quincy, July 1993. In the days preceding the flood, he was always on a walkie-talkie. Here, he speaks in one while holding another.

Volunteers stack sandbags along the West Quincy levee three days before the break, West Quincy, Missouri, 1993.

Illinois and Missouri National Guardsmen erect the West Quincy levee
to stem the rising river, West Quincy, Missouri, July 13, 1993.

The chaotic scene on the West Quincy levee three days before the break. Volunteers
came from the furthest reaches of America, West Quincy, Missouri, 1993.

The Mississippi River threatens to flood US-24
in West Quincy, Missouri, July 13, 1993.

A platoon of Illinois National Guardsmen receive instructions
for that day's patrol, West Quincy, Missouri, July 1993.

On July 17, 1993, one day after the West Quincy levee break, 14,000 acres of land flooded. In the foreground, the Memorial Bridge had been underwater for over a week. Just north of that, the Bayview Bridge—the only means of crossing the Mississippi between St. Louis and Keokuk, Iowa—succumbs to the river.

Shortly after the levee break, a giant barge broke free from its harness on the Mississippi River and floated inland. A massive explosion ensued when it struck the Ayerco Gas Station, West Quincy, Missouri, July 16, 1993.

Dan Leake and his family, Fowler, Illinois, 2005. Dan died in his sleep a year later.

The Scott Family. Back row: Sharon, Robert, unidentified woman
Front row: Mike, Jimmy, and Jeff, 1981. This is the only family photo.

University of Missouri soil scientist Dr. R. David Hammer says that any one of six parameters can deem a levee fallible. The levee in West Quincy met all six.

Adams County (Illinois) Sheriff Bob Nall standing in the county jail in 1990. This is where James Scott was housed each time he was arrested.

Quincy Detective Neal Baker stands by the Bayview Bridge, Quincy, Illinois, 2007.

A cellblock inside the old Jefferson City Correctional Center (a.k.a. The Walls), which was open from 1836 until 2004. James Scott was one of the last inmates here, Jefferson City, Missouri, 2007.

(*left*) The exact spot where the West Quincy levee broke in 1993. The white riprap was only placed over the area that broke in 1995 as a reinforcement, even though officially the levee wouldn't have failed were it not for James Scott, West Quincy, Missouri, 2007.

This barge and two others like it came rushing through the levee breach on July 16, 1993. Today, it sits decaying along US-24 in West Quincy, Missouri, as it's too large to move.

Sharon and Robert Scott on their front porch, Quincy, Illinois, 2007.

James Scott, inmate #1001364, inside the Jefferson City
Correctional Center, Jefferson City, Missouri, 2007.

into the table, using her nails to chisel away pieces of splintering wood. Then without warning, Tina started crying. Jimmy scooted his chair around until it met hers and he put his arms around her. The awkward teen ran his fingers through her hair and kissed the top of her head.

"There, there," he said. "I know it's hard to see me in here. I need you to be strong. I won't be here forever." She sniffled repeatedly and surrendered to his embrace. Tina started sobbing deeply. Her moans reverberated off the visiting room walls and some inmates turned in their seats to see a girl crying on the shoulder of that random guy who never said a word to anyone. Jimmy noticed them looking and tried to avert his eyes. They welled up with emotion, a sign of humanity in such an inhumane setting—but it was a sign of weakness for those who might want to sever an Achilles heel for their own pleasure or gain.

Tina gradually pulled herself together. "I've got something to tell you," she said at long last. Jimmy held her shoulders and gently pushed his girl off him. He lowered his head to meet her eyes and raised his eyebrows in a timid, inviting manner. When he was sure he had her attention, he gave her another grin. She started slowly. "This is hard for me to say, so I'll just say it. I'm pregnant."

The inmate's grin crept into a full-blown smile. He started to giggle. "Really!" he exclaimed excitedly. "Are you sure?"

"I'd been getting sick for the last few weeks so I went to the doctor the other day and he said I'm pregnant. Are you mad at me?" she asked with a hint of shame on her face. Tina was a Catholic, and even though she behaved very recklessly in her personal life, she was imbued with the idea that premarital sex was a sin, and a baby born out of wedlock was an even greater, more visible one. Similar tenets were instilled over the years in Jimmy, but his jubilation at the news far outweighed his concern over their transgression.

"Hell no I'm not mad!" he cried out. And he wasn't. This news was the only positive he had in his world. Jimmy Scott helped to create a life. He would be a father. All of those grand visions he shared with Tina when they'd laid together in bed were happening now. He hugged her again, this time not caring what wandering eyes thought of him. As he squeezed her chest against his, Jimmy searched for the right words to say. He needed to assure the frightened pregnant teenager that he'd be there for her and the baby, even if he was still locked up. He'd make it work. She wouldn't be all alone, not just another statistic. He wanted to convince her that this child would always have a father.

Jimmy was never much of a talker as words didn't come easy. Perhaps it was this special moment, or maybe the promise of a new, clean-slated life, but Jimmy could only harness a few words to say all that was in his heart. He planted another kiss on Tina's forehead, then another one on the tip of her red nose. She relaxed and sighed as he licked his lips and began to speak. A mild squeak proceeded his blurting out.

"I love you."

Jimmy smiled to himself the rest of the morning. He sat on his cot in his blue prison jumpsuit, lost in thought, and blocked out the negative influences in his head. He couldn't fathom what it would mean to be a daddy; he just liked the idea that he had a hand in creating a life.

After lunch and the afternoon count, a corrections officer summoned him for yet another visitor. This one was Gary Farha, his court-appointed defense attorney. He introduced himself and shook Jimmy's hand. Then he laid out the gloomy situation.

The teen would be going to the penitentiary; there was no getting around it. He'd signed confessions to his crimes, almost all of which were felonies. Adams County and the state of Illinois now needed to punish him for breaking her laws.

Farha said he'd speak with the prosecuting attorney and try to arrange a deal. It wouldn't be easy because Jimmy had a record.

"How much time we talking about here?" Jimmy asked. Farha told him it could be up to a 20-year sentence, out in 10.

He struggled to wrap his head around that daunting figure. In ten years he'd be 28, and to an 18-year-old, 28 was a dinosaur. Ten years earlier, he was only eight, and he couldn't really remember what it meant to be eight—that's how long 10 years was.

Jimmy implored his attorney to see what he could do. "Please," he said to the stranger. "I'm begging you. I just found out I'm gonna be a father. Ten years is too much time. Please see if you can get that reduced."

Farha said he'd do his best and that he'd be in touch. They shook hands, and the defense attorney left. Jimmy no longer reveled in the idea of his unborn child. His second visitor of the day deflated his sense of accomplishment. All Jimmy could think about for the rest of the day was that he'd be stuck in jail for a decade. There'd be no more parties, no Marine Corps, no more family, and he wouldn't get to see his son or daughter's birth.

He languished in jail for more than a month. Farah made brief appearances from time to time and Tina made even less frequent ones. She couldn't stand to see her baby's father locked up, so she limited her visits.

In May 1988, Farha came to prison with a deal in hand. The district attorney agreed to drop some of the counts against Jimmy because he'd been relatively clean since he was 12. He had to agree to pay for the $1,000 in damage done to the apartment on North Eighth Street and he had to repay an insurance agency $5,600. The DA would drop one of the arson charges, one of the Lind Street garage charges, and the Q Car Care Center charges altogether. In return, Judge Dennis Cashman sentenced Jimmy to seven years in state prison. He'd be up for parole in three and a half years.

Jimmy reluctantly agreed to the deal. Seven years was still a long time, but the possibility of only serving half that time was somewhat encouraging. Farha instructed him to stay out of trouble any way he could while in prison. He told his client to get involved with any programs they offered, anything that would make a case for his rehabilitation come parole hearing number-one. The defense attorney also wanted to impart some words of wisdom to his client. Farha did a good job getting Jimmy's sentence pared down. Now he wanted to ready the teen for life on the inside of adult prison.

"James," he said, "when you get there, you get in where you fit in." It was a saying used by people familiar with the penal system, loosely translated to mean that prisons were cliquey. You need to have a friend or two on the inside to watch your back. The underlying message was that in the county jail, inmates still have a glimmer of hope that their sentence will be light. As such, they stay out of trouble. In prison, however, the men were already convicted. They knew exactly how much time they had left, and the long-timers often looked upon young, handsome 18-year-old short-timers like Jimmy as easy marks.

"You get in where you fit in," Farha said again.

◄o►

The first place he went was the Dixon Correctional Center, a high-medium security prison. The Aryans were a force there and they actually approached Jimmy rather than the other way around. He requested a job in the prison's kitchen and received it. He was one of the men who controlled the portions of food each inmate received. The Aryans always received an extra slice of roast beef or some extra French fries when they passed Jimmy's station. He now had allies.

On a personal level, Jimmy enrolled in the prison's version of Alcoholics Anonymous. He didn't think it'd cure him long term because he desperately wanted a beer, but for the time being, it helped stifle his cravings. Moreover, the system often looked favorably on inmates electing to help themselves with voluntary enrollment in counseling programs.

He did good time there and as a result was transferred to Mt. Sterling Correctional Center, a medium security prison. Because of the state's constant influx of inmates, those deemed not to be a threat were bussed around the state to joints that were less restrictive. If a convict kept his nose clean, he was rewarded with a transfer to a lower security facility. Jimmy welcomed his transfer to Mt. Sterling. It was also a pleasant change of scenery and kept him from going stir crazy in his eight-by-twelve cell.

There was still a white gang presence at his new residence, but it wasn't as pronounced as in Dixon. He applied for a job as a clerk in the cold storage room and was granted the privilege to work. Every once in a while, some errant ice cream bars made their way into the hands of the white gang leaders, and as a result, Jimmy's back was covered daily.

The prison brass weren't ready to downgrade him to a low-medium just yet, despite his stellar internal record. Jimmy had a high school diploma so he didn't have to register for his GED. Instead, he was allowed to register and take college correspondence courses, classes that were meant to make him smarter. A quest for knowledge would bode well with the parole board. He didn't like to read and study, but the more he immersed himself in the material, the more time seemed to fly by.

Just when he was getting used to a routine, he was transferred to the Graham Correctional Center in the south-central corridor of the state. This medium security prison had an active sports program that piqued Jimmy's interest. He continued with his college courses and got a job as a clerk in central receiving: A great gig because it meant he had contact with outsiders. Truck drivers, the mail carrier—anyone who wasn't wearing a prison jumpsuit or an IDOC uniform was a welcome sight. He also tried out for the prison softball team and his prowess as a second baseman was instantly recognized.

He no longer had to curry favor only with the Aryans. Now he had a multiracial baseball team to run with. In prison, sports are often the only activities that allow the racial barriers to come down. Sure, Jimmy worked with African American and Mexican inmates at his various duties throughout the prisons, but on coffee breaks, they talked amongst their own.

He was asked to join the volleyball team. Jimmy was becoming known around Graham as a standout athlete. The guards noticed too and some would ask him to shoot pool in the rec room with them after their shift ended.

Visits from Tina became more sporadic, and he didn't actually mind because not knowing what was going on made the time more bearable. She sent him a letter in November 1988 congratulating him: He was the father of a healthy baby girl.

Jimmy tried to suppress his jubilation. Tina sent pictures and asked when she could bring the baby up to the prison so he could see his daughter for the first time. He practically cried out loud when he wrote her back instructing her not to bring his child to the stir: He didn't want the first glimpse of his daughter to be inside a correctional facility. That's when Tina's visits stopped altogether.

She understood his position, and yet she was quite frustrated with the predicament. Tina had to rely on her parents for help all throughout her pregnancy. She was often sick and laid-up. The baby was a kicker, and her frail body struggled with the extra weight and the frequent jolts to her organs. The night she delivered, it was her mother holding her hand, not her boyfriend.

He posted the pictures of his daughter on the cell wall. They were the only ones he hung. Just those few photographs seemed to make the day brighter. Yet they also made his time seem longer.

Jimmy learned from a case worker that he'd receive his tentative parole date in a few months. That dominated his thought process most of his days. He kept trying to show demonstrable evidence of rehabilitation for anyone who cared to take notice. A prison case worker continued to encourage his progress, which he interpreted to mean he was on the right road to parole. His mental state was as good as it could have been until June 1989, when he received a visit from his mother.

Sharon Scott made the three hour drive alone to break some hard news to her middle son. It was the sort of thing she couldn't bring herself to do in a letter, and she was due for a visit anyway. Jimmy was ecstatic to see his mother. They had mended fences through correspondence and he was over-joyed at the prospect of a loving, familiar face. But the face that stared back at him in the visiting room was swelled and tear-stained.

He hugged his mother and the two took their seats. Much like Tina's demeanor when breaking the news of her pregnancy, Sharon exhibited similar mannerisms. She scratched at the table and lowered her head. Without looking at her son, she blurted out the news: Jeff went and got himself in trouble with the law. He was sentenced to 14 years in prison, but that wasn't all.

Sharon explained in lengthy detail about the downward spiral Jeff's life had taken since Jimmy got incarcerated. He was angry at society when his older brother got clipped. That anger transformed into severe depression, much like Mike's had years earlier. Five months ago, Jeff overdosed on sleeping pills. The kid was trying to kill himself. He was rushed to Memorial Hospital, where his stomach was pumped. From there, he was admitted to St. Mary's Hospital and placed in the psychiatric ward.

Sharon spoke solemnly as Jimmy absorbed her words. "I was told if he didn't get help then he might be institutionalized for the rest of his life," she said. Sharon relayed how hard she'd pleaded with the hospital to keep Jeffrey and cure him. Her son was a good kid who had a real rough run at life. He wanted to be helped—he begged her to find him help. "But they released him anyway."

Jeff tried to be proactive. He went to a local counseling center where he requested an evaluation. "He warned them that he was a danger to himself and others," his mother said. The center was already at capacity. Jeff was told he'd be considered when a spot opened up a month or two down the line. Sharon got involved, beseeching the managers that her son needed help now, not in four to eight weeks. Her pleas went unanswered.

Jeff withdrew from society in much the same way that Mike and Jimmy had before him. He stopped being social and started marauding around town alone. And then he started setting fires. Arson was a way to get attention—that much he learned from his older brother. He began casing the town for abandoned buildings, four of which he ultimately lit. No one was injured in the blazes, but the town was at its wits end. Neal and Bruce Baker, through even more exemplary detective work, were now responsible for arresting another Scott and sending him upstate.

At trial, Jeff had asked to address the court. In a rambling statement, the 18-year-old read two poems for the judge. In one of them, he owned up to his delinquency. "I built this prison myself. These are the walls I built. With God's help, I can break these walls."

His court appointed attorney asked the judge to give Jeff probation and assign him counseling. Public defender J. Devin Cashman, brother of Judge Dennis Cashman who had sentenced Jimmy, tried to use his well-known name in Adams County to influence the court's sentence. "We see a young man drawing attention to himself, crying out for help," Cashman explained. "When he can't deal with a problem, he resorts to this behavior. Give him an opportunity to get the help he needs. He has serious emotional problems which need to be addressed." Now another set of brothers were mixed up in the affairs of the Scott boys—the Bakers *and* the Cashmans.

The district attorney asked for a 20-year sentence. The judge compromised and gave Jeff 14. Jimmy received the news with a heavy heart. He blamed himself for not being a better role model for the kid whom he knew idolized him. Jimmy liked to set fires to get attention, and unsurprisingly, Jeff, the little guy who wanted to try smoking so badly because his big brother was smoking back in the early '80s, was now sentenced to even more time than Jim for the same crime.

Jimmy assured his mother that he'd try to take care of him the best he could. He'd send messages through the prison grapevine that his "friends" should look out for Jeff Scott. Sharon appreciated the gesture. She just hoped her older incarcerated son had enough clout among the cons to protect her younger one.

◄○►

Two years into his sentence, Jimmy received a tentative release date: April 1, 1991. April Fools'. He'd accrued so much good behavior time that he would be released two years and eleven months into his seven year sentence. Provided, of course, that he wasn't written up for an infraction in the next year.

He was placed in a high minimum security facility in Taylorville, Illinois. It was a clean and sanitary place, a far cry from the rotting prisons he'd been in. Jimmy was one of the inaugural inmates for Taylorville Correctional Center's grand opening in 1990. He marveled at just how technically advanced everything was. The cells opened electronically from a central command center. Better still, the windows actually yielded a view of the yard and of the generally well-manicured campus. Best of all, the varied insects and rodents that he'd grown accustomed to in the other places were absent. The new prison, he figured, was a fine place to start the waning days of the time he owed the state. In addition, with a new prison came new grounds. Taylorville had brand new baseball diamonds, a volleyball net, two basketball courts, and even a horseshoe pit. For a sports nut like Jimmy, this place was the best he could have hoped for.

He became quite popular at Taylorville, mostly because of his athletic ability. All the inmates were recent transfers, so they weren't nearly as clannish as in the older institutions. Prisoners in the Illinois Department of Corrections are not allowed to correspond with other inmates, so Jimmy received updates on his brother from his mother as well as by word-of-mouth from fellow cons. Jeff told Sharon he was doing well and that she needn't worry about him. Jimmy was pretty sure he was only saying that for her benefit. The prison pipeline provided more detailed—and ironically, more reliable and accurate—information.

He learned that Jeff was having a hard time. The kid hadn't figured out the rules of the game and was wandering through the system as a loner. Jimmy figured it was because of the sheer length of the sentence: 14 years is so much time that the number alone is daunting. Big brother sent word that Jeff should try to get a kitchen job. If he wasn't going to seek out friends, at the very least, he could perhaps come into the Aryan's good graces by doing good deeds.

For his part, Jimmy continued on the straight and narrow. He had a couple guys he called friends, and some of the corrections officers regularly engaged him in conversation. Save for the fact that he missed home and wanted to see his baby for the first time, Taylorville took his mind off of his circumstance. His softball team was chosen to participate in a new DOC program, where different penal complexes competed for bragging rights and trophies against each other in competitive play. Jimmy's Taylorville team had some former high school letterman and even a couple of ex-college baseball players. They slaughtered most of the other teams. His cell became a shrine of accomplishment: He had his trophies and his baby pictures.

Abruptly and without warning though, his ideal prison atmosphere disappeared. He was transferred to another high minimum facility, the Jacksonville Correctional center. Luckily, he only had about six months left on his sentence, which by now, he could do standing on his head. Rather than working, he put his time and efforts into his studies. Jimmy wanted to get his college degree before being paroled because he knew he'd never go to college once on the outside.

With only two months to go until the April Fools' Day benchmark, Jimmy received his last transfer to the East Moline Correctional Center three hours north of Quincy. He took some more classes but fell short of earning a college degree. By then, he didn't care. He was going home—to his mother's house and to his baby girl's mother's house. As a condition of his parole, he wouldn't be able to correspond directly with inmates in the system.

Being brotherly, he once again sent a message through the grapevine to see how Jeff was doing. The day before Jimmy stepped foot outside of prison for the first time in nearly three years, he received the news that Jeff got a job in the kitchen.

Jimmy was satisfied on all fronts. He came of age in prison unlike many before him who became hardened criminals. Long ago, he wanted to find discipline and direction in the Marine Corps. That dream would never happen. The Marines don't take ex-cons into their fold. Jimmy found his manhood not at Paris Island, the South Carolina-based Marine boot camp, but within the confines of six different prisons in the Illinois Department of Corrections.

PART THREE
When the Levee Breaks

CHAPTER THIRTEEN

◄○►

Detective Bruce Baker was eating a late supper in his Quincy home on July 16, 1993, when the phone rang. It was his big brother, just back from Advanced Hostage Negotiation training at the FBI's headquarters in Quantico, Virginia.

Bruce was genuinely delighted to hear from Neal. As most kid brothers are, he was proud of his elder brother being invited to FBI training as a result of a dangerous bust.

But Bruce didn't have time to ask Neal about Quantico. The moment he said "hello," Neal instructed him to turn on WGEM-TV news. Bruce assented.

"You seein' what I'm seein'?" the older brother asked.

"I sure as shit am, and I sure as shit don't believe my eyes."

"Look how clean he is," Neal continued. "Does he look like he's been working on a levee all day? Because that's what he just told Michelle McCormack."

"No, sure doesn't. He looks like he's been out walkin' around in the heat."

"And listen to the questions McCormack is asking. They're not prying at all, but he can't name names. He doesn't know times. And he's lookin' around a little too nervously for my liking," Neal stated.

"You think he might be more than just a volunteer?" Bruce asked the senior lawman. They were in full-fledged detective mode now. Any brotherly catching-up would have to wait.

"Well let me ask you this: Does that seem like the Jimmy Scott you know?"

In the background, James Scott wrapped up his second interview of the evening with the pretty reporter. Ordinarily, the Bakers—and many other men in town—watched WGEM-TV because McCormack was without doubt the best-looking newsperson in the area. Even in the muggy, stifling temperature, with gnats and mosquitoes buzzing around her long, brown frizzy hair, she managed to look attractive. Nevertheless, on this evening, it was Jimmy the Bakers couldn't peal their eyes away from.

He stood there in a white T-shirt—the collar rolling inward from sweat—blue trucker's hat, and blue jeans, boasting he'd seen the actual break. "Water was just gushing through," Jimmy told Michelle during the live feed.

"How big did the break look?" the reporter asked.

"Probably about 2 to 3 feet."

"Now you had seen a problem earlier in the day and reported it. What exactly did you see?"

"I seen sand boils toward the top and the bottom," he declared, pausing briefly to wipe sweat off the tip of his nose and to shoe away bugs. "I informed people about them."

"Do you normally take breaks at a certain hour so it's very well that everybody was on a break, or do you know that people patrol all the time?"

"That I'm not sure," he said. "I know they have four-wheelers."

"Okay. Well when you were here yesterday, did they take a break around this time?"

"I'm not sure," he said again. "I wasn't here this late last night."

Neal Baker smelled a rat. He knew Jimmy's mannerisms, like whenever he looked around skittishly, he was lying. He told Bruce to meet him at the station early the next morning for a strategy session, and Bruce agreed.

After they hung up, Neal watched the rest of the interview. As far as he was concerned, Jimmy was implicating himself in some capacity for the West Quincy levee break. One of the fundamental elements of detective work is placing your suspect at the scene of the crime. The 10 o'clock evening news did that parcel of work for him. There was James Scott at the levee. He believed that Michelle McCormack's videotape was physical evidence. It wasn't necessarily a smoking gun, but at the very least, it negated the possibility of James Scott saying he was somewhere else on the evening of July 16, 1993.

—◄o►—

While the Baker brothers discussed the boastful volunteer recounting his heroics on their televisions, a similar scenario among neighboring law enforcement officials played out 15 minutes down the road.

Adams County, Illinois, Sheriff Bob Nall was at home talking to the 911 dispatcher. She informed the county's top cop that the Quincy emergency service was being inundated with calls from residents trying to get more information about the levee break. Most of the callers were frantic wives who weren't able to communicate with their husbands and sons across the river and who were fearing the worst, like the giant current had carried them away. Many others were asking about transportation over to Missouri and still others were calling in to volunteer their help with boat evacuations and the like.

Nall told the operator to tell callers to sit tight in their homes and stay away from the floodplain. He also said that he wanted to be informed immediately if any county folks were still unaccounted for by midnight.

Nall's 9-year-old daughter was in the den playing with her dolls as WGEM-TV news came on in the background. Nall tried to catch sound bites intermittently. As soon as he hung up with 911, he rang his deputy sheriff, John McCoy, but the phone was busy. He hung up the receiver just as a familiar voice broadcasted from his family room.

"Honey," he hollered to his daughter. "Who's that on the TV?"

"I don't know, daddy," she replied and recommended playing with her dolls. Bob walked into the room and saw the same picture Neal and Bruce Baker were seeing in town. A man in a white cotton T-shirt, blue hat, and blue jeans spoke in a simple Midwestern drawl to the lovely Michelle McCormack. The man looked really familiar to the sheriff, but he couldn't figure why, nor could he place a name with the face. He listened for a few moments to the man and immediately suspected something was wrong with this picture: The image of the man, the way he looked around, and the tremulous tone in his voice made for a visceral reaction. "This guy's lying," Nall said aloud.

"What, daddy?" his daughter asked. She assumed he was speaking to her, as she was the only other person in the room. The sheriff was deep in thought. He spoke to his daughter as though he was speaking to a legal peer. "This guy," he said again, keeping his eyes trained on the television. "He's not telling the truth. I can just tell. He had something to do with the break of this levee. He had something to do with it."

As if on cue, the telephone rang. Nall left his daughter, went back to his study, and picked up the call.

"Sheriff Nall," he said.

"Bob, you watching this?" the caller said without introduction. And he didn't need to. It was his deputy, John McCoy.

McCoy was sitting at home in his recliner and watching Michelle McCormack talk to a known felon, too. Known, that is, to almost everybody watching the newscast except for Michelle McCormack herself.

"Yeah, I just said to my daughter that this guy is lying through his teeth. I think we're watching the guy who broke the levee on purpose."

"You know who that guy is, don't you?" McCoy asked almost rhetorically.

"He sure looks familiar, but I can't remember how I know him."

"You know him because it's Jimmy Scott!"

"Jimmy Scott . . ." he said probingly. "Where do I know that name from?" McCoy's reply was only one word, but it was the only word needed to jar the boss's memory.

"Webster."

"Well I'll be," Nall declared. "Jimmy Scott is a big hero, eh? John, this don't add up."

"Think we might need to pay a visit to ol' Jim. Meet you at the station in an hour," Deputy Sheriff John McCoy said and hung up.

Nall stood in his study thinking for a moment. He'd been swamped the previous week with flood prevention. The added workload and strain were beginning to wear on him, but seeing Jimmy Scott on television describing how he was there to help was the second most bizarre spectacle he'd witnessed that season.

Months earlier in April, Nall made his contribution to the relief effort by ringing his buddies in Springfield. He sat on the Adult Advisor Board of the Department of Corrections and tellingly, the old boy network of veteran law enforcement officials within the DOC was a much quicker, more efficient way of getting things done than going through the governor's office, especially at that time. Illinois Governor Jim Edgar was busy shuttling between the state's capitol and the nation's capitol, requesting federal emergency funds for all the levee districts upriver from Quincy that were deluged with Mississippi River water.

Nall spoke to DOC brass and basically said, "We need help." Boils had been spotted all along the levees in the Lima Lake Drainage District north of Quincy, and Durgin's Creek was starting to show signs of severe strain. The National Guard was just starting to filter in, and the Fabius River Drainage District and volunteers from both sides of the river were spearheading the sandbagging effort. He needed more boots on the ground, even if those boots were state-issued and the chattel of Illinois' convicts.

Nall received more than 100 inmates ready to work. He was nervous when the prison's converted school bus arrived in Adams County and its passengers filed off. Ninety percent of them were black, and the majority of them were from Cook County, Chicago's parent county. He was mostly worried because Adams County consisted mostly of white, rural farmers. It wasn't that they were racist, but the arrival of these jailbirds threw one more uncertain wrench in an already uncertain equation. Nall recognized that the tension was palpable and potentially explosive.

The sheriff became an intermediary between the convict work crew and the anxious local volunteers. The former didn't cause any problems, and in fairness, they were some of the stronger workers on the riverbanks. After one pleasant April morning of sandbagging, the convicts broke for lunch. They came off the levee singing their prison chants and eyeballing the locals, which was the first most bizarre and potentially explosive occurrence Nall had witnessed in all his years of law enforcement, let alone the strangest that flood season. The farmers froze in their tracks. It was a scene right out of *The Bridge on the River Kwai*.

Nall approached a group of them to extend his gratitude for their help. Much to his surprise, they said they couldn't wait to get the hell out of

Dodge. Ordinarily, wards of the state jump at the chance to join a work detail. It means being outdoors among the general population and more importantly, it means a change of scenery. Yet these men told the sheriff they were scared to death to be in Adams County. "You're scared to death?" was the sheriff's stunned reply. "How do you think the folks around here feel?"

"We've heard about you farmers and your shotguns," one inmate exclaimed. "You shoot first and then ask questions. We're afraid if we say or do something wrong, they'll get their gats and pop us!" The prisoners eventually left with no more holes in their bodies than when they arrived and the National Guard came on the scene.

But on July 16, as he stood there in his study, he couldn't believe that the levee had failed. It was just unfathomable given the sheer manpower out there on the river bottoms.

After a while, he got in his car and drove to the Adams County police station. Deputy Sheriff McCoy was already there. The plan was to go over to Jimmy Scott's Fowler residence and bring him in for questioning. McCoy reported to Nall that prior to arriving at the station, he paid a visit to WGEM and spoke with Michelle McCormack. He questioned her as to why, out of thousands of people on the floodplain, she chose to interview James Scott. Her response was simply "because he was there." McCormack wasn't a Quincy native, so she didn't know about Webster Elementary. Nor did she know that two years earlier, Jimmy was paroled from the joint where he served time for arson. She seemed surprised because her interviewee had such a pleasant disposition when they spoke, especially considering the circumstances.

The sheriff and his deputy headed out to the TV star's Fowler residence. The streets were practically empty. Everyone was holed up watching the news or talking on the phone. They arrived at Jimmy's modest ranch house and knocked firmly on his plywood door. No lights were on in the house and not surprisingly, nobody answered.

They knocked on a neighbor's door—a house that still had lights on at 11:15 p.m. A woman in a bathrobe answered the door reluctantly, as she wasn't used to receiving visitors at such an hour. She recognized Sheriff Nall though and opened up.

He asked her if she had any idea where James Scott might be. She said she didn't, and he kindly asked her to call him if she saw him around in the next day or two. She agreed.

Rather than rousing people from their slumber, Bob Nall and John McCoy called it a night. They decided to reconvene in the morning and try Jimmy's house again.

Ironically, Jimmy was en route home in a buddy's car just as the lawmen were leaving. He'd lost his car keys while helping the Coast Guard load boats into the water and had to have a friend tow his car across the Bayview Bridge right before it was submerged. They dropped Jimmy's car off at a garage so that it could get a new starter in the morning. The friend drove Jimmy back home where he showered, changed, and then walked the two blocks to Dan's party, where he could regale guests with stories of being a television star.

◄o►

The Alcoholics Anonymous classes he attended in prison were forgotten once he set foot in the outside world—five hours later, to be exact. It would have been sooner, but the drive from Jacksonville was an hour and a half and he wanted to spend *some* catch-up time with his parents.

Robert called in sick to the Pepsi plant—something he hadn't done in over a decade—and picked his son up outside the institution's steel doors. Father and son used the time during the drive back to Quincy to speak openly and honestly. Robert warned Jimmy about his drinking: "It's booze that got you into this mess in the first place." Jimmy recognized that his father was right. It wasn't idle talk, either. Robert had battled with his own demons for decades. Drinking didn't affect his work, but it did affect his interaction with his kids. Yet when he found his son's stash of beer bottles behind some garbage cans in the garage when Jimmy was only 16, he quit cold turkey.

Robert told his son he'd already spoken to a friend over at the County Market who said he would give Jimmy a job as a floor maintenance manager, which meant he'd be the head janitor. That was fine by Jimmy. As a condition of his early parole, he needed to demonstrate gainful employment and he needed to report to a parole officer once a week.

Jimmy was extremely excited at the prospect of finally seeing his daughter for the first time. Tina hadn't been in touch, but he knew where she lived and figured he'd just pop in after he caught up with his family.

Surprisingly, no one was home when the car pulled up. Jimmy figured everyone would be waiting around for his return, but Sharon and Mike were still at work. Robert used his time off to get some things done around the house. He told Jimmy he didn't need to help: Today was his special day. The ex-con could use his first day of free time however he wanted. All the 21-year-old really wanted to do was be around family, so he asked to borrow the car to drive out to Fowler and see Dan. Robert didn't want to contribute to lawless behavior, which is what he would be doing by lending Jimmy the car keys. Parolees need to get their paperwork in order before they can get their driver's licenses reinstated. That would be tomorrow. Robert volunteered to drop Jim off at Dan's house.

Dan was perhaps the most excited of all the Scott clan for Jimmy's release. It meant he'd have his sidekick back. Not more than a minute after Robert maneuvered the car out of the driveway and back toward town did Dan pop the tops off of two Buds. They toasted Jimmy's freedom and chugged.

The liquid tasted sweet to Jimmy. He had missed beer so much. Dan obliged his half brother. He produced a full case from a cooler with a red ribbon tied around it. "Welcome Home," Dan said, from one partier to another.

Jimmy didn't see his daughter that day. Rather, he spent the next several hours jumping head-first off the wagon. He consumed his entire present and then dipped into Dan's stash later that night.

He awoke the next morning in bed with an old high school girlfriend. Jimmy couldn't remember if they'd messed around or not. He was just happy to have female companionship again. Dan was already awake when Jimmy stumbled out of the all-too-familiar bedroom. He volunteered to give Jimmy a ride back home. Surely Mom, Dad, and Mike wanted to see him, and Dan didn't need an earful from his mother about how irresponsible he was by keeping Jimmy all to himself.

Sharon took the day off and spent it shuttling her middle son around town. Jimmy bought some new clothes with his mother's credit card. When he went to prison, the then 18-year-old was still growing and filling out.

Now he weighed close to 175 pounds and was a good 2 inches taller. All day long, as he moved between racks at Wal-Mart, his daughter was foursquare on his mind.

Come nightfall, he received the visit he'd longed for over the last three years. Tina stood at the threshold of his parent's house with a beautiful brown-haired, blue-eyed toddler gripping her hand. Jimmy knelt down low and gave the little girl a brilliant smile. She smiled back and then buried her head in her mother's pant leg.

"This is your daddy," Tina said warmly. "Is there something you want to say to him?"

The girl smiled shyly and gripped harder at her mother's leg. Jimmy spoke first. "Hi there," he said, still keeping his head at her level. "You sure are pretty."

"Go on," Tina coaxed. "It's alright."

The little girl looked at her father and slowly eased up her hold. "Hi, Daddy," she said at long last. "I love you." Then she jumped into her father's arms.

Jimmy lifted his daughter off the ground and hugged her tightly. He put a hand on the back of her head and stroked her long, flowing hair. "Hello, baby," he uttered through tearful gasps. "I love you, too." In that moment, Jimmy said a silent prayer to a God he hadn't recognized in years. He thanked the Lord for delivering him from prison and for blessing him with a beautiful, healthy daughter. And also for a new start at life.

Tina was moved by the moment as well. But she kept quiet, partly because she wanted to give her baby's father a chance to bond with his child and partly because she had some bad news for him: While Jimmy was in prison, she'd met a man. They'd been seeing each other exclusively for almost a year, and she was considering a move to Missouri. Jim's daughter would be coming with them. Tina thought best not to spring the information on her old boyfriend right then. That time would come.

It did. Jimmy received a telephone call from Tina the very next day. Her tone was mature and civil: It was time to grow up. She had domestic responsibilities and a new beau.

Jimmy was furious. He asked how she could do this to him—how she could even consider taking his daughter from him after they'd just met. Tina was unyielding. He'd be allowed to see his girl from time to time, but she wasn't convinced that he was on the straight and narrow just yet. Jimmy threatened to take her to court, but that didn't faze her. She knew that no judge would award a 3-year-old to an ex-con. He knew it, too. He hung up in disgust and tried to push them both out of his mind. And in his experience, there was only one way to elude a problem. And there was also only one place to do it. Jimmy put a call into a couple of friends until he located one who was available to give him a ride to Dan's.

The parolee fell right back into the same rut he was in prior to being incarcerated. He did take that job at County Market and made his weekly visits to a parole officer. Those were his daily and weekly obligations. Almost every evening, however, concluded at Dan's. Some good did come out of his drunken behavior. He met a cool party girl named Susan Nelson. Suzie, as he came to call her, lived with her parents in Palmyra, Missouri, and worked at the 18 Wheeler Truck Stop in Taylor. She'd made friends with this Illinois crew during some of their frequent visits to the truck stop. One night, a Quincy local invited her to one of Dan's parties. Jimmy noticed her from across the room and thought she was pretty. They got to talking.

A year later, he proposed to her almost as an afterthought, and she casually accepted. They married on the steps of the courthouse—the same courthouse that had handed down two arson convictions at two different points in James Scott's life.

These were the salad days for the 20-year-old. Jimmy snagged a second job at Burger King in 1992, and managed to save a big enough portion of his two incomes to put a down payment on a house just a spit from Dan's. He'd alternate his days between jobs and conclude each evening at his half brother's. The best part about his life was he'd never have to worry about getting a DUI. Jimmy wasn't much of a bar guy anymore, choosing instead to party at a familiar house and then walk home. When he bought a car later that year, Jimmy faithfully drove to Tina's new home in Missouri, and spent an hour at a time with his daughter on a weekly basis. He'd calmed down and stopped laying guilt trips on his former fling, so she permitted brief visits between father and child.

As time started passing, the town started to seem more forgiving: Or at the very least, Quincy wasn't as vocal about their loathing of the Webster fire starter. Jimmy was staying out of trouble while within city limits, and there hadn't been any arsons since he left prison. Jimmy thought he'd been forgiven. He also thought life couldn't get much better than it was. Though as had been the case throughout his life, as soon as things seemed to be going in the right direction, something would derail him.

Jeff Scott was having a real hard time in prison. He started fighting with the other inmates and being an all-around discipline problem for the corrections officers. The multiple violations earned him a one-way ticket to the Menard Correctional Center, a maximum security facility that held some of the state's worst and most violent offenders. Jeff managed to score a job working in the kitchen, but the wayward inmate who had slowly learned over time how to stand up for himself was no match physically and mentally for Menard's crafty, violent population.

Jimmy got word that there was an incident in the prison kitchen. Jeff was washing dishes. He made it halfway through the dirty crockery when he ran out of detergent. While opening a new bin, he used too much torque and the powder flung up in his face. At least that was the official story. The unofficial version that worked its way out of the penitentiary and onto the streets of Quincy was that Jeff got in a fight with an inmate armed with a fork. They scuffled for a couple of minutes before the fork found its way into Jeff's eye. Whichever account people chose to believe, the endgame was that young Jeff would serve out the rest of his sentence—and live out the rest of his life—with only one eye.

The news stunned Jimmy. *He* was the aggressive one according to officials, and yet *he* managed to make it through his time unscathed. Poor Jeff was now even more vulnerable with just one eye for protection. But there was nothing Jimmy could do for his brother, which made him feel helpless. His only recourse, he determined, was to drink away his sorrow and numb the pain.

◄o►

Jimmy walked into Dan's house just before midnight on July 16, 1993, to a hero's welcome. All the party people had seen him on television that night and they were dying to hear the skinny on the levee break. After all, it was purported—by Jimmy himself and reaffirmed by Michelle McCormack—that he was one of the few eye-witnesses to the disaster. He was also one of the only people, according to WGEM-TV, that observed trouble spots earlier that day.

Jimmy told his story ad nauseam. Some of the guys, like Eric Epping and Cory Anderson—guys he had joked to in recent weeks about the extraordinary fishing conditions that would present themselves should the levee break—were now much more preoccupied with finding out how hot Michelle McCormack was in person.

Sitting in the corner listening to the banter was 16-year-old Joe Flachs. He too had engaged Jimmy in conversation at a party earlier in the week. They'd spoken about what would happen if the levee broke, when Jimmy drunkenly mentioned to young Joe how cool it would be to party without Suzie around and flirt with other women.

Joe saw Jimmy on television earlier that night also but he didn't crowd the man like the others did. He thought Jimmy was lying. What the ex-con had said to him a week ago—about how he wouldn't mind if the levee broke—and what he was saying at that moment were effectively two different stories. And true to form, Suzie was indeed stranded in Missouri.

Jimmy noticed Joe sitting by himself and eavesdropping. He shot the teen a smile and nodded his head as if to say "hi." Joe looked at him with revulsion and turned away.

What had Joe miffed that night was a rumor he'd heard from someone at the party. Apparently, Jimmy and Kathy Flachs, Joe's mother, had become quite friendly in recent weeks. In fact, someone told Joe that Jimmy and Joe's 40-year-old mother purportedly had sex. Joe never confronted the ex-con, partially because he was afraid of him. Joe was a skinny 16-year-old to the muscular, 21-year-old Jimmy. Jimmy had done time and was also a notorious criminal. That's not to say Joe hadn't crossed the legal line a few times. When he was nine, he was sent to a youth home for a series of behavioral problems. Joe learned what it meant to be a real delinquent while inside: How to do a robbery, how to pick a pocket, and he also learned some of the tenets of criminal life, like never rat on your friends. Because he didn't get much attention at home, Joe started acting out. Much like Jimmy did a decade ago, Joe started sneaking out of the house at 11, 12, and 13 years old. He also started dabbling in petty vandalism.

The more he heard Jimmy's voice that night, the angrier he became. He wanted to lash out at the man who was supposedly screwing his mother. He wanted to kick his ass. He hated the fact that this guy—who said he wanted his wife stranded—was now the life of the party, just because of a lousy couple minutes on television. Joe couldn't stand the sight of Jimmy anymore. He moved to a different part of the house.

-◄o►-

On July 17, Neal and Bruce Baker met at the new police headquarters on South Eighth Street. It was an old bank that had been converted into a station while Jimmy was in the joint. Neal and Bruce crammed into an office and started discussing a plan of attack.

They were convinced that James Scott, one of their first collars as detectives, was behind the levee break across the Mississippi River in West Quincy. In order to proceed with an investigation, they outlined who needed to be questioned. They also had to inform some of the locals to keep their eyes and ears open to Jimmy's movements and conversations.

Neal suggested that they check in with the Army Corps of Engineers at their emergency operations center on Broadway. The detective wanted to query whether any of the government workers had seen a lone figure atop the levee in the hour before it broke.

A smattering of Corps employees were on radios and telephones with Fabius River Drainage District personnel and National Guardsmen when the Bakers arrived. They were neck-deep in questions about the levee break and the extent of the damage.

The Corps was on edge. They were initially catching a tremendous amount of heat for the levee break. Farmers and other residents of the river bottoms lost everything and not all of them had flood insurance. In fact, most of them didn't. They were looking for someone to point a finger at, and the Corps seemed like the most logical candidate.

Neal and Bruce Baker carefully broached the subject of their hunch. They knew it was a touchy subject for Corps workers, especially because the flood was so recent and they were still trying to figure out a way of shoring up the broken levee. Neal got in a huddle with some people and told them that in his opinion, the West Quincy levee didn't just blow out. He was fairly certain that someone—a local bad boy—had played a hand in this catastrophe.

For their part, the Corps employees were floored by this information. Just hearing that one man may have purposefully sabotaged a levee was all but unthinkable. In their line of work, they were kept segregated from matters of criminal conduct, so this struck them to the core on both a personal and professional level.

As the Bakers explained their theory about Jimmy Scott being a saboteur, the Corps employees listened with rapt intent. These weren't Quincy people, so they'd never heard of James Scott, but they were completely surprised to learn of the local miscreant's past. They pledged their help to the investigation on all fronts and asked the cops to keep them informed of developments as well.

One Corps employee, however, rose from his station and approached Neal Baker. He was one of the Mississippi River Rangers—an elite team of engineers within the Corps, who were similar to the elite Army special forces unit. The River Ranger had almost 20 years of experience working on river systems. And he was also the lone local among them, born and raised in Quincy.

Earl Basswood[1] knew all about the Webster fire, and he knew about both of the Scott brothers' other arson convictions. He didn't think very highly of the kids. Truth be told, Earl Basswood thought society might be better off with the whole Scott family behind bars. By the same token, he'd been intimately involved in monitoring the West Quincy levee, as well as levees up and down the Mississippi River ever since the rains started coming down in March. He personally saw trouble spots—specifically, boils—all over Marion County, Missouri, where the break occurred. He had actually walked right over the spot that would eventually fail on that day.

---

[1] This is a pseudonym. The real Corps employee spoke to the author under conditions of anonymity. Only the man's name has been changed. All the information is presented as told to the author.

Just yesterday, Basswood trudged the stretch of saturated dam with some other Corps employees. He didn't notice any boils per se, but he noted to his partner that the whole levee was in bad shape. It was wet, it was soggy, and there was tremendous pressure against the levee walls. The water level was a little bit lower, which signaled to Basswood that overtopping was not the biggest danger, but seepage was occurring all along the levee: He saw it with his own eyes. Because of this, Earl could only be convinced of any one man's involvement in the break if he heard specific evidence. That's what he asked of Neal Baker: Just how sure was he about James Scott?

According to Basswood, Neal Baker told him that there was no doubt in his mind that Jimmy broke the levee. The River Ranger asked what sort of facts the detective had gathered that made him come to such a definite conclusion, to which Baker responded that it was an ongoing investigation, so he couldn't comment on the status. Earl knew from his own government experiences that detectives could not talk to ordinary people about ongoing investigations. But he also adhered to a precept of the American justice system: A man is innocent until proven guilty. From what Baker was not telling him, Earl Basswood grew immediately suspicious of his intentions. The detective was way too convinced of guilt less than 24 hours after the levee broke. And he was way too motivated to find evidence before he had even questioned any witnesses. As far as the River Ranger was concerned, local law enforcement was absolutely certain that James Scott broke the levee at West Quincy. Now they just needed to find enough evidence to prove it.

◄○►

After the raging party the night of the break, Jimmy woke up first thing the next morning and asked Dan to drop him off at the mechanic's shop in town, where he'd dropped his car off the night before. The mechanic replaced his starter and as soon as he did, Jimmy fired the ignition and headed north along Highway 96 toward Iowa. He'd called his wife's parents house in Palmyra, Missouri, and spoke with Suzie for about 20 minutes while waiting for repairs. She was sitting around biding time. Palmyra was out of harm's way, but she was reluctant to drive nevertheless because of the hoopla surrounding the flood. No one knew just how bad the damage was yet. Arial photos shown on TV made the entire region look as if it was under water. All she knew was she wanted to be with her husband. Jimmy told her that as soon as his car was fixed, he'd drive an hour north to Keokuk, Iowa—since that was the only open bridge between Iowa and St. Louis roughly 200 miles due south—and then another hour and forty-five minutes back south toward Palmyra to pick her up.

When he got on the road, he was awestruck by the vista out his driver's side window. The horizon looked like an ocean. Everything was gone. Only rooftops and treetops were visible. Several barges were scattered about though nary a person was in sight. The drive took almost five hours, partly because all the other cars were doing the exact same thing, and partly because of all the rubbernecking that was going on along Highway 96. As soon as he picked Suzie up, he turned right back around and drove five more hours on the return trip to Quincy.

They made it back to town just as the sun was setting on the Missouri horizon. The couple decided to watch the sunset from their favorite hangout, the Villa Kathrine Castle on Front Street. Jimmy and Suzie held each other as a fiery amber orb descended over the Great Midwestern Flood. They marveled at the spectacle of so much water as Jimmy hugged his wife from behind. They peered west over the disaster, watching as red and orange hues reflected off the vast Mississippi River and shimmered in the gentle ripples. When all was dark, they packed up and headed home.

Jimmy and Suzie pulled into their driveway as the stars began to appear. Suzie dropped her husband off and drove back to town to grab them some food. Jimmy went into the backyard and cracked open a beer.

As he lounged unsuspectingly in the yard, Jimmy's neighbor picked up her phone and called the county police station. Sheriff Bob Nall and Deputy John McCoy were informed that a light was on in Jimmy's house. The two lawmen quickly jumped into Nall's car and headed out to the Columbus Heights subdivision.

They pulled into the driveway just as Suzie returned from Taco Bell. She was surprised to see a car in her spot. Suzie parked on the street and marched right up to the strange vehicle.

"Is there something I can help you with?" she asked the man emerging from the driver's seat. Just then, another man exited the vehicle on the passenger side. They were in plain clothes and she had no way of knowing they were lawmen, save for the badges they wore on their belts.

"Yes ma'am," Sheriff Nall said. "Do you by any chance know where Jim is at?"

"What you want Jim for?" she probed suspiciously.

"We want to talk to him about the levee break."

Before Suzie had a chance to answer, Jimmy came walking from around the back of the house. He'd heard men's voices talking to his wife and came to check on her. Deputy McCoy saw him first and spoke.

"Mr. Scott, I'm Deputy McCoy of the Adams County Sheriff's Department. I was wondering if you'd mind accompanying us down to the courthouse for some questioning."

"What's this about?" he asked. Jimmy was completely taken off guard by these uninvited visitors. He was exhausted from spending more than 10 hours in the car, and he was already a little tipsy from the beer, not to mention how worn out he was from partying the night before.

"It's about the levee break," Sheriff Nall said.

He thought they wanted to talk about what he'd seen, to give them a more detailed explanation of what he said to TV reporter Michelle McCormack.

Jimmy hopped in the passenger seat of his Monte Carlo and Suzie got behind the wheel as they followed Nall and McCoy to the courthouse. Jimmy wasn't worried. He had no indication from the men that he was a suspect in an act of sabotage. He munched his three tacos as Suzie drove. It wasn't until he got out of the car and into the station that he realized something was up.

They left Suzie in the reception area and went into an interview room. Right off the bat, Sheriff Nall read the man his Miranda Rights. Then he asked Jimmy if he understood the rights as they were read to him. He answered in the affirmative—it wasn't the first time he'd been read them. Still, he wasn't worried. Nall asked him if he wanted to exercise his right to have an attorney present.

"Naw," Jimmy replied out-of-hand. "Don't need one."

Nall and McCoy didn't merely ask Jimmy about his take on events. They turned on a tape recorder and launched into a full-blown interrogation. The tone in which they asked questions threw the suspect. He didn't understand why they were raising their voices. Nall led the inquiry with questions designed to trip Jimmy up. He asked about where Jimmy worked while volunteering in the relief effort, where he noticed the trouble spots, whom he flagged down, why he walked on the plastic tarp, and why he threw sandbags. Jimmy fielded each question as it came and never so much as broke stride. He used terms like "boils" and "trouble spots" as though they were long a part of his vocabulary. Both Nall and McCoy interpreted Jimmy's reference to these terms as nothing more than words he'd heard broadcasted at least 20 times a day for the last month on WGEM. Everything Scott said was mulled over by the sheriff and the deputy. After about an hour, Nall asked the million dollar question: "Did you break the levee." Jimmy looked the man straight in the eye and answered a split second later. "No, sheriff. I did not."

This conversation wasn't going anywhere. The sheriff hadn't spoken to Detective Neal Baker of the QPD since the flood, but he too was convinced that Jimmy Scott was no innocent bystander. At 10 o'clock, Nall turned off the tape recorder. "Okay, Jim. You're free to go."

Jimmy stood up and walked to the waiting room, where Suzie sat anxiously. She asked him if he was in trouble, to which he responded that he wasn't. "They was just talking to me. It's no big deal."

That was the first official questioning of James Scott for his role in the Great Midwestern Floods of 1993. Nall had the entire conversation on tape, which could be used as evidence should a prosecutor decide to charge him with a crime later down the line.

As Jimmy left the station, Nall and McCoy stayed and chatted for a few more minutes. Then they replayed portions of the tape. Jimmy confirmed that he saw a trouble spot, and that he moved a few sandbags around in order to shore up the seepage. In addition, under direct questioning, he denied having anything to do with the West Quincy levee break.

The sheriff pondered all this information. He didn't have anything to go on, but he was still convinced of Jimmy's guilt: There was more to this story than what the notorious fire starter said. He was, after all, the person responsible for burning down Webster Elementary. No man that would willingly and knowingly torch his own former school could be capable of civic mindedness. Jimmy was there the night the levee broke and Michelle McCormack was kind enough to place him on the scene. Nall thought the interview was a roadblock, but he was in no way ready to give up.

The sheriff, with 21 years of experience under his belt, listened to the tape one more time for good measure. Nothing jumped out at him. Rather than hold onto the tape for use later in the future, Sheriff Bob Nall decided that even though the investigation of James Scott was corresponding to the investigation of hundreds of millions of dollars in deliberate property damage, the information on the tape wasn't worth the dollar it had cost the taxpayers of Adams County to purchase it. Sheriff Nall walked back to the storage room and stuck the tape back in the equipment pool for another officer to reuse on someone else at a later date.

The first police interview with James Scott was now lost forever.

CHAPTER FOURTEEN

◄○►

J immy and Suzie returned home and retreated to their modest den. It was
late and the couple was exhausted. They were in no mood to party on the
evening of July 17, 1993, as most of their region was treading water and
overwhelmed with dread. As he reflected on the interview, Jimmy had the
sneaking suspicion that county law enforcement was looking to pin the flood
on him.

He knew how this game was played. The interview with Sheriff Nall and
Deputy McCoy was a preliminary one. Now the lawmen would delve into a
fact-finding expedition, casting the net wide, to see if they could find any
more dirt on James Scott. He knew people in the community still hated him
and would stand idly by as the cops tried to nail him. The men in blue had
nothing he figured, yet every time he'd thought that in the past, he wound
up in the county jail.

For all the inclement weather over the past four months, as soon as the
levee burst in West Quincy, the skies cleared and the rains subsided.
Temperatures dropped to the low 80s, which made the humidity more tolerable. A radiant sun still cooked the terrain from on high, though it was
mitigated by a gentle eastward breeze. Jimmy wanted to be outdoors since
many businesses closed shop immediately after the flood. County Market
decided to open for half a day, but Jimmy was not on the schedule. People
in the area didn't know how to react to the disaster, so many stayed indoors
and tuned in to national and local newscasts. They were waiting for the
official word from President Clinton—for some comforting dialogue to allay

their pain. Mostly, though, they wanted to hear that they'd be compensated with federal money, or at the very least, insurance money, for their losses.

Jimmy took to the streets to do some shopping a week after the flood. He parked on Broadway and walked along the thoroughfare. The first stop on the list was Wal-Mart. He needed to buy some new clothes, and the super center was one of few stores that stayed open throughout the ordeal. After that, he wanted to make an obligatory stop at the liquor store. Jimmy hadn't partied in a couple of days—not since the barn burner at Dan's house the night of the levee break. He figured a free-for-all would spring up sooner or later, and he wanted to be prepared.

Wal-Mart was practically empty, which was odd considering it was the busiest retailer in town on a regular day, let alone a day when the rest of the community had battened down. The paltry crowd wasn't even the strangest sight. What had Jimmy perplexed as he walked around Wal-Mart were the very peculiar looks cast his way. He didn't know any of these people. Wal-Mart had only been open three years, yet it drew customers from all the neighboring counties and cities. As such, there were a lot of unfamiliar faces—but they all recognized him. Jimmy chalked it up to his television spot and dismissed their gazes as mere gawking. "Is that the guy I saw on TV?" he figured they asked themselves. "He sure looks familiar."

Indeed the people were asking themselves that question. Almost the entire town watched Michelle McCormack reporting from the Bayview Bridge, and thus, almost the entire town saw and heard James Scott rattle off answers as though he alone tried to fend off the mighty Mississippi River. The local's first reaction was utter disgust. They'd all been out there sand-bagging, too, day in and day out.

Collectively, *they* were the real heroes of July 16, 1993. They managed to stave off the river for four long months. There'd been levee breaks upstream—almost one per day (and sometimes two)—for the past 14 days, but the West Quincy levee hadn't breeched. The townspeople credited this circumstance to their own resolve and teamwork. They were right. The West Quincy levee wasn't built stronger than the ones in any other districts. In fact, some local farmers figured that the West Quincy levee was actually weaker than the ones in the Indian Grave district, Union, and Lima Lake. Those levees were more regularly maintained and refurbished by the Corps of Engineers because of Lock and Dam 20, a channel system that enables barges and other large watercraft to navigate the river. Despite the extra attention, those levees burst. But not the one at West Quincy. Hell, even the South Levee broke near Hannibal, which was, tellingly, south of Quincy. That was two days after their own dike gave way. The South district had Lock and Dam 21, which meant that they too received more attention. Actually, every levee in the surrounding region broke. After each one failed, tens of thousands of acres took on water and washed away all traces of existence. The landscape of those Midwestern states straddling the Mississippi River in the spring and summer months of 1993 looked more like Pangea than of industrialized society. By July 16, 1993, more than 400 levees broke on the Mississippi and another 400 on other rivers in America's midsection. No community had the resources or the wherewithal to pose a counteroffensive against the weather. None, that is, except one.

West Quincy and the Fabius River Drainage District had hit every curveball thrown their way. General consensus held that the other Midwestern towns simply didn't mobilize as quickly and with as much sheer force as those in the Fabius river bottoms. Of course, the people at the Indian Grave, Union, Lima Lake, and South districts demonstrated a farmer's work ethic, and if they had as many volunteers and as much fervor for the task at hand, perhaps they could have also saved their levees. But they didn't. And they couldn't. Not like West Quincy. That town fought the river and had won, at least for awhile.

In all, more than a million man hours were put into saving the West Quincy levee. Now all they had to show for it was 14,000 acres of Lake Mississippi. How come nobody commended them on holding back the river for so long? Where were Harry Smith and Paula Zahn now? Why didn't Michelle McCormack ask *them* about *their* heroic efforts to save the levee? And what the hell was the Webster Elementary School fire starter doing on television? Those were the questions Jimmy thought Wal-Mart customers were asking themselves as he casually strolled down the aisles.

When he exited the store, Jimmy noticed an unmarked Crown Victoria parked in the distance. He attempted to focus and see who was inside, but the sun's glare blinded him. Jimmy started to walk toward the car but then decided not to. Prison paranoia took hold. He tried not to follow his hunch too much. After all, this was the parking lot at Wal-Mart, not the B-Wing at Dixon Correctional Center.

Jimmy continued to walk along Broadway. Next stop: County Market, his stomping grounds. That's where he'd left his car before hoofing it to Wal-Mart. Jimmy decided to buy a warm case of Budweiser, which he planned to put on ice—if Dan had a party later that night—and one cold six-pack to drink when he got home.

County Market was also mostly deserted. He felt a little guilty buying beer in front of coworkers who couldn't kick a few back themselves. At the same time, he sort of enjoyed the subtle dig. Jimmy was, after all, a TV star. The other baggers and checkout girls must have seen his broadcast. He looked forward to the attention.

Much to his chagrin, not a single person mentioned his 15 minutes of fame. A couple of employees said hello, but even more looked away when he walked toward the beer section. The same questions were on their minds as the folks in Wal-Mart. To boot, they felt even closer to the precarious predicament James Scott went and got himself into because they had to work with the ex-con. He kept his nose clean on the job, but they were reminded daily just by his presence that Jimmy had been a fire-starting malefactor. Don't piss him off or you might wake up in a burning house.

He bought the alcohol without incident and left as abruptly as he arrived. Jimmy walked toward his Monte Carlo with beer in tow and surveyed the scene once more. There was that unmarked Crown Vic again. He was sure of it. Whoever was driving was going to some lengths to avoid detection. But he parked it at such a strange angle, and it was so shiny and clean, that the image jumped out at the man who had honed his surveillance skills in prison.

Jimmy quickly threw his beer in the back seat and hopped in the car. He made sure to fasten his seatbelt before he slowly eased into first gear. He also used his turn signals and assiduously followed the posted speed limit, just in case that Crown Victoria was for him and wasn't coincidently wherever he appeared.

Each changing stoplight made him edgy. He waited for dash lights to flash in his rearview mirror as soon as he accelerated. The 15-minute drive seemed to take hours. Jimmy made it home to Fowler undisturbed and pretty sure that no one followed him. The unmarked Crown Vic didn't pull out when he did, as far as he knew. Just to be safe, he left his purchases of socks, underwear, and beer in the car while he sat in wait on his front porch. Sure enough, five minutes later, the Crown Vic made a pass by his house.

Jimmy rushed inside to tell Suzie that someone was watching him. She was annoyed but not surprised. That last unexpected visit planted a suspicious seed in her head. She'd also been hearing strange rumors around town about her husband.

"Stay inside today," she suggested. "If it is the cops, they're looking to bust you for something."

"Yeah, I know," he replied. "But I didn't do nothing. This is harassment!"

Jimmy grew panicky. Ordinarily, if a strange car followed you around, the cops were your remedy. But what do you do when it's the cops that are following you? He couldn't call the cops to report the cops. So he did the next best thing. Jimmy pulled out the phonebook and hastily searched for the number.

A receptionist answered on the first ring. "WGEM-TV. How may I direct your call?"

"Michelle McCormack," a shaky voice said into the receiver.

"One moment please."

The reporter picked up the phone and barely had enough time to hear the caller identify himself when Jimmy started into a paranoid rambling about being followed.

"Who's following you?" McCormack asked. "What are you talking about?"

"I think it's the FBI. Or some kind of cop. They're following me around, wherever I go. They're saying I did it."

Michelle listened intently but offered no advice. She was a reporter, an objective observer of news and events. It wasn't her job to counsel people in legal matters: She was there to broadcast information. At the same time, though, McCormack was intrigued with Jimmy's fearful premonitions. Strange things had been happening around the station ever since her interview with him on July 16.

When she first returned to the newsroom, the other reporters served up a dose of grief. They brought her up to speed on whom she'd interviewed and wanted to know why she'd chosen *him*. Jimmy wasn't her first choice, she'd said. There was a Department of Transportation worker on the Bayview Bridge's flank whom she initially approached. McCormack identified herself and asked him what happened. The DOT worker said he just arrived on the scene and didn't know. "Why don't you ask that guy?" he said pointing to a lone figure walking in the vicinity. It was James Scott.

One WGEM coworker piped up that James Scott wasn't simply a bystander. He actually broke the levee. "Oh yeah?" McCormack asked. "Says who?" The coworker pointed to the glass doors in the newsroom. Standing in WGEM's nerve center and talking to a producer was Deputy John McCoy. He asked to speak with the reporter, and she agreed. He was quite interested in why Jimmy was her sole interviewee. Had she also suspected him? McCoy was principally concerned with whether Jimmy told her why he was on the levee to begin with. McCormack wasn't trying to be coy; she just didn't know. "What I know is exactly what you saw," she said.

Both McCormack and the rest of WGEM news continued to report on the West Quincy levee break as an act of Mother Nature, even though the intrepid journalist knew something else was brewing. A couple of days after she received a visit from John McCoy, she received an ominous phone call from some men across the river in Missouri. Norman Haerr and Herald Knapheide, chairman and co-chair of the Fabius River Drainage District, requested a meeting with the reporter. Their questions were no different than the ones posed by McCoy, but they were acting peculiar. Knapheide, who also doubled as the owner of Knapheide Manufacturing Company—now under 8 feet of water—told her to keep quiet about the meeting. He said the commissioners were assembling in secret, but would she please meet with them. She did: What they were alluding to was potentially newsworthy.

So when Jimmy Scott called her to say that he was being followed, the week's activities seemed to confirm his suspicion. McCormick told him there was nothing she could do, but to keep her posted if any new developments occurred.

Almost instantly, as the reporter hung up the phone, two more policemen—twins, she thought—showed up at the news station to ask her a few questions.

◄○►

The farmers and the families who lived on the river bottoms for generations in Marion County, Missouri, were all safe and sound, thank God. And that's just what Roy Grimm did as he grabbed a handheld video camera and loaded into his bass boat.

Reverend Grimm served as the minister of Apostolic Christian Church in Taylor for the past 21 years. His family roots went even deeper still. Grimm's grandfather was one of the first farmers to buy a chunk of Missouri land across the Mississippi River from Quincy, Illinois, back in the 1920s. Soil in that region was fertile and could produce a strong, healthy crop, but the Mississippi River was a long, meandering question mark from season to season. Prolonged rain—no matter how severe—often caused Old Man River to breach its natural banks and flood out the vegetation. In fact, 40 years earlier, Mark Twain wrote at length about that very area in Marion County in his book, *Life on the Mississippi*.

> *One who knows the Mississippi will promptly aver—not aloud, but to himself—that ten thousand River Commissions, with the mines of the world at their back, cannot tame that lawless stream, cannot curb it or confine it, cannot say to it, Go here, or Go there, and make it obey; cannot save a shore which it has sentenced; cannot bar its path with an obstruction which it will not tear down, dance over, and laugh at. But a discreet man will not put these things into spoken words.*

Grimm's grandfather had Twain in mind when he and a band of like-minded farmers helped to raise the first levee in Marion County. In 1926, after the farmers managed to prove Twain wrong and construct a levee that held back the waters of the mighty Mississippi, Grandpa Grimm established the Apostolic Christian Church in the river bottoms. He also wrote the house of worship's trademark song, "Come to the Church on the Levee." The song and the role of a Grimm as Apostolic Christian Church minister remained unchanged nearly 70 years later.

The families that had uncanny foresight and saw the potential in Marion County farmland in the 1920s became a part of the lore of the land. Once they established themselves, they rooted their kin in the earth. Grimm wasn't the only multigenerational family on the river bottoms. Most of his church congregants were farming ancestors of those 1920s pioneers and many of them were related.

Grimm lived on the high ground. His house and property remained intact. He helped Norman Haerr—a church member as well as the Fabius River Drainage District commissioner—and other West Quincy residents coordinate relief efforts, and he helped sandbag for a time until he sprained his foot and had to adhere to a strictly clerical role. On July 16, the day of the flood, Grimm was driving to the staging area at Knapheide Manufacturing when he remembers seeing a lone figure walking off the dam. He thought it strange that a man would be by himself, as volunteers were ordered to patrol in pairs. But apparently he didn't think it strange enough to report it at the time.

Then the levee broke.

The minister helped coordinate evacuation efforts, making sure his parishioners made it inland and to a distance unreachable by the high watermark. He spent the days immediately following the deluge comforting the people. They weren't able to return to the area and assess property damage, and they were overwrought with fear and worry. The minister decided to take action and do whatever he could to at the very least curb speculation on the part of the farmers and their families. Grimm felt it his duty, both as a man of God and as the owner of a boat, to take a voyage on the newly formed lake and document the damage. He knew the landscape would be devastated based on the aerial shots shown on television, but he couldn't discern just how bad with the camera rolling from 200 feet in the sky.

Grimm towed his boat to where the water met the land and shoved off, praying to the Lord, who delivered his flock unharmed, that he'd see it in his heart to deliver their homes and crops with only minimal damage. Yet what he saw in the first few minutes of his journey made Roy Grimm come closer than he ever had to taking the name of the Lord in vain.

As in the Bible, when God unleashed his fury on the heathens and spared Noah and the animals, West Quincy was consumed by a flood that all but wiped it off the map. Highway 61 was erased from existence. The only telltale sign that a major thoroughfare had once passed through was a sign emerging from beneath 7 feet of water. "Keep Right" was visible, as were a couple of telephone poles in the distance, and the golden arches of the nearby McDonalds, but not too much else. Grimm videotaped these startling scenes and made a somber audio commentary as his rickety boat maneuvered along a lake that wasn't on any state map.

He passed a huge red sign that advertised the "Mississippi Grill" in white cursive type. The red catfish sat atop the billboard in a pose that looked natural for the conditions, as if it was actually jumping out of the water, but there was no restaurant. The doublewide trailer was now buried treasure. As he continued along the floodplain, the waters deepened. The Shell Gas Station was now just a sign and a roof. The big brown barn that housed the Mini Mart was two-stories underwater. Worst of all were the homes. Giant king-sized beds and full sofas capsized and floated within arms reach of the gutted residences. Dead animals floated face-down in the water, but some lucky dogs and cats clung to roofs. They literally floated out of an upper-level bedroom window and clawed themselves 6 inches out of the water to safe haven. They were out of harm's way, but the pets were marooned for the foreseeable future. Roy Grimm did indeed become Noah. He rescued as many strays as his 18-foot bass boat would permit.

As he maneuvered over the yards of his parishioners, the air started to become stale. A heavy, pungent stench surrounded the modest farmhouses and lingered on the water's surface. Wispy plants swayed atop the gentle current. Grimm steered the boat through the vegetation, which looked like algae, only algae had no place on a rural Midwestern farm. It was corn. Giant eight-foot stalks were underwater with only the stalk's silky heads showing themselves. The warm water ate away at the crop. What Grimm smelled was corn fermenting. The disgusting odor was so overpowering that he pulled his handkerchief from his suspenders and covered his nose and mouth.

He continued on his path, looking for some good news to report: Perhaps a car or a house on high enough ground to survive the millions of gallons. But there was nothing left, no sign of life, save for the pets. Roy Grimm drove his boat for several hours until he came dangerously close to running out of gas. By the time he arrived back at his truck, Grimm had covered more than 10,000 acres of farmland by boat. He never even came close to running aground.

Detective Neal Baker was having all sorts of difficulty launching his investigation. He had one large piece of the puzzle—Jimmy himself at the scene of the crime when he went on television—which is usually cause enough for a police chief to give his assent to start investigating. In the past, Baker commenced with much less evidence, and he still managed to get the bad guys. He was naturally agitated when the chief of the Quincy Police Department told him to slow down and think about what he was asking. He also reminded Baker that the flood was in Missouri.

Detective Baker was getting a little too much limelight as far as some in the Quincy Police Department were concerned. The brass didn't want to let a guilty man roam free, but they also didn't necessarily want Neal Baker getting credit for a collar that would have been the biggest his town had ever seen. The QPD executives had an out: When Baker asked if he could have a shot at interrogating James Scott about the flood in West Quincy, the lieutenant told him not to bother. "It's a Missouri problem, not an Illinois one," he informed Baker.

The detective wasn't about to give up so easily. He certainly wasn't going to let something as ugly as departmental jealousy stand in his way. Sure, the alleged crime happened across state lines, but an Illinois resident, one that Baker had a history with, was the one who'd broken the Missouri law. What was more, there was no way for the Missouri authorities to conduct an investigation in Illinois—even if they had permission from the local authorities—because they had no way of getting across the river. The Marion County Sheriff's Office was not as sophisticated as the Adams County Sheriff's Office, and neither were as sophisticated as the Quincy Police Department.

No other cop in the region had as much experience with career criminals as Neal Baker, and with the sole exception of the juvenile officers a decade earlier, no other man in the region had been able to extract a confession out of James Scott.

Baker thought long and hard about his next move. He was convinced of Jimmy's guilt and felt certain that if given the chance to question him again, he'd be able to get the canary to sing. If he wasn't going to have the department's permission to pursue this, then he needed to broach the matter tactically after doing some surreptitious detective work on his own time. He needed to talk to Marion County's head lawman, Sheriff Dan Campbell. The two knew each other by name only, but that didn't prevent Detective Baker from giving Sheriff Campbell a call several days after the flood.

Campbell was another career sheriff, much like his eponymous peer across the river in Adams County. He'd been a lawman since 1980 and Sheriff of Marion County for the last decade. The farmers out in the rural reaches of Missouri, as well as the local businessmen in Hannibal, held Campbell in very high esteem. He and his staff managed to maintain law and order during the 1980s population surge, and Campbell kept the riffraff out of town during the peak tourist seasons. Visitors to Mark Twain's boyhood home, as well as to the Becky Thatcher Café, felt comfortable while strolling around the antique shops, and they felt safe carrying wads of cash to spend on Tom Sawyer memorabilia.

Rumors and innuendo spread fast, though. The Missouri residents and especially the farmers who lost everything were hearing gossip about a known felon who broke the levee on purpose. They too had seen Jimmy Scott on television and they too were privy to the informal investigation. They started calling Sheriff Campbell around the clock and badgering him for information. His constituency wanted to know why an arrest hadn't been made yet. After all, their friends and neighbors in Illinois spoke adamantly about the need for police action—both on the city and county level—and Missourians were bothered that *they* were the ones who suffered from the actions of this local bad boy yet their sheriff wasn't doing anything to apprehend him.

He was in a pickle. Even if Sheriff Campbell had been able to investigate the matter extensively, he'd need an eyewitness of James Scott breaking the levee to get an indictment. And he'd need a motive. Simply being a bad seed didn't in and of itself mean a man was capable of causing a natural disaster and millions of dollars of damage, and even if a motive did arise, in legalese, motive is not an element of an offense. If he arrested James Scott, what would he charge him with? Vandalism? That's a misdemeanor. Negligence? He'd have to prove that James Scott was the only amateur on the scene not following the Corps of Engineers' manual of levee maintenance. But most of all, assuming all the chips fell into place, whether or not the state had enough evidence to bring the case to trial was up to John Jackson, the prosecuting attorney. During a casual conversation with Campbell, Jackson indicated that he wasn't planning on filing criminal charges against James Scott—or anyone, for that matter—unless he had an iron-clad confession. In fact, he didn't know what to charge Scott with anyway since no one had ever stood trial for breaking a levee. Campbell would have to nail Jimmy cold for a case to be brought before the Missouri courts, and he didn't have the time, the resources, or the wherewithal to investigate a man across the Mississippi River when the only lead to go on was that James Scott had been there.

Sheriff Campbell called Sheriff Nall in Illinois and relayed the sentiments of the locals. Sheriff Nall assured his counterpart that Adams County was on it: They'd already questioned Jimmy once and they were fixing to speak to some of the local youths who might have information regarding Jimmy's penchant for blabbering. Campbell was pleased with this information. He decided to stay on the sidelines and let Adams County take care of the detective work. Because his prior dealings with Illinois law enforcement had been primarily with Sheriff Nall, Campbell had no way of knowing that the Quincy Police Department and the Adams County Sheriff's Department worked independently of each other. Bob Nall rarely corroborated with Quincy detectives. He didn't need to. So when Marion County Sheriff Dan Campbell received a phone call from Quincy Detective Neal Baker, the top Missouri cop said he'd already given Nall his blessing to forge ahead. Campbell also said that because this was a matter that concerned the Army Corps of Engineers, a federal agency, the FBI was dispatching several agents from their field office in St. Louis. What Campbell didn't say was that he, Sheriff Nall, Deputy Sheriff McCoy, Marion County Prosecutor John Jackson, and the FBI recently had a meeting at Quincy's

City Hall. It was a standard meeting about how the investigation would proceed. Because Campbell never said it, Baker had no way of knowing that Missouri considered James Scott a prime suspect. The cop with the most James Scott experience would have to sit this one out.

Sheriff Campbell thanked Neal Baker for his interest in the matter, but he should rest assured that someone was on the case. Right then, it was clear to Detective Baker that he'd have little help coming out of Missouri. There'd be little help coming out of the Quincy Police Department and the Adams County Sheriff's Department in Illinois, too. Just the same, Baker was a career competitor. A lone wolf. Despite his lack of resources, he felt as though the advantage was still his. Sheriff Nall would practice his own technique and despite his many years as the sheriff, Baker was convinced that Nall hadn't done as much detective work. As for Campbell, there was no way a Marion County sheriff would get his much-needed confession from a savvy ex-con like Jimmy Scott. Baker knew that if he was going to solve the case of the sabotaged levee, he'd have to do it himself.

CHAPTER FIFTEEN

—◄◦►—

Sheriff Nall and Deputy McCoy were following the senior sheriff's hunch into late July. The two men became fixtures in and around Jimmy's Columbus Heights neighborhood. McCoy personally went door-to-door, interviewing the underage Fowler youths who he learned were regulars at Dan Leake's house.

The teenagers were nervous. An unwritten edict of their culture was that the law was out to get them, especially because they were engaging in underage drinking almost nightly. Three teens in particular, Eric Epping, Cory Anderson, and Eric Wagy—all of whom were good buddies—shared stories of McCoy's visits. They felt fortunate that the interviews occurred at their homes rather than at the police station, but they were afraid that they'd become the subject of later investigations.

McCoy was a genial-enough person, as was Nall, but on follow-up interviews, they were accompanied by two men in brown suits and sunglasses that made the boys feel uneasy. Perhaps it was because they never identified themselves, or perhaps it was because the two FBI agents were outsiders.

All three boys informed the deputy during separate interviews about the comments Jimmy had made a week prior to the flood: How if the levee broke, there'd be good fishing over in West Quincy. Cory Anderson and Eric Epping were more forthcoming with their answers, so McCoy focused more on them than the third boy. He didn't lean too hard on them. McCoy was the good cop in the equation. Besides, the FBI's imposing presence was more than enough bad cop for troubled teenagers. The deputy overlooked their underage drinking in exchange for their cooperation. McCoy wouldn't be so understanding, however, with the enabler: The man who knowingly contributed to the delinquency of minors.

In late July, Deputy McCoy visited Dan Leake's house. The two had never met before, which was a relief to Dan. Now that an officer was at his door though, Dan grew immediately panicky. He'd had legal run-ins before. Dan learned over time that the best living was done anonymously. So when McCoy knocked on his door on July 23, 1993, and asked to speak with Jimmy, the lawman didn't accept Dan's simple answer of "he's not here."

McCoy had been with the sheriff's department for 20 years. He knew how to deal with these simpletons, especially the "white trash" head bangers who were hard drinkers and ungovernable, untrustworthy characters. It was textbook questioning for a seasoned deputy, coupled with a little something extra he'd learned at the FBI academy in Quantico, Virginia, a decade earlier. McCoy gave Dan a hard stare. His eyes widened and sunk back in his head. Conversely, his mouth maintained a warm, positive expression. He was careful to maintain eye contact with his source and to enunciate each spoken word vigilantly. As McCoy made mention of Dan's late night parties where teenagers were permitted to drink beer and smoke cigarettes, he spoke in a friendly tone. There was no judgment in his voice because his eyes handled that part. And there were no obvious threats because the subversive phrasing handled that. "Tell you what," Deputy McCoy said as he wrapped up their front-porch exchange, "it'd probably be a good idea to call me the next time you see Jimmy. I'll see you soon." As he walked back to his Crown Vic, McCoy put a delicate exclamation point on his message: "You stay outta trouble now, ya here."

Dan got the message loud and clear. Jimmy was the one they wanted, and unless Dan gave him up, the Adams County Sheriff's Department might start putting his own actions under a microscope. He figured he could serve Jimmy on a platter without raising his half brother's suspicions. Dan would call the cops when Jimmy came over, and when they arrived, he'd act surprised. He'd be a tipster, but nothing more. Besides, they'd catch up with the 23-year-old suspect sooner or later. Dan would do his civic duty and appease McCoy without actually doing anything all that terrible. Nevertheless, that wasn't the most troubling thought on his mind after the deputy's visit.

Dan had watched Jimmy on television the night the levee broke, along with everyone else in town. In the same vein as Detective Neal Baker, Sheriff Bob Nall, and Deputy John McCoy, Dan also grew immediately suspicious of Jimmy. Not because of his presence on the levee and his past, but because of aberrant comments made a week before the break. Jimmy told Dan that he *wanted* that levee to break. He hoped Suzie would be stranded for a spell. He thought it'd be neat to fish for big cats in a boat right next to the Mississippi Grill and that big red catfish figurine on their billboard. Dan was also mystified by Jimmy's reaction to his own direct questioning. He asked Jimmy after the fact if he had a hand in the catastrophe. Jimmy never said yes or no. Instead, he walked away in an angry huff. Dan figured it was either out of guilt or out of disgust. The law was haranguing him about his television appearance and the events of July 16. That was burdensome enough. The last person Jimmy needed doubting him was his own blood, or half blood, anyway.

At 12:30 a.m. on the morning of July 24, Jimmy turned up at Dan's house. There wasn't a party that night, but Suzie was out with her girlfriends and Jimmy was bored. Despite the late hour, Jimmy figured Dan would be up and could offer some light conversation. It was, after all, Friday night. An hour earlier, Jimmy was home watching the Cardinals on television. They were playing the Colorado Rockies in Denver, and with the time delay, the game went late. He polished off a 12-pack as St. Louis snapped a three game losing streak with a monster eight-run sixth inning. Jimmy was delighted: Those pesky Rockies, the dregs of the National League, had managed to beat the mediocre Red Birds four of their last nine meetings. Not this time, though. Jimmy wanted someone to talk ball with. Dan was a huge Ozzie Smith fan, and surely he'd have a mouthful to say about Smith's 415-foot ground-rule double.

Jimmy locked up and walked a block to Dan's house in the darkness. The door was open and Jimmy swung the screen and let himself in. Dan was sitting in his recliner, watching Letterman and making a beer can pyramid on his tray table. They exchanged greetings and spoke briefly about the Cardinals before Dan excused himself to use the bathroom. He took his cordless phone with him and briefly contemplated the call he was about to make. It was late, and he didn't know the number to the Sheriff's

Department off the top of his head. He didn't want to start thumbing through the phonebook. That would arouse Jimmy's suspicion. He also started to question his rationalization for tipping the authorities off to Jimmy's whereabouts. It was bad outlaw etiquette.

"Aw, fuck it," he thought. "Let's just get this over with." Dan pressed the Talk button and dialed 911.

The dispatcher received the phone call with anticipation. She'd been advised to call Deputy McCoy the second someone rang with information regarding James Scott. Although usually a conduit between the police, fire department, or paramedics, the 911 dispatcher served as a secretary at that moment. She jotted down a message from Dan—Jimmy was at his place right now if McCoy wanted to talk to him.

Dan and the operator exchanged goodbyes and Dan flushed the toilet after he pressed the End button so he could sell the deception. He emerged from the bathroom and plopped back down in his recliner. Jimmy thought and said nothing.

As the half brothers popped the tops off of a couple more Buds, Deputy McCoy's pager started chirping and vibrating on his nightstand. It was coming from 911. He rang dispatch headquarters, where the lone operator working the switchboard announced that the phone call he'd been awaiting just came in.

McCoy quickly sprung into action. He donned his utilities and shot down the stairs. Within the half hour, Deputy McCoy pulled into Dan Leake's driveway and knocked on the door.

Dan rose from his recliner and scrunched up his forehead. "Who the hell could that be?" he asked Jimmy, who stayed seated on the sofa. Dan opened the door and John McCoy asked if Jimmy was there. "Sure, come on in," Dan replied. And that, Dan figured, would conclude his participation in the investigation while at the same time fulfilling the deputy's "required" subtext.

Jimmy thought for a moment that he was hallucinating. What was the sheriff's deputy doing at Dan's house at one o'clock in the morning? At first, he figured he was drunk and he misplaced the face. As he focused more and realized that McCoy was actually making a middle-of-the-night house call, he became instantly jittery. McCoy walked right past Dan and planted his feet a few inches from where Jimmy sat.

"Mr. Scott?" he began.

"Yes."

"I'm Deputy McCoy."

"I know."

"What have you been up to tonight?" the lawman began.

"Not a whole lot. Just watched the Cardinals game earlier. I was at home. Been there and here all night. Why? Something wrong?"

McCoy studied Jimmy's tone. He'd asked a rather undemanding question, yet the 23-year-old seemed uneasy. He didn't want to put Jimmy on high alert just yet—not until he got the information he was seeking. "Well, I was just wondering if you'd mind accompanying me down to the sheriff's department for an interview."

"Am I under arrest?" Jimmy asked immediately.

"Oh, no," the deputy said. "Not at the moment. Just had some questions I wanted to ask you. Whaddaya say we go for a little ride?"

Dan stood there in the entry way listening. He regretted making the phone call. "I'll drive you down there, Jim," Dan offered.

Jimmy thought for a moment. He wondered if he should request an attorney, as this was now the second time in as many weeks that the sheriff's department wanted to question him. At the same time, he speculated whether bringing a lawyer in would signal to McCoy that he had a guilty conscience.

Jimmy was tired and his guard was down. McCoy had been a fixture around the county forever, and Jimmy worried that the Adams County cop might trick him into saying something damning. All this went through his mind in a matter of seconds. The one recurring theme was that he had been through the sheriff department's questioning once already. He'd managed to slip the hangman's noose when Sheriff Bob Nall questioned him last week. Jimmy's story wouldn't change this time either; he'd been staying out of trouble ever since he was paroled in 1991. Also, McCoy didn't seem nearly as cagey as Detective Baker with the Quincy Police Department. McCoy was the lesser of two evils. Jimmy was actually relieved that he hadn't heard from Baker. "Just this one last time," Jimmy said to himself. "Jump through their hoops and get on with your life."

"Yeah, let's go," the suspect blurted out. All three men exited the house. Dan was so anxious that he forgot to lock his door.

Jimmy and Dan got into Dan's car and followed McCoy's Crown Vic to Vermont Street. When they arrived, all three marched single file into the station with McCoy in the lead. He escorted the men to an interview room and asked Jimmy to have a seat. For an informal meeting, Jimmy thought, McCoy sure seemed rigid.

Dan stood in the corner of the room. Before he had a chance to take his own seat, the deputy looked down at his suspect and spoke. "James Scott, you have the right to remain silent. Anything you say . . ."

"Jesus Christ," Jimmy muttered to no one in particular. He'd been sand-bagged. This was a formal interrogation, not some late-night get-together.

McCoy finished reading Jimmy his rights and then asked Dan to go have a seat in the waiting room, which he did. The interview commenced at 1:30 a.m. Deputy McCoy asked specific questions about Jimmy's work on the levee on July 16. Once again, Jimmy walked a member of the sheriff's department through his day. He said he talked to a guy named Duke from the Missouri National Guard, but he couldn't remember his last name. He and the sergeant walked halfway to the trouble spot and the sergeant walked back after awhile. Then Jimmy went back to where he thought he saw a problem—alone—and grabbed some sandbags from one section of the levee and threw them on the problem area. He finished at about 5:30 p.m. and made his way off the dam and back toward the Bayview Bridge, just as the levee broke.

Each time Jimmy answered a question, Deputy McCoy carefully jotted down notes. He brought up tidbits of factual information to try and trip Jimmy up. He asked if the volunteer noticed a helicopter hovering right over the break. Jimmy said he did notice it and he waived his arms in its direction to signal for help. Jimmy hadn't mentioned a word of that to Michelle McCormack. The lawman asked if Jimmy was aware that a fixed-wing air-craft also flew over the break at the same time, and that it taped Jimmy down on the levee. The tape had been submitted to the sheriff's department as evidence. Jimmy then made an addendum to his story. McCoy asked Jimmy if he knew what the tape revealed. Jimmy said he leaned over the side of the levee—to the water-side—and tried to repair the plastic tarp.

There was a video: of that McCoy spoke the truth. It didn't, however, show Jimmy. McCoy tried to get the career criminal to implicate himself, which he did to an extent. He asked him point blank if he tried to break the levee. Jimmy's eyes looked around the room, a reaction that McCoy interpreted as being a nervous tell. "No," Jimmy said. "I had nothing to do with that levee break."

McCoy tried to pull a confession out of him for the next several hours. He was convinced of Jimmy's guilt by his body language and by his seemingly evolving answers. The deputy brought up the three teenagers he'd questioned earlier in the week. They all said the same thing: Jimmy told them he was going to break the levee. Jimmy refuted their statements and said that Eric Epping and Cory Anderson had an ax to grind with him. That, too, was damning. McCoy never said their names. Jimmy had broached the subject first.

The deputy questioned him into the early morning hours, but Jimmy never said the one phrase that would have convinced Missouri's prosecuting attorney across the river to bring charges. And because he never said "I did it," McCoy knew Hannibal Prosecutor John Jackson wouldn't touch this case. That was unequivocally clear when they'd met in Quincy's City Hall a few days earlier.

At 4:30 in the morning, the deputy dismissed his suspect. Jimmy wearily stood and walked to the waiting room, where Dan was out cold. Jimmy shook Dan's shoulder, making sure not to startle him. The two trudged to the parking lot and drove off while McCoy stayed around for another half-hour filling out his report.

He detailed everything the suspect said, even though he too was having a hard time staying awake. Whether it was the hour or the heated exchange, veteran McCoy failed to flag Jimmy's inconsistencies in his report. Nor did he make any mention of the peculiar body language. The lawman wrote in the report that he suspected foul play, but he didn't describe what about his interview indicated such a feeling.

◄o►

Detective Neal Baker sat at his desk and pored over his notes. He had obtained a videotape of James Scott speaking with Michelle McCormack from their television interview, and he meticulously dissected Jimmy's statements while looking for inconsistencies. He was trying to garner enough evidence so that his superior would allow him to bring Jimmy in for questioning. Something about Jimmy's story just wasn't jibing. Something just didn't add up, though he couldn't put his finger on it—not yet anyway.

In the late afternoon, after the detective had put about four hours into his investigation, a skinny, disheveled youth walked into the new police headquarters on South Eighth Street. He looked frightened to be there, as if there was something preternatural about the stationhouse and all those men walking around in blue uniforms and shiny gold badges.

The teen had messy, greasy brown hair and bushy eyebrows. His long, pointy, acne-pocked nose jutted from the center of a pale gaunt face. His lips drew together closer on the left side of his mouth, which was the side of his mouth that he spoke from. He was missing a couple of teeth, and all the teeth from his left front tooth back were broken.

Joe Flachs had no use for cops, and he certainly felt he had no business in a cop shop. He abhorred these men who had sent him to juvenile home when he was nine. Joe apprehensively trudged to the desk of the watch commander. Then he asked to speak with Detective Neal Baker.

The teen had no way of knowing that at that very moment, Baker was constructing a fact pattern in the case of James Scott. Nor did Joe know that the Adams County Sheriff's Department had launched a full-scale investigation. He was a Fowler youth, and had he known, he probably would have approached the Fowler authorities rather than the cops in the "city." He asked to speak with Baker because Baker was the only name he knew on the Quincy Police force. And the only reason he knew Baker's name was because Jimmy used to bitch about all the trouble Baker had caused him over the years.

Baker was paged over the station's PA system but wasn't available at the time. Officer Dennis Boden responded to the page and came out to the front desk. He looked the scraggly boy over before addressing him. Joe introduced himself and said he had information about James Scott.

"What sort of information?" Boden quizzed.

"Information about the levee break," Joe said, avoiding eye contact.

"I see. Why don't you come and sit down."

For the next 45 minutes, Joe Flachs described to Officer Boden the events immediately following the flood. He spoke of being at Dan Leake's house and of having a conversation with Jimmy. Jimmy, Joe said, told him that the levee break in West Quincy was no accident. Joe relayed information that Jimmy bragged about walking out onto the floodplain with a shovel and piercing the industrial strength plastic tarp with his spade. He said Jimmy dug around in the saturated sand until the Mississippi River first trickled and then burst through the breach. Then he made the statement that hit the cop like a brick: Jimmy, he said, intentionally broke the levee to strand his wife in Missouri so he could party in Illinois without her.

Boden's jaw literally dropped. His chin tilted to the floor and his eyes fixed on the teen. "Are you kidding me?" he asked in sheer disbelief.

"That's what he said."

"He wanted to strand his wife in Missouri so he could party in Illinois?"

"Uh-huh."

"Well hell, I've heard it all!" the cop exclaimed. Boden, like the rest of the officers in the QPD, knew Jimmy had criminal tendencies, and he was certainly capable of causing little disasters, but this was the most ridiculous motive in the history of detective work. He struggled to wrap his head around such a fantastic story. Still, it confirmed what he thought on July 16 as he too watched Michelle McCormack reporting from the levee: Jimmy Scott wasn't down there sandbagging out of his love for mankind. He went down there to sabotage the dike. Period.

Boden took a statement from Joe, and Joe signed the bottom of it, indicating that he made it willingly, that he wasn't coerced, and that it was he who approached the QPD rather than the other way around.

Detective Neal Baker arrived back at the police station shortly after Joe left. Officer Boden briefed Baker on what had just transpired. He knew the detective was working the case. Baker, who was usually all-business, smiled ear to ear, for he had smelled a rat the moment Jimmy's face appeared on TV. He employed standard police work coupled with his own sixth sense to make a confident deduction. Now that deduction had a witness. The cop didn't like to boast, so he didn't sprint into his superior's office and brag on his news. Baker decided to continue his plodding investigation and bide his time until the right moment arose. He'd have his crack at Jimmy Scott, and when he did, he'd be ready. He'd question his man only when the facts were all in place, not like the Sheriff's Department, running all over town with their half-baked leads.

There was no denying it: Baker was good.

—◄o►—

It took more than a month, but the waters of the Mississippi River disappeared from the Missouri interior. Every farmer's crop was destroyed within a 14,000 acre radius, and while tragic, the porous, absorbent earth that earned them a living slowly swallowed the excess water and replenished the nutrients deep in the soil's alluvial layer. Then it trickled further down, past the humus and topsoil, into the subsoil, regolith, and finally the Midwest's 4 billion-year-old bedrock, where it became just another relic of the past.

The damage left, however, was anything but forgettable. Gutted homes and buildings, rusted cars, tractors and grain elevators, and saturated, destroyed crops gradually emerged from the river's depths. The devastation was so pervasive from the events of July 16 that hardworking farmers could do nothing but scratch their heads. There was no way of knowing how or where to begin the cleanup. Their machinery was rendered useless; their soil still too soggy to plant. Insurance companies hadn't come to a firm decision on how to dole out money—if they were to dole it out at all—because surprisingly, not everyone living and farming the river bottoms had federal flood insurance. Most companies balked at the homeowners' requests for new homes. Farmers had crop insurance, so at least they'd farm again, but unless the indemnity clauses worked in their favor, they'd have nowhere to live. There were so many questions and so much destruction.

In mid-August, over the now-repaired Bayview Bridge, Quincy life returned to normal, save for the people that plied their trades in Marion County. Factories and commercial businesses operated at full steam. Children returned to South Park and to Bicentennial Park, people filled Wal-Mart and the mall again, and over in Fowler, Dan Leake reopened his doors to the late summer party crew.

Jimmy continued to move through town somewhat cautiously. He noticed the occasional Crown Victoria cruising past his house, and sometimes it appeared in the parking lots of Burger King and County Market. Even though no one ever drove the car in his path and hindered his forward progress, he figured someone was still looking to nail him. The local authorities—both city and county—demonstrated over time that they were nothing if not tenacious. Nevertheless, Jimmy grew more comfortable as every day ticked by without the cops meddling in his personal affairs. The more comfortable he became, the more he shed his heightened sense of awareness and reverted back to his old self.

Seldom a hot August night went by that he didn't down a 12-pack of Budweiser. In fact, he drank so much so quickly and so often that the 23-year-old built up an immunity to beer. Some of the metal-heads started bringing Jack Daniels whisky around. Guns N' Roses curly-haired guitar player, Slash, had done more for the Tennessee spirit than any team of advertising executives could ever have. For five years, the paparazzi photographed him lipping a fifth of JD. Quincy 20-somethings followed suit.

Beer became an appetizer. Whisky became the main course. Jimmy reached a state of inebriation from the charcoal-aged sour mash that no brew could match. But Jack Daniels also made for loose lips. The more Jimmy consumed, the more vocal he became. He stumbled around Dan's house—bottle in hand, banging into other people and into finger-marked sheetrock—just like Slash when he stumbled around backstage. He hugged-up on women when Suzie wasn't looking and he bullshitted with the men about how bad the Cardinals sucked and how he was sure they'd lose to the Dodgers on that August night, inevitably slipping into a seven game losing streak.

He continued to entertain questions about his television appearance. Jimmy Scott face-to-face with Michelle McCormack was passé to most of the locals, but not the party people. They still wanted to know what she looked like in person, what she smelled like, whether the rumors were true about how she liked to date people she interviewed.

Jimmy embellished his answers. All of a sudden, McCormack had a crush on him and they might get together for drinks. The party people were enthralled. Not often did a member of their clique get the chance to rub elbows with Quincy's social elite.

Three people at the party listened attentively though said nothing. They observed Jimmy with nervous eyes and tried to keep their sheer disgust for his words at bay. Eric Epping, Cory Anderson, and Joe Flachs didn't believe a word Jimmy said. They sat quietly in lifeless arrest and purposefully averted their gazes. They thought about conversations with Jimmy prior to—and in Joe's case after—the West Quincy levee broke. Their minds were on Adams County cops and on the investigation that proceeded unbeknownst to anyone in the room. They wanted to stand up and shout. "LIAR!" Yet not even a syllable was uttered, not because they were scared of James Scott, but because they were terrified of the authorities.

Jimmy longed for attention and it didn't matter that he was spinning yarns. Nor did it matter that he only told lies when he drank. Jimmy by now was a full-fledged alcoholic. He couldn't function physically without either a drink in hand or the prospect of one in the future. Likewise, he couldn't socialize without being under the influence. Jimmy was the party crowd's prankster, the joker. They fed his persona and shaped the image he so ardently desired. So much so that in September 1993, when he and Dan decided to get tattoos after a long day of binge drinking, the 23-year-old chose to have a joker inked on his right arm for the rest of time.

Oddly, despite the fun he was having, Jimmy realized his life was spinning out of control. He had an older brother who was still living in the past, a baby brother, now with only one eye, who was serving 14 years in the state pen, a wife that he loved but who he struggled to provide for, a daughter somewhere in Missouri that he slowly learned to live without, and a beer-swilling half brother who was both his best friend and his worst demon. There was no endgame to his plight, no light at the end of the tunnel. The only moments in Jimmy's life that weren't completely consumed with self-loathing were the fleeting hours between when he tied a buzz on and when he became so intoxicated that he was unable to control his actions or he'd simply black out. Either way, he felt hollow the next day. A couple of times, when he wasn't lucky enough to black out, he woke up with a piercing headache and some strange cuts and scratches on his hands and arms. Jimmy spent those days meticulously retracing his steps in an effort to remember what he'd done. He remembered places he went—or intended to go—but not necessarily what transpired. Like the morning he woke up with a backpack that he knew didn't belong to him.

After each occasion, Jimmy swore to himself that he wouldn't get that drunk anymore. Of course, he never kept that promise. There was no other way to stem the depression. In the meantime, he went through the strange backpack, pocketed the $200 inside, and stashed it in the trunk of his car. He'd throw it out tomorrow.

<o>

September was a particularly crime-ridden month in Quincy. Perhaps it was because of the Indian summer, which kept people out later than usual, or just mere coincidence. In any event, many of the crimes landed on Detective Neal Baker's desk, and he diligently pursued each lead. Four offenses made him stop and scratch his head. Somebody had written some bad checks, snatched a woman's purse, robbed a man at knifepoint, and broken in to a man's truck and stole his backpack.

During the course of questioning witnesses and matching descriptions, a Caucasian male, medium height, medium build with long, blond hair and a mustache was implicated as a suspect four different times. In Baker's past dealings with Quincy's criminal element, one man matched this description, except for the mustache. Baker figured Jimmy grew one to look regal.

He didn't go after Scott right away. The Adams County Sheriff's Department was still tailing Jimmy. The detective was surprised that Jimmy could commit so many crimes with so much heat already on him. He carefully went over departmental paperwork and followed procedure right down to the last detail. Whether Jimmy had done all four crimes was a moot point. Baker had a history with him and he'd get to the truth sooner than anyone. More importantly, the detective had probable cause to haul Jimmy in, and that meant he had an excuse to question him about the levee.

On September 30, 1993, Neal called his brother and scheduled a meeting for nine o'clock the following morning. A bust was about to go down, and as was his style when dealing with perpetrators who had nothing to gain and everything to lose, the detective needed some backup.

They met at McDonalds and discussed how the afternoon's events would unfold. Bruce was brought up to speed on the four crimes in which

James Scott was a suspect. Neal harped on the point that this was their opportunity to discuss the levee break. Bruce listened attentively as his brother described the stellar police work he'd done behind the scenes. The four crimes Jimmy was suspected of committing were interesting to say the least, but Bruce couldn't get past this crazy story Neal had unearthed. Jimmy Scott broke that levee so he could get it on with another woman in Illinois while Suzie was marooned in Missouri.

"That's absurd!" Bruce announced. "Did he really think he'd get away with it?"

"He might have, had he not told this Flachs kid about taking a shovel and digging the thing up. And if he wouldn't have talked to Michelle."

Despite Neal's enthusiasm for the afternoon "conversation" he was going to have with Jimmy, the seasoned detective knew that this case was anything but shut. Neal wasn't the lead investigator. In fact, his department wasn't even supposed to be working on the investigation. Marion County's legal crew would need something exceptional from the Baker interview if they were going to move forward with an indictment. Truth be told, the feeling Neal got from Marion County Sheriff Dan Campbell was that anything short of a confession would be worthless for the prosecuting attorney's office.

Neal instructed Bruce on how the bust would go down. He became familiar with Jimmy's work schedule and knew that the 23-year-old would be at Burger King on Broadway in a few hours.

They could have stormed into the restaurant, talked tough, and slapped cuffs on the suspicious fast food employee; they'd be well within their right as lawmen to do so. Though Neal had other plans. And even more importantly, a guy like James Scott didn't respond well to police intimidation. He was a career confessor—someone who liked other people to know his handiwork—and embarrassing him in front of his coworkers and the store's customers would most likely make him clam up.

No, this interview would have to be conducted with kid gloves. Jimmy broke the levee, of that they were sure. Jimmy was proud of the chaos he'd caused, evidenced by the comments he made to Joe Flachs. Now Neal Baker needed to make him comfortable enough to confess his crime while at the same time exerting his authority.

The brothers finished their coffee as they plotted the various elements of the imminent inquiry. "Make no mistake," Neal told his brother, "this'll be the toughest interview we've ever done."

CHAPTER SIXTEEN

◄○►

The evening of September 29 was a rough one for Jimmy. He partied hard at Dan's house, arriving home in the wee hours of September 30. Jimmy slept off his hangover until around noon when he woke up and started paying some bills. It was a Thursday and the power company was threatening to shut off the juice. With all the previous month's activities, Jimmy was suddenly consumed by the desire to make sure that his house was not thrown into perpetual darkness.

Dan was planning yet another get together that night, and Jimmy thought about ways to back out of work. No such luck, though. He drew the nightshift at Burger King, which meant that he'd be responsible for cleaning out the fryers, mopping the floor, and emptying the godforsaken grease trap. It also meant he'd be dragging ass all night long because he was operating on little sleep and just couldn't shake his headache.

Jimmy drove to the restaurant, parked his Monte Carlo behind the drive-through window, and punched in at 10:26 p.m., four minutes earlier than scheduled. He grabbed a broom and a mop, then meticulously went over the floor, first with one and then with the other. As dawn approached, Jimmy continued his cleaning regimen. He stopped often for cigarette breaks, taking breathers five minutes at a time to enjoy a Camel in the cool fall night. He thought about what was going on across town at Dan's house and little else. Jimmy flicked his cigarette butt into the empty parking lot and headed back inside, where he addressed the grease trap, the most disgusting of chores.

He was supposed to punch out at seven o'clock, a full hour and a half after the morning shift arrived. Right before he was to leave, the Burger King supply truck pulled up with a shipment of beef patties, buns, and a parcel of French fries. A morning manager coaxed Jimmy into helping unload the truck. He was promised a free meal in addition to time-and-a-half in exchange, so the weary worker agreed.

Unloading the eighteen-wheeler was always a pain. The patties were packed in ice, which froze his hands. The French fries—in their raw state— weighed a ton, and the crates of buns always made him hungry. They finished the task three hours after they started when Jimmy collapsed into one of the restaurant's booths. The manager brought him a sausage Croissan'wich meal, complete with an extra hash brown and a large coffee. Jimmy hungrily grabbed the sandwich with two hands and began to scarf it down. He chewed at a frenzied pace as he looked out the window. Then on a dime, he slowed down and leisurely ate his meal. It was already pretty late in the morning and he didn't have anything to do except sleep that day, so there was no longer any reason to rush.

Jimmy observed carloads of workers lined up outside the drive-through. Senior citizens casually walked across a sun-streaked parking lot and into the restaurant, where they mulled over the menu and eventually ordered "the usual." He smiled to himself: The old folks always read the board as if they were at a fine dining establishment and deciding between filet and prime rib. An old lady gave her husband an earful after he ordered coffee. "You know coffee gives you gas!" she scolded. Jimmy giggled as the old man stood there annoyed.

Eleven o'clock in the morning rolled around and Jimmy took one last sip from his half-full coffee cup. Fatigue set in all at once. He'd been up for 23 hours and he had another headache—this one from a combination of exhaustion and strain rather than alcohol. He wanted to go home, change out of that oily uniform and slip beneath his warm covers. Suzie would be at work and he'd have several hours of undisturbed sleep.

He eased out of the booth and waved to the cute girl working the register. "See ya, Jimmy," she said above an order. The manager briefly stopped loading a tray and waved. Jimmy pushed open the now-fingerprinted glass doors and ambled across the parking lot to his car. The ex-con must have been much more tired than he thought because he shuffled right past an unmarked Crown Victoria without even noticing the two men—twins, maybe—that sat in the front seats. They shared the same stoic expression and wore similar brown suits.

The Baker brothers had been sitting there for almost three hours. They had arrived at Burger King shortly after seven o'clock, fully prepared to execute their plan of apprehending James Scott and hauling him in for questioning, when the delivery truck showed up. As Jimmy scampered out of the restaurant, they were ready to chase him across the parking lot. Ex-cons, especially this one, would be none to happy to see Neal and Bruce. He might try to bolt across the shopping complex and beat the 250-plus pounders in a footrace. But not on that day. This guy, the Bakers silently observed, was in no shape to evade arrest.

Jimmy unlocked the door of his Monte Carlo and eased into the driver's seat. He started the ignition and literally strained to turn around and look for oncoming traffic. The moment Neal Baker saw Jimmy's reverse lights go on, he quickly started his own car and moved it into position behind his prey. Jim slammed on the breaks to avoid a collision. The close call abruptly shook him from his daze. He was still too tired to figure out that the car he'd almost hit was a Crown Vic carrying the Bakers.

Neal shifted into park and the two emerged from their seats. Jimmy knew exactly what was going on now. He even recognized which brother was which.

He put his own automobile in park and shut off the engine. The Bakers stood behind his car and Neal motioned Jimmy out. The 23-year-old slowly emerged and walked halfway toward his old nemesis.

"Hey, Jim," Neal said quite matter-of-factly.

"Hiya, detective. A little early to be staking me out, don't ya think?"

"Well, we've got a little bit of a problem. We need you to come with us to the station."

Jimmy's conversational tone instantly vanished. He stuck his hands in his Burger King-issued trouser pockets and alternated glances between the asphalt and the cop. "You want to talk to me about that fucking levee, don't you?" he volunteered. Bruce shot his brother a glance while Neal kept his eyes trained on Jimmy.

"Actually, we've got a few things to talk about. Why don't you jump in the back seat there and we'll get under way." Neal's voice never trembled. And he never scowled, not even when Jimmy muttered an expletive about a topic that the cop didn't raise.

"Mind if we search your car here real quick, Jimmy?" The suspect shook his head. He watched from the back seat of the Crown Vic as the brothers rummaged through his Monte Carlo. Neal was looking for evidence of the levee break—perhaps the shovel still covered with dirt—that the man used to unleash the awesome power of the Mississippi River. He didn't find a shovel, but there was a gray Jansport knapsack in his trunk, which matched the description of one reported stolen a couple weeks earlier. And a crowbar.

"Want me to grab your bag for you?" Neal asked. Jimmy completely forgot about the pack. It was too late for him to trash it now. "Yeah, go ahead," Jimmy said. Neal fought back a grin. If the looming interview should go awry—like if the suspect started lying to him—that piece of evidence might come in handy.

They drove in silence to the station and pulled into the underground garage. The men maneuvered through the whitewashed hallway and entered a waiting room with no windows. Jimmy was instructed to take the lone seat, which he did. Neal spoke up. "We're gonna go get the interview room ready, Jimmy."

Jimmy had the door closed on him and was left to contemplate what the Bakers had in store. His head felt as though it was splitting down the center and he was bleary-eyed from sleep deprivation. Taken together, Jimmy couldn't wrap his head around why he was there. Neal Baker didn't tell him exactly why he waited all morning long outside Burger King. Jimmy supposed it was the levee, but then he started replaying the last hazy month in his equally hazy head. Jack Daniels dulled his memory for the most part. He knew he'd been lawless, but to what extent he honestly did not know. He struggled to stay awake and to think what sort of evidence Neal might have on him. Jimmy fought back the sandman with all his strength for at least a half hour. As the time passed, he began to wonder where the Bakers were and why this was taking so long.

Jimmy's best efforts to stay awake ultimately failed him. His head buoyed up and down and his breathing became slow and labored. The only reason he wasn't out cold was because of the fear clutching him in the gut. If the Bakers did in fact have him, they'd violate him right back to prison. He had one year left on his parole, and criminal activity was the most surefire way to get sent upstate. He was so nervous and yet so tired. Neal Baker was a thorough cop and Jimmy wasn't prepared to deal with him. A half hour had ticked by already. The suspect figured he had at least another half hour until the questioning started. That was the QPD's style: They liked to sweat their perps and make them contemplate their lot. He needed a nap, even if it meant sleeping while sitting in a chair. There was just no way he could mentally spar with Baker in his current physical and mental state. Jimmy lowered his chin to his pulsating chest and closed his eyes. He breathed deeply and steadily, like he imagined pregnant women in labor do, as he tried to tamp down his apprehension. The Bakers were making him wait, so he was going to make them wait, too. He hummed James Taylor's "Sweet Baby James" softly to himself and meditated on his favorite lyrics. When he juxtaposed his own young life with the young cowboy in Taylor's song, his mien calmed instantly.

Baker wouldn't get him this time, he thought. He wasn't some scared 18-year-old kid anymore. Nor was he some 12-year-old delinquent running rampant around Webster Elementary School. Jimmy was 23, and he was street smart. He'd been around. He transported himself to the northeastern Shangri-la Taylor spoke of: Jimmy pictured himself sitting by an open fire as the moon shown on high. He thought about the women he'd had and about beer after beer, about a peaceful song in his head and an unfettered heart, and the possibility that someone somewhere might save his soul.

Jimmy reflexively mumbled the words as he slowly drifted off into a peaceful snooze. Cliché after cliché played out in his head as his utterances manifested into mellifluous, guttural moans. "No reason to worry until there's something to worry about," he said aloud. "Baker's just an old skeleton. His bark is worse than his bite. What's done is done. Wrong me once, it's your fault; wrong me twice, it's my fault. I'll just give him what he wants. He's reasonable. Let sleeping dogs lie. Easy now, man. Easy. Deep breaths. Rock-a-bye, baby. Rock-a-bye Sweet Baby James."

—◄o►—

A thunderous boom roused Jimmy from his repose. He jerked his head up so violently that it smacked against the cinderblock wall. As he came to, Jimmy looked around trying to remember where he was. The first face he saw was that of Detective Neal Baker. As always, kid brother Bruce was at his side.

"Sorry to scare you, Jimmy," the elder cop said. He wasn't really sorry. Neal was just gaining the upper hand by jarring his suspect without actually intimidating him. It worked. Jimmy was confused and struggled to respond in a manly manner.

"Hey, Neal. That's okay. What's going on?" It was a puzzling response from both men's point of views.

"Not a whole lot, Jim. We're ready for you now. Why don't you follow us?"

Jimmy rose to his feet and followed Bruce, who followed Neal outside the waiting room and down the corridor. He caught a glimpse of a clock as they walked down the whitewashed hallway: 1:11 p.m. He'd been asleep a little over an hour, which served more as an inhibitor than a refresher. Jimmy was so exhausted that he struggled to walk straight and his head hurt from smacking against the wall. He hadn't achieved REM sleep yet and his body reacted sluggishly.

Neal paused at a door with a brushed aluminum plaque on it: Interview Room 4. The room was small, maybe 9 feet by 12 feet. A tape recorder and a telephone were the lone instruments on a standard-sized wooden desk. There were three chairs for the three men. Jimmy took a seat that faced a giant mirror. He figured it was a one-way mirror and that someone was on the other side watching what went down. Before the Baker brothers took their seats, Neal unplugged the tape recorder and the telephone. He wrapped the chords around each one and handed them to his brother. "Do me a favor, Bruce, and put these in my office, will ya?" Bruce snapped to without question. It was a calculated move. The detective knew that a man measured his words when he was being recorded. Jimmy always had, even back in the day, and should the telephone ring in the middle of questioning, the clang could bring any momentum he'd built up to a screeching halt. He wanted Jimmy to feel comfortable, like he could speak easy without fear of incriminating himself on tape. Only after he heard what he wanted would the tape recorder be brought back in. Then Baker would have the same conversation again, for posterity's sake. That time would come, he hoped. For now, James Scott needed to feel like this was just a conversation. Bruce returned a minute later and the brother's occupied the other two steel chairs.

Neal began. "Jimmy, your name has come up in a series of crimes we've been investigating. I want us to just talk and see what you know about these incidents. That sound all right by you?"

Jimmy avoided making eye contact. He knew Neal was a master at reading body language and he was too tired to hold the cop's unflinching stare. "Sure, detective," was his moderate response.

Neal broached the subject of the violent crimes first. They brought with them the most serious penalties. If Jimmy copped to purse snatching and armed robbery, the other two crimes would essentially be formalities. Plus, Jimmy wouldn't mind confessing to bad checks and breaking into a car if they already had him on two felonies. The detective was careful not to mention the levee until the other offenses were discussed. If he did, he could possibly be on the hook for wrongful arrest.

Neal used his patented technique of open-ended questions with the ex-con. He fed Jimmy misinformation and skewed details in the hopes that his culprit would correct the record. Jimmy thought long and hard after each question and answered in frank, level tones. He had no earthly idea what Baker was talking about. Jimmy adamantly denied the purse-snatching and armed robbery out of hand. He wasn't a violent man—not since those high school fights with bullies who tormented his handicapped brother had he so much as raised a finger to another man. Not even in prison.

Baker listened and nodded his head in agreement. He continued to probe deeper into Jimmy's answers, though the detective seemed inclined to believe his suspect. Nothing about Jimmy's criminal profile or his past transgressions matched those of a vicious offender. Jimmy broke laws to get attention and to impress others. Still, the detective proceeded cautiously. It wasn't unthinkable for Jimmy to have an as-yet-to-be-exposed dual personality. After all, before John Wilkes Booth became Lincoln's assassin, he was popularly regarded as the best actor of his day, and the most handsome man in America, north or south.

The detective then brought up the subject of a truck vandalism/burglary in which a backpack was stolen. Jimmy played dumb at first. The details Neal fed him didn't ring any bells, but when Neal described the backpack, Jimmy gritted his teeth. The detective was describing the same backpack he'd confiscated from the trunk of Jimmy's Monte Carlo earlier that day. The suspect kowtowed to the detective. He *did* break into the truck and steal the knapsack. His admission didn't change the tenor of the interview. Neal simply said, "okay," and then moved on to the fourth and presumably last crime Jimmy was on the hook for, bad checks.

Although the 23-year-old worked two jobs, his lifestyle never allowed him to save any money. His existence was one lived hand-to-mouth. Jimmy wrote several hot checks that bounced. Taken together, the amounts were enough to make his crime a felony. The detective sensed the apprehension on Jimmy's face: He wanted to confess, but not to a more severe charge. Neal made the suspect a promise—admit to the checks, and he'll make sure to tell the state's attorney that during questioning, Jimmy was truthful and cooperative. Jimmy agreed.

The admitted criminal looked frazzled. He and Quincy's top cop had been sparring for close to seven hours already, and he was not only tired but hungry. Jimmy asked Neal if he could call his parents, to which the detective replied he could in a little while. There was one more thing he wanted to discuss. Neal casually brought up the West Quincy levee break. "I want to go over the story you told the news," he started. Jimmy shifted uncomfortably in his chair. This would take some time.

"Mind if I have a cigarette?" he asked.

"There's no smoking in the station," Bruce chimed in. Neal could tell by his suspect's edgy demeanor that there was something he wanted to say about the levee: He was about to shed light on something previously undisclosed. "Yeah," Neal said, "now's a good time for a smoke break. Let's step outside for a minute and then we'll come back in."

They left the room, which now smelled quite funky. Especially because one of them hadn't showered in over 30 hours. As they made their way down the whitewashed hallway, Neal ducked into his office and grabbed two cigars, one for him and one for Bruce. The Baker brothers were far too athletic to smoke cigarettes. Neither would be able to suck one down while maintaining his composure.

The three men stood behind police headquarters. Jimmy drew a Camel from his pack and Neal Baker produced the two cigars. Neal lit himself and then he lit Jimmy and his brother. The smoke break made Jimmy more relaxed, and Neal too for that matter.

Neal made some light conversation. He knew Jimmy was a sports nut from past meetings, so he brought up the Chicago Bears rout of the Tampa Bay Buccaneers from Sunday. Jimmy immediately bit. They talked about how Bears quarterback Jim Harbaugh was finally playing to his ability, as demonstrated by the 47–17 score. The defense was finally pulling their own also. Maybe this would be another Cinderella year, like back in 1986 when Jim McMahon led the Bears to a Super Bowl drumming of the New England Patriots.

They wrapped up and stamped out their butts on the sidewalk. Neal then led the man back into the station and back to Interview Room 4, where everyone was seated. Jimmy started telling the same story he'd told Michelle McCormack, Sheriff Bob Nall, and Deputy John McCoy. The detective sat passively while maintaining direct eye contact. He questioned Jimmy as much with his glare as with his mouth. After Jimmy concluded, Neal looked at Bruce and then back at the suspect. "Jim, I don't think you're being truthful," he said at long last.

"That's the way it happened," Jimmy replied. He felt as if he'd told the story so many times that there wasn't any possible way he could have left out details.

"What was the name of the man from Missouri National Guard that you say you told about trouble spots?"

"I don't remember his name. Duke something."

"Do you remember what he looks like?"

"Not really. He was wearing camouflage and all the guys were asking him questions."

"I've gotta tell you, Jim, he sounds made up."

"Well, he's not."

Baker switched gears. "Where did you get the shovel from?" Jimmy stared back at him blankly.

"What shovel?"

"The shovel you had with you when you were up on the levee by yourself. A few people have said you had a shovel." Baker employed his technique of misinformation to make Jimmy stumble. The only person who'd mentioned the shovel was young Joe Flachs. That was the lead Baker had to go on though—that and the wife-stranding motive.

"I never used no shovel," Jimmy stated emphatically. "I just moved a couple of sandbags."

"How many sandbags?"

"I don't know, three or four. I was trying to draw attention to the trouble spot."

"Okay, when did you first notice the problem?" Baker asked. The cop was on to something. Jimmy had just made an admission to moving sandbags, which most likely caused the levee to fail. Neal abandoned the shovel statement because there was no physical evidence of a shovel found at the scene. Moreover, Joe's statement would have been considered hearsay in court. He began probing the 23-year-old about moving sandbags.

"Probably about 9 a.m.," Jimmy said.

"On that day? July 16? Did you tell anybody?"

"Yes I did. I knew there was a problem. I didn't mean to cause a bigger problem. That was my least intentions. I just wanted somebody to come and see that there was a problem. I pulled three or four sandbags."

"Could it have been more than three or four sandbags? Could it have been a few more than that? Is that possible?"

"No."

"Okay. What you told us earlier I think was at least four or five. Could it have been four or five?"

"It could have been."

He was so tired. And hungry. Jimmy had been up for more than 35 hours now and hadn't eaten since his complimentary meal that morning. He asked Baker again if he could call his parents.

The detective was brimming with excitement even though he was careful to keep all signs of happiness masked. Jimmy had just confessed to breaking the West Quincy levee. He'd admitted to moving sandbags on the area where the levee broke. He'd also said he didn't mean to make it worse, which translated to he made it worse, even if he *said* he didn't mean to. There were still some procedural moves the detective needed to make, like getting the statement on tape. He also had to make a couple of phone calls to the other players in the investigation, and he couldn't wait to see their reactions.

Baker had done it again: He solved a giant case. In so doing, he was still batting .1000 against James Scott.

He looked Jimmy over and saw a portrait of a broken man. Only eight hours earlier, this guy was finishing up a shift at work and thinking ahead to sleep and a late-night party. Eight hours from now, he'd be sitting in the Adams County Jail awaiting extradition to Missouri, where he'd be booked, charged, and later tried for a crime. He'd also have to deal with the Illinois state's attorney for the two crimes he copped to at the beginning of the interview.

Baker felt sorry for his suspect. He liked Jimmy Scott—always had. That didn't mean he would let him slide, though. Baker thought back to a piece of advice he learned a decade earlier: A veteran police officer told him that he can't worry about what'll happen to the people he arrests. He can't dwell on the length of their prison sentence, and he can't think about their future. Cops concentrate on the task at hand. They follow leads and make sure to arrest the right person. That's their due diligence. Once they've done their job, the suspect is the system's problem.

James Scott would certainly be at the mercy of the state of Missouri, and right quick. Still, the detective wanted to give Jimmy one last taste of freedom—one last semblance of humanity. Instead of bringing the telephone back into the interview room so he could call his parents, Neal, Bruce, and Jimmy left the station and piled into the same Crown Victoria that hauled him in earlier. A few turns later, they arrived at his old residence on Elm Street.

When they walked to the door and knocked, it was Sharon Scott who answered. She lowered her head and started crying when she saw that Jimmy was once again in the custody of the Quincy Police Department. He tried to console her by telling her that everything was going to be all right and that it wasn't as bad as it looked. Neal and Bruce said nothing.

The three men entered the house and Jimmy made a beeline for the bathroom, where he immediately stripped and showered. Neal and Bruce took seats on the couch in the living room and patiently waited for their man to finish in the lavatory. Sharon offered to make them coffee. They politely declined in unison. Neal thought it best not to burden the woman. He realized none of this was her fault and that as rough of a ride as she'd already had, it was about to get a lot rougher.

Jimmy emerged from the bathroom with a head of combed, wet blond hair and shaved cheeks. His mustache looked trimmed also. In prison, a simple shower and shave lifted a man's spirits. Jimmy knew that he'd be making a stop in the county jail later that night, so he groomed himself one last time as a free man.

He kept the parting scene with his mother to a minimum. She asked how long he'd be gone, to which he replied he didn't know. "But I don't think it'll be too long," he told her. "With what I did, I can't see my sentence being any longer than a year or so." Jimmy was referring to the stolen backpack and the bad checks. He hadn't been charged with breaking the levee. Sharon told him to be careful. "It will be short time, mom," he said. "I can do a year standing on my head if I have to!" She managed a laugh. Neal and Bruce found the comment funny, but given the dubious circumstances, they didn't so much as crack a smile.

As the car pulled out of Jimmy's old neighborhood, Neal suggested they make a pit stop at Wendy's for some takeout dinner. Jimmy fumbled in his pockets and made sure he had enough money to cover a double-cheeseburger and large fry. He had $6, just enough to eat one last meal as a free man.

They went up to the drive-through window and Neal ordered for everyone. As they pulled around to pay, Jimmy produced his $6. The detective refused his money. "This one's on me, Jim." Neal recognized also that this would be Jim's last free meal for awhile, figuratively and literally.

Neal carried the bags into the station and each man carried his Coke. They filed back to Interview Room 4 and had an impromptu picnic. Neal finished eating first and excused himself to make a phone call. Jimmy and Bruce stayed behind. They finished their meals and then kicked back a little, resuming the earlier conversation about Jim Harbaugh's Chicago Bears.

When the detective returned, he rejoined the conversation. Bruce did a good job diverting Jimmy's attention to the unfortunate situation he was in and kept him occupied while Big Brother attended to details. Neal was in the other room calling his superior officer, who reluctantly congratulated him and demanded that he get something on tape. Then he called Sheriff Dan Campbell of Marion County, Missouri, where the crime occurred. Campbell was genuinely elated when Baker broke the news of a confession he'd just retrieved from none other than the elusive James Scott.

Campbell said he'd be right over. The Missouri sheriff arrived 40 minutes later to a scene of the Baker brothers and Jimmy sipping sodas and lollygagging in Interview Room 4. The sudden presence of an additional lawman, whom Jimmy had never met, eclipsed the lighthearted mood. Jimmy instantly realized the severity of the situation. Bruce ran across the hallway and returned with a tape recorder. Neal Baker's premonition was correct: Jimmy clammed up the minute Bruce plugged in the machine and set it on the desk.

Neal introduced the man. "This is Sheriff Dan Campbell with the Marion County Sheriff's Department. We're going to go over your statement one last time and record it for the record."

Jimmy thought back to his last meeting with Bob Nall two and a half months earlier and remembered how he had been asked if he wanted a lawyer present. He didn't then but he did now. Jimmy asked Neal Baker if he could get a defense attorney in for the taped statement. Baker was ready for such a request: Tape recorders made people nervous. But before he had a chance to answer, Campbell chimed in and told Jimmy that because this was a Missouri crime, he must wait until a Missouri court appointed a Missouri defense attorney. And anyway, since he had already confessed to his role in the flood, Baker just needed to get something on the record to prove that their earlier conversation had actually happened.

Jimmy walked them through the story one last time. He admitted to moving sandbags and said again that he never intended to make the levee worse. He never came right out and said "I broke the thing on purpose," but he did confess to being there, to seeing a trouble spot, to moving at least four or five sandbags. Most damning, Jimmy said he knew there was a problem and that he did what he did to raise a red flag to get attention. Whether he wanted to draw attention to the problem he alleged to have seen or whether he just wanted attention for attention's sake—as he had in the past with the fires—was unclear.

◄○►

Neal Baker made a copy of the tape and handed it off to Sheriff Dan Campbell. The Missouri lawman thanked him, pocketed it, and got back in his cruiser. He hurriedly drove over the repaired Bayview Bridge and back into his home state, past the remnants of the Great Midwestern Floods. Everything was still in shambles, except for the Ayerco gas station. Its external tanks exploded when struck by a barge on July 16, sending streaming flames and plumes of toxic black smoke—fueled by 62,000 gallons of gasoline—into the air. Those tanks had since been replaced, and the station was once again open for business.

Campbell's plan was to listen to the tape once more when he got home that evening. Then he'd place a call into Marion County Prosecuting Attorney John Jackson. Campbell would arrange a meeting and they'd discuss extradition papers and formal charges.

Campbell couldn't help but think of the irony of the situation. Two and a half months of fruitless investigations by his proxy in the Adams County

Sheriff's Department had produced no results. The heat did keep coming from Campbell's constituency, though. In fact, that very morning, Campbell spoke with Marion County Prosecutor John Jackson to check whether he was ready to issue a warrant for James Scott's arrest. Jackson put the question back on Campbell: "How's your investigation going?" When Campbell replied that he was deferring the pursuit to the more-sophisticated Adams County Sheriff's Department, Jackson said that he was calling off the investigation. The State of Missouri couldn't wait around for Illinois law enforcement to get their act together.

At the exact same time that Neal Baker pulled his Crown Vic behind Jimmy's Monte Carlo, Jackson made the decision to call off a criminal inquiry into the West Quincy levee break. Too much time had elapsed with too little headway, and Jackson reiterated that morning that because there'd been no confession—despite the several runs Illinois law enforcement made at James Scott—the state's attorney had no choice but to drop the case. The Great Midwestern Floods of 1993 in Marion County, Missouri, would go down in the annals of Missouri history as an act of God and not an act of sabotage.

"Strange," Campbell thought. Only a few hours had elapsed since that conversation. Now, as the sheriff drove back to his home on the opposite side of the Mississippi River with a single cassette tape in his jacket pocket, he realized that John Jackson's earlier sentiments were moot. Sheriff Campbell realized during his 30-minute drive that thanks to a detective in Quincy and not the Adams County sheriff, he was playing in a whole new ballgame.

Neal Baker wrapped up his questioning shortly after Campbell left the station. Once again, Jimmy, Bruce, and Neal had Interview Room 4 all to themselves. The elder detective produced some paperwork for Jimmy to fill out, the gist of which stated that he'd made his statements on his own volition and not under duress. Jimmy signed, and then he signed the confessions for the truck vandalism/burglary and the bad checks. He didn't sign anything that said he broke the West Quincy levee. Since it was a Missouri crime, he'd have to do Missouri paperwork.

Unceremoniously, Neal and Bruce escorted Jimmy to a holding cell. He'd be arraigned in the morning on the two confessed Illinois crimes, and he'd most likely be charged with something pertaining to the levee. Jimmy felt dejected. He knew prison lay on the horizon. But he didn't feel hopeless. As far as he was concerned, he admitted no wrongdoing in the levee investigation. Breaking into a truck and writing hot checks were bad, but they were mere bumps on life's road and not a life sentence.

He used that night in jail to ready his mind for a prison stretch. He thought about the jobs he'd apply for in either the kitchen or the factory. He considered whether he'd put all of his efforts into working, which usually impressed the parole board, or if he'd try to eek out some enjoyment by playing any and all sports. Regardless, he held on to one glimmer of hope— one that would make any sentence tolerable. He prayed that night to the God he had long abandoned that the State of Illinois would incarcerate him in the same penitentiary as his brother. Whatever time they gave him would be minuscule compared to the hard time Jeff was serving. Best case scenario, Jimmy would be able to steady his younger brother for the comparatively brief stint he was about to serve. He thought about Jeff long into the night until he forced himself to address the grimmest reality, one that he shuttered to think about.

Jimmy came to grips with the fact that he wouldn't get to come home to his wife for a little while. He could bear that easily enough. And since he hadn't seen his daughter in almost a year, he could stomach one more year with her out of his life. Hardest though was the thought that he'd taken his last drink for the foreseeable future. Jimmy could live without family. He didn't know how he'd survive without Budweiser or Jack Daniels.

CHAPTER SEVENTEEN

Marion County Prosecuting Attorney John Jackson got thrown for a loop. He was at home, preparing to retire early on the evening on October 1, 1993, when he received an urgent call.

It wasn't unheard of for Sheriff Dan Campbell to ring the state's attorney after hours. Sometimes, evidence in a particular case surfaced after five o'clock—and this was evidence he would like to see.

James Scott did it. He sabotaged the West Quincy levee, Campbell told him. He was in possession of a cassette tape that detailed blow-for-blow the steps Scott took on July 16. The sheriff requested a meeting early the next morning so that Jackson could consider the new evidence and mull over what charges to level against the Illinois man.

Jackson queried the sheriff on how he managed to get Jimmy to own up. Campbell, an honest cop, admitted that he had nothing to do with the confession. It was the Illinois authorities who coaxed it out of him. The state's attorney made a note out loud: He'd have to call Sheriff Nall in the morning and thank him for such fine detective work.

"It wasn't Nall," Campbell said. "It was Neal Baker over at the QPD."

"Really? I didn't know the Quincy police were pursuing the case."

"Baker needed to question him about some other local crimes, and he also questioned him about the levee."

They agreed to meet at nine o'clock the next morning at the Marion County Courthouse.

Jackson spent the rest of the night pouring over his law books. This was a delicate situation for all parties involved. He'd only been the prosecutor for two years, though he had the ear of the court. In that time, Jackson had brought many criminal investigations and many vandalism cases, but this was the most extraordinary vandalism case in Marion County history, if not Missouri history. He knew the community would be gunning for a conviction. West Quincy wasn't the only town in Marion County that exhausted thousands of man hours only to see their labors wash away with so much water. Parts of Hannibal succumbed to the mighty Mississippi River not long after West Quincy, which was no great surprise since Hannibal is downriver from West Quincy. The Sny levee also broke downriver in Pike County, Illinois, across the river from Hannibal. When the Fabius River Drainage District's levee broke, the Mississippi River water levels dropped because so much volume was displaced into the mainland. Resilient Hannibal residents stepped up their own sandbagging efforts as a result. Jackson himself was tossing bags in Hannibal the night of West Quincy's break, and still, Jackson's town, his county, and his state as well as many of the eight states that border Missouri flooded.

How would the neophyte prosecutor charge James Scott? What precedent could he use for causing a flood? Had this sort of thing ever happened before?

Jackson scoured his numerous law books looking for direction. He analyzed case after case in his volume of the *South Western Reporter Second Edition* as well as various Missouri statutes and penal codes.

In all his reading that night, Jackson kept returning to a single historical event, one that was as synonymous with flooding in the United States as Noah's ark in the Bible. It happened in another part of the county in a different era, yet the parallels seemed uncanny.

In the late 1800s, a small coal mining town nestled deep in the heart of Appalachia lured American families to undeveloped and picturesque central Pennsylvania. President Grover Cleveland signed the Interstate Commerce Act (ICA) into law in 1887, thereby regulating the railroads and ensuring fair rates regardless of geography. As such, Johnstown, Pennsylvania's coal and steel could be transported to all points throughout the United States. Tycoons of industry profited greatly off the ICA, and many of them decided to set up a kind of exclusive summer camp in the hills above Johnstown.

Henry Clay Frick, Andrew Carnegie, and Andrew Mellon funded the remodeling of a long-neglected earthen dam in order to create pristine Lake Conemaugh. The industrialists received many warnings from engineers and locals familiar with the area to cease and desist their construction: If the dam should ever break, Johnstown would be doomed.

Much like the Midwestern spring rains of 1993, Pennsylvania spring rains of 1889 raised the lake above Johnstown to new heights. In turn, tremendous pressure built up against the dam.

On the afternoon of May 31, 1889, the inevitable happened: The dam burst, sending waters from three-mile-wide Lake Conemaugh blazing down the hillside and smashing into the industrial hamlet of Johnstown. The city was wiped off the face of the map in a matter of hours. More than 2,200 people drowned as a result of the horrific flood, including 300 children. Ninety-nine entire families died: The Johnstown Flood erased their legacies and progeny for all time.

In the years to follow, public outcry called for the heads of Frick, Carnegie, and Mellon. So many dead bodies and a bill of more than $200 million in damages naturally shocked the country. A lawsuit was filed on behalf of the survivors, though the courts ultimately held that the Johnstown Flood was an "Act of God." The survivors received no compensation.

To John Jackson, the flood in West Quincy was similar to Johnston in terms of sheer property damage. Fourteen thousand acres were submerged under 10 feet of water. The main difference was that not a single human life had been lost during the West Quincy flood. Plenty of animals died, but he'd have a hard time selling a jury on a Johnstown argument when all 600 residents of West Quincy made it out alive. Moreover, the courts held that God and no other mitigating factor had caused the Johnstown Flood. That was the sort of precedent that could really work against Jackson.

The next morning, John Jackson arrived at his Hannibal office an hour and a half before his scheduled meeting with Sheriff Dan Campbell. He used the early morning hours to study some newspaper clippings from around Missouri and see how other municipalities dealt with the swollen Mississippi River. One article from the previous day's *St. Charles Post* stopped the state's attorney dead in his tracks. One hundred and twenty miles due south, in a St. Louis suburb called West Alton, a 34-year-old man was charged with a levee break that inundated West Alton with 3 feet of water.

On July 7, 1993, nine days before the West Quincy levee broke, Timothy O. Steinmann was cruising the Mississippi River in his 20-foot johnboat. West Alton, a city 20 miles north of St. Louis, was also at the mercy of the river, and a tremendous sandbagging effort was underway to raise the levee 18 inches. The Army Corps of Engineers said that without a hefty barrier of sandbags, the Mississippi River would overtop the dam and flood the town.

And just like in West Quincy, everybody turned out to help save West Alton. At nine o'clock in the evening of July 7, Timothy Steinmann steered his boat into the middle of the river and turned the bow toward the levee. He sat silently at the stern with his hand on the tiller while studying the volunteers and the mountain of sandbags before him. Then without warning, Steinmann gunned his motor and piloted his light watercraft directly toward the built-up dike. The West Alton man rammed the levee with such force that he blew clear through it. Instantaneously, the Mississippi River raged through the breach, ultimately causing a hole in the levee 40 feet deep and 200 feet wide. West Alton was completely under water 12 hours later.

That situation had the markings of the one northward in West Quincy. The *Post* article did more than merely provide John Jackson with ammo for his own imminent case. It mapped out a criminal statute he could use on James Scott. Just to be sure, Jackson put a phone call into Missouri Attorney General Jay Nixon and ran the scenario by him.

West Alton prosecutors charged Steinmann with violating an obscure law that had been on the Missouri books since 1979, but which had never—up until that time—been used in an indictment. The crime was "Intentionally Causing a Catastrophe," a Class A felony punishable by 10 years to life in prison. Because no one died in the West Alton flood, the Causing a Catastrophe charge was the best way of nailing Steinmann with a felony and getting him the harshest possible prison term. Prosecutors in that part of the state were also catching lots of flack from their community, much like Jackson and Campbell in Marion County. West Alton authorities decided to go after their levee breaker hard.

Jackson mulled over his colleague's decision 120 miles away as Sheriff Campbell arrived in his office at nine o'clock. Without delay, the sheriff produced the cassette tape and loaded it into a portable player. Marion County's top legal officials listened while James Scott walked Quincy Detective Neal Baker through the events that led up to the flood. Jackson listened closely as this career bad boy from across the river spoke about moving sandbags in order to draw attention to a trouble spot. Jackson's ears honed in on the statement Jimmy made about not intending to make matters worse with his actions. When the interview concluded, Campbell pushed Stop.

The state's attorney was far from floored by the recording. At best, James Scott gave Baker *somewhat* of a confession. It was hardly the smoking gun he'd been hoping for.

Jackson raised the issue of a newspaper story he read prior to the sheriff's arrival. A West Alton man did what amounted to the same crime, only authorities there had him cold, or much colder than Campbell and he had James Scott. Down there, Timothy Steinmann was charged with Intentionally Causing a Catastrophe. He faced up to life in prison. The question for Marion County was whether they should follow suit and file the same charges? It was either that or to go after Jimmy with First Degree Property Damage, especially because proving intent in Jimmy's case would be exceedingly difficult. First Degree Property Damage was a much lighter crime, punishable by a maximum of five years in prison and a $5,000 fine. Or more realistically, should Jackson charge him with the former and eventually allow Jimmy's attorney to plea-bargain down to the latter? That's when Sheriff Campbell dropped the bombshell. He told the prosecuting attorney about a Fowler, Illinois, teenager named Joe Flachs, who had come forward voluntarily a few weeks earlier. Joe told the QPD that Jimmy admitted breaking the West Quincy levee, that he had done it on purpose. And get this: His intent was to keep his wife in Missouri so he could party without her in Illinois.

John Jackson took a step backward and sat down in his leather chair. He'd heard some whoppers in his brief tenure as state's attorney—crazy criminal motives came with the job description—but this was sheer insanity. The explanation would have been laughable had Jackson not spent several nights sweltering in the summer heat throwing sandbags. It would have been comical had scores of other volunteers from around the country not descended on their river bank and labored with such dedication and heroism.

James Scott's quasi-confession might be able to set the stage for a trial under this obscure law that had never been used in Missouri before (it had only been dusted off a day earlier 120 miles away). Joe Flachs would be a star witness: He'd provide Jackson with the motive he needed to make the charge stick.

◄○►

Jimmy was arraigned in Illinois while Missouri officials were deciding what to charge him with. Bail was set at $20,000, a rather high sum for bad checks and vehicle vandalism.

He was furious. That's a king's ransom, he figured, and only because he was a suspect in the West Quincy levee break. Worst of all, none of his friends or family—or his friends and family combined—had the requisite $2,000 needed to bond him out. Jimmy would have to sit in the Adams County Jail until the justice system decided what they were going to do. He spent the next few days contemplating a reunion with his younger brother, Jeff. Any prison time is bad, but it'd be so much easier if he had his running mate by his side, like when they were kids.

The thought of two Scott brothers doing time together was fleeting, however. A Marion County police car rolled up to the Adams County Jail a couple days later. Two officers emerged with extradition papers in hand, requesting permission from Illinois authorities to transport James Scott across the Mississippi River. John Jackson had filed his warrant for the 23-year-old's arrest.

Jimmy was processed and handed over to the two men, who along with a couple of Adams County officers walked Jimmy out to a waiting squad car. As he made his way out of the station's double doors, he caught a glimpse of the *Quincy Herald-Whig* sitting in a newsstand with a glaring headline atop the paper's fold. It declared that a local man was being held for allegedly causing the levee break. The story stated that a Fowler, Illinois, man named

James Scott was implicated in a criminal scheme to purposefully break open a hole in the dike.

Usually, Jimmy liked controlling the front page headlines. He welcomed attention—good or bad—because it meant he was noteworthy, at least in Quincy and the surrounding areas. This headline, however, made his stomach drop. It didn't mention the other two crimes he'd copped to, the ones that he assumed he was going to prison for. Only the levee. He knew that there were scores of local residents who were convicting him already. Too many still clung to the memory of the Webster Elementary School fire to forgive and forget James Scott. What he didn't know was that WGEM-TV, the *St. Louis Post-Dispatch*, the *Associated Press* and a host of other news outlets were gearing up for one crazy news cycle. The story in the *Herald-Whig* alluded to the wife-stranding motive introduced to authorities by Joe Flachs. Jimmy didn't know that because he only saw the words above the fold as the officers escorted him to a waiting cruiser. Tellingly, he couldn't foresee the awesome power of newswires and of the media in general. Once the *AP* moved the story onto its national wire, Americans in the furthest reaches of the country—California, Vermont, Maine, Alaska, Hawaii—knew of the Great Midwestern Floods of 1993, and now they had a name to associate with the disaster. All the biggies ran with the news. It was, in media parlance, a "sexy" story: A story about a man who caused a flood so his wife couldn't return home. Every news outlet—including all of the national nightly news broadcasts—descended on sleepy Adams County and Marion County to dig up more dirt on James Scott.

Oddly, though, Neal Baker wasn't getting credit for the bust. Marion County's sheriff emerged as the authoritative voice on the story. "I believe he acted alone," Campbell told the *AP.*

The Marion County squad car arrived at the jail and Jimmy was formally charged with Intentionally Causing a Catastrophe. He was read his Miranda Rights and taken into custody. When he was arraigned later that day, Jimmy asked the judge for a public defender. Bail was set at $1 million. That's when James Scott realized the severity of what was happening. This was no longer a scare tactic or some sort of puppet show for the locals and the media. The State of Missouri was preparing to place blame for the West Quincy flood foursquare on Jimmy's head. John Jackson was furiously gathering evidence against the Illinois man in hopes of sending him to prison for a minimum of 10 years. If the state got her way though, Jimmy would be going away for good.

He sat in jail on October 4, 1993, awaiting a visit from the public defender. The all-too-familiar setting, albeit in a different state, made Jimmy's eyes well up with tears. He quickly wiped them away with his state-issued jumpsuit sleeve and then buried his head in his arm. "Do they *really* think I broke the levee?" he asked himself. "I'll bet Neal Baker is all over the news right now, bragging about how he nailed me again. I bet the cops over in Quincy are getting a good laugh out of this."

The Illinois authorities were indeed making the collar of James Scott known, but it wasn't Neal Baker doing the talking. Missouri sheriff Dan Campbell handled the *AP* while Illinois sheriff Bob Nall handled *USA Today.* Nall told America's daily that he informed Missouri about the suspect, and that he did all the fact-gathering in the investigation. "There's no way to describe the severity of what he did," Nall was quoted as saying in *USA Today.* "My assumption was, he thought he was going to be a hero, that he'd find this break and save the town, but he underestimated the river. I don't know that he feels remorse."

For the first time since they repaired the giant hole in the levee, the Mississippi River Rangers and their parent organization, the Army Corps of Engineers, sprung to life with renewed activity. Hundreds of calls from news organizations across the country overwhelmed their one phone line and drew their attention away from the real work. Everybody, it seemed, wanted to learn about river systems and about the particular stretch of dam that ultimately broke and flooded 14,000 acres. Reporters, in their quest for fair and accurate coverage, tried to determine just how one man could cause so much destruction. For the engineers, these callers were pesky, like the mosquitoes that swarmed around them in the summer.

Reporters weren't the only people descending on their Quincy headquarters. Missouri investigators, including State's Attorney John Jackson and Marion County Sheriff Dan Campbell, made unscheduled visits to their neighbors to the east. They were gathering evidence and asking questions, assuming the reins of the investigation from Illinois law enforcement.

Corps employees answered the questions in turn. They spoke about a fight with the river that they were winning, evidenced by the fact that they staved off the worst of the rains three days before the levee broke. They said that no major trouble spots had been reported on the now-infamous stretch of levee and that as far as they were concerned, the thing would have held if it weren't for James Scott. That's why they were so interested in the back story of Quincy's meddling local bad boy. Any outside interference would thereby alleviate their own culpability in the disaster.

As his colleagues answered the investigators' questions, Earl Basswood sat quietly stewing on that October 5th afternoon. He'd been around too long and worked that stretch of levee far too many times over his 20-year career to buy the line the investigators were selling. He remembered all too well cops showing up at HQ hours after the levee broke, minutes after James Scott appeared on television. And he remembered the exchange he had with Detective Neal Baker. Being a local, he knew that there was far too much damage for these hard-working people to take a financial loss sitting down. Hell, the law was ready to convict James Scott on July 16. Now here they were three months later gathering evidence for a trial that was based on the hunches of Detective Neal Baker and Sheriff Bob Nall.

Back on July 16, Earl Basswood concluded that local law enforcement, local farmers, businessmen, and the good ol' boys from the Fabius River Drainage District were on a witch hunt. They were far too invested in the relief effort to admit defeat. Initially on July 16, the River Ranger thought the cops came to headquarters in order to blame the Corps for building and maintaining a bad levee; much as Henry Clay Frick, Andrew Carnegie, and Andrew Mellon bore the brunt of blame in the waning days of the Johnstown Flood. Basswood changed his mind when the name James Scott started getting batted around.

Three months later, as he listened to Missouri lawmen doing their own investigation and legwork for the first time since the disaster, Earl Basswood began to question the entire justice system. What was happening in this little pocket of America contradicted everything that the country stood for. Nailing Jimmy Scott because he'd committed crimes in the past wasn't a far stretch from nailing anyone who the authorities simply didn't like. He listened to the questions and answers and realized that the two events of time—July 16 and October 5—had become neatly tied together. But there was something else at play here.

Because Basswood was a local, he was intimately familiar with many of the farmers and small business owners who lost everything. They had crop insurance, but Basswood knew that most of them didn't have federal flood insurance. They were betting that the levees would hold and that their homes and businesses would not be lost to a flood. West Quincy was gambling their livelihood, just like their parents, grandparents, and great-grandparents did before them. And the stakes couldn't be higher. The only way that they'd be compensated in a flood was if the disaster was manmade. Acts of God weren't covered in their homeowners' policies; acts of vandalism were. "Looks like they found their witch," Basswood thought.

Basswood patiently waited for the investigators to question him. In fact, he secretly wished that he'd be approached. If they wanted to take a statement, he'd be sworn in and legally-bound to tell them what he knew. It was the sort of insurance policy he needed to avoid any sort of professional repercussions from the Corps of Engineers. He wanted to tell them about the unorthodox scene down at headquarters immediately following the break. He wanted to tell them about Neal Baker. He wanted them to investigate the insurance claims that were coming out of Marion County, and he wanted to tell them the one piece of evidence he felt was instrumental to the case. Earl Basswood had been on that very spot where the levee broke on the day that it broke—and truth be told, he wasn't surprised when it did.

July 16 was like any other day that month prior to the disaster. Basswood was making a patrol as he did every day throughout the month of July. He was on a four-wheeler scanning the levee for problems. He didn't see the trouble spot that Jimmy told authorities about, but he made mental notes about the overall condition of the section of levee between the Bayview Bridge and the railroad bridge to the north. The whole thing was bad: No section was worse off than another. Everything was just plain bad. He knew he wasn't the only one whot felt that way because of all the National Guard helicopters hovering overhead, monitoring that exact stretch. In addition, the stepped-up media helicopters indicated that the news was expecting a break that day. Basswood figured that everyone on the levee shared his sentiment: The levee could go at any time. And when it did—and because business and commerce were halted for a 200-mile stretch for 74 days when the Bayview Bridge closed—somebody would have to answer.

But no Missouri official approached him on October 5. Not a single question was posed to Earl Basswood, so he kept quiet. His mind, though, would not stop racing.

"I hope for that boy's sake that he has a damn good lawyer," he mumbled to himself as the Missouri officials left his headquarters. "They're coming for him. And it looks like they won't sleep until he's tied to the stake."

◄o►

Marion County Public Defender Jeff Estes drew a hell of a case. By court order, he would defend James R. Scott of Fowler, Illinois, for a crime that he admitted to but now said he was innocent of.

Estes had no idea how to argue this one before a jury. Not only were Jimmy's statements seemingly inconsistent, but the state was putting all their weight behind this case, submitting a witness list half a mile long that included Corps workers, local interests, and local government entities.

There was no precedent: No one in Missouri had ever been sentenced to Intentionally Causing a Catastrophe. Yes, there was Timothy Steinmann in West Alton who stood accused of the same crime, but that case hadn't gone to court yet. Estes figured Steinmann's attorney was probably hoping James Scott would go on trial first so he'd know how to argue on his own client's behalf. Estes wished for the opposite. He couldn't afford to spin the wheel and hope the West Alton man drew an earlier docket number. Jimmy's own had already come up: October 31, 1994.

Estes couldn't help but shake his head at the ominous dates in Jimmy's life. He was paroled from prison on April Fools' Day 1991, and he'd be on trial for his life this coming Halloween. Some guys are just cursed, he mused.

Estes' first order of business was to file for a change of venue. With all the news coverage, he was convinced Jimmy wouldn't get a fair shake anywhere in Missouri, let alone Marion County. It would still be a tough acquittal anywhere in the United States given the media's insatiable appetite for this story. He petitioned to have the case tried out of state, preferably in Arizona or New Mexico. He told the judge that those western outposts were the only places he'd found that hadn't been overly diluted with pretrial coverage. That was a half-truth: Estes just wanted the case tried in a geographically dry part of the country, a place where jurors couldn't fathom just how destructive the Mississippi River was.

Judge Bruce Normile agreed that a change of venue would ensure an impartial jury, but he wasn't about to pack his bags. He moved the case to Kirksville, Missouri, in Adair County, about 95 miles northwest of West Quincy. Both parties agreed upon the October 31 trial date—they figured it would give them plenty of time to build a case and stockpile evidence.

In January 1994, six months after the flood, Jimmy was removed from the Marion County Jail and taken back over the Mississippi River, where he was remanded to the custody of the Illinois Department of Corrections. In the course of Estes sifting through the case and filing for a change of venue, an Illinois court sentenced Jimmy to 10 years in prison for the truck vandalism/burglary and the bad checks.

Jimmy drew Judge Cashman again, the same judge who meted out his arson sentence. Even though Jimmy hadn't stood trial for his alleged Missouri crime, Cashman made reference to the impending case at sentencing. "With his bare hands, he perhaps removed a few sandbags, but tore apart the lives of hundreds perhaps thousands of people." Jimmy's court-appointed attorney raised no legal objections to a sitting judge citing an as-yet-to-be-tried case in Missouri at an Illinois sentencing.

It was a big chunk of time all things considered, but Jimmy knew the rules: With good behavior, he'd be out in half that time, if not less. Plus, should he be sentenced in Missouri, the court would most likely run his sentences concurrently. He was by no means happy to be back in the joint, the one place he'd sworn off for good, but Jimmy took cold comfort in knowing that he'd be better able to keep a watchful eye on his younger brother. Unfortunately, IDOC didn't put the men in the same prison, but Jimmy fell right back into his routine of prison work and sports. He made enough "friends" with guards and guys that he could send messages to Jeff and receive information on his situation.

For Marion County Public Defender Estes, however, Jimmy's prison stint in Illinois made his own job twice as difficult. IDOC adhered to its policy of continuously transferring inmates within its institutions every six months. Each time he was moved, Jimmy's physical location became a longer drive for the already overworked public defender.

Through the course of discovery, Estes carefully questioned all the witnesses on the prosecution's list. Their stories were consistent and seemingly airtight. The public defender made a stop over to the Mississippi River Rangers and painstakingly went over rudimentary elements of levee maintenance. The men cooperated but no one gave Estes information he could use in Scott's defense. Overlooked again was Earl Basswood. Because he wasn't on the prosecution's witness list, he was an unknown variable to the defense. More time passed and the urge to tell someone what he knew about the levee and what he suspected about the witch hunt intensified. It gnawed at Basswood like the river rats that feasted on dredged debris. Yet he just couldn't come forward: He had a family to feed and he was still a decade removed from his pension.

With no one stepping forward from the River Rangers, the public defender decided he needed an expert. John Jackson had a laundry list of professionals familiar with river systems, and Estes had none.

Several possibilities crossed his mind. Truman State University in Kirksville, where the trial would be held, had one of the premiere agriculture departments in the state. He put a call into the university and chummed the waters for an expert witness. Much to his chagrin, none of the tenured faculty felt comfortable testifying on behalf of the defense. Most had heard of James Scott through the media. Based on what they'd read and heard, he was guilty. Moreover, a PhD in the field of agricultural sciences wasn't the best expert to speak on behalf of a flood, unless they were going to testify about how too much water ruins a crop.

Estes took his search on the road. He drove southwest from Hannibal to Rolla, Missouri, and the home of the University of Missouri-Rolla, one of the best engineering schools in the entire country. He asked around the department for a lead on who was the most distinguished, notable civil engineer. All fingers pointed to Dr. Charles Morris, a professor of civil, architectural, and environmental engineering.

Estes walked into Morris' office and introduced himself. Morris reciprocated the greeting and asked how he might be of service.

"I need someone to help me defend a guilty man," Estes bluntly replied. Morris shot him a puzzled look.

"Come again?" the professor said.

"I need an expert to help me defend someone who's guilty in causing a flood. He confessed to breaking a levee."

"With all do respect, counselor," Morris began, "I'm not interested in helping someone who is guilty."

"Well, he says he's innocent despite the confession. It's not really a confession inasmuch as it's an admission to being at the scene of the disaster." Estes had the esteemed professor's ear. He spent the next 20 minutes explaining the particulars and the bizarre circumstances surrounding the charges against James Scott. Morris slowly realized what Estes was talking about. He'd read about this man in the *Post-Dispatch*. It was an intriguing story, one worthy of a romance novel gone bad, but Morris wasn't so much interested in the motive of wife-stranding as he was in the science of the disaster.

Dr. Charles Morris had been a tenured professor at the University of Missouri-Rolla for 25 years. For 10 of those years, he also served as a consultant with the Army Corps of Engineers. He grew up in Jefferson City, Missouri, right on the banks of the Missouri River. Morris saw many a flood firsthand. When he was a boy back in 1950, he remembered the Missouri River creeping up onto his front porch. In later years, he did some work in the Hannibal area, so he was vaguely familiar with the West Quincy levee and the Fabius River Drainage District. But in present times, he was obsessed with the Great Floods of '93. For a scientist, this was the 500-year flood that had long been anticipated and predicted. How any one man could be held responsible for a levee breach in an area where almost every single levee had given out was beyond him.

"Tell you what, Mr. Estes: Let me read the confession, and show me the photographs you've obtained of the West Quincy levee before, the day of, during, and after the flood, and I'll consider being a witness for the defense."

Estes eagerly agreed to the professor's terms. He arranged for all the material to be sent to Morris at his UM-Rolla office, and he followed up a few days later with a phone call.

The evidence troubled the professor. He thought the confession was as loose as they came, though admittedly, he wasn't a forensics expert. He'd testified in lots of trials over the years, but only twice in criminal court. What had him so baffled in this case was the appearance of the levee in question. Large sheets of plastic tarp stretched for hundreds of yards in each direction on both the land and water sides of the levee. Yet there wasn't a huge wall of sandbags in the specific area that eventually broke, as the news had led him to believe. Indeed, some stretches of dam were walled with burlap sacks to keep the Mississippi River from overtopping, but not in this section. The photo, taken on the same day but before the break, showed the occasional sandbag along the plastic tarp. They were being used more as paperweights than anything else. Morris also saw straw spread along the backside of the levee.

Levees are porous. They're built to intentionally let a small, steady flow of water pass through in order to alleviate pressure on the levee walls. On West Quincy's levee, straw was placed on the backside—or the land side— because the protecting sod had been bulldozed, exposing bare soil. Rain was constant for days in mid-July, so the exposed soil on the land side was highly susceptible to erosion. The straw helped hinder that erosion. Nevertheless, straw can't help internal erosion, known as "piping." Piping is saturated flow through a continuous opening. Saturated flow means the pore in the earthen dam was completely filled. As water moves rapidly through an earthen dam, the dam can erode, enlarging the "pipe" inside the levee, which increases flow, which increases erosion, and so on. Eventually, the pipe becomes so large that it can no longer support the weight of the overlying soil (levee), which then collapses into the pipe. When the levee collapses into the pipe, the levee surface is lowered. If the surface is lowered sufficiently for the river to overtop it, the rapidly moving river quickly erodes a gully into the levee at that point. Therefore, the levee appears to have been overtopped, but it actually failed prior to the overtopping. It failed due to collapse on the internal pipe. Here, no sandbag wall kept the river out while the levee collapsed on itself. That's what Professor Morris concluded. And that's why he agreed to testify.

Estes also managed to procure an ace witness. The elusive Missouri Guardsman whom Jimmy approached when he noticed a trouble spot on the levee—the guy he could only identify as "Duke" and who Detective Neal Baker thought sounded made up—was in fact a real person. Duke Kelly was the noncommissioned officer in charge that day, and he did remember a man approaching him and talking about trouble spots. Estes subpoenaed the man from his home outside of St. Louis. At the very least, Duke could demonstrate that Jimmy wasn't lying to investigators.

◄○►

State's Attorney John Jackson trucked along with his own investigation. He had some stars on his starting lineup: Fabius River Drainage District Chairman Norman Haerr, Knapheide Manufacturing Company President Harold Knapheide, Sheriff Bob Nall, Deputy John McCoy, and Don Bawmann from the Corps of Engineers. He was still a tad bit reluctant with his case because he believed that Jimmy's confession wasn't exactly ironclad. Moreover, there was no physical evidence left at the scene of the crime, like footprints or a shovel.

His most effective weapon would be this teenage kid named Joe Flachs. Joe would provide the motive: A firsthand account and admission from James Scott about how he broke the levee and partied like a fiend—wifeless—on July 16.

Suddenly, in early 1994, Jackson's star witness disappeared. He rang the kid's home on several occasions but never seemed to be able to get a hold of someone. It took a drive over the bridge and a visit to Sheriff Nall before Jackson learned what had happened to Joe Flachs.

It seemed that young Joe just couldn't stay out of trouble, and he obviously hadn't learned anything during the juvenile stretch when he was nine. At 17, he went and committed a burglary. In so doing, he was also charged with obstructing justice. Joe was sentenced to three years in prison. He'd serve half that time and then most likely be on parole until he was 21.

Jackson wrestled with whether to pull the kid out of prison and have him testify in open court. If he did, Jeff Estes wouldn't have too much trouble discrediting his testimony. After all, why should any jury of sound mind believe the word of one felon over another? Jackson decided he'd subpoena the kid if he felt the trial slipping away.

He planned to do the same with Cory Anderson due to the boy's age. Cory had told the Adams County Sheriff's Department that James Scott confessed to breaking the levee. Jackson didn't want to subject a juvenile to a criminal proceeding if he didn't have to, especially one almost 100 miles away from his home.

As Halloween 1994 drew near, Jackson put the finishing touches on the state's case. All the players would be arriving throughout the course of the trial, which he anticipated lasting two weeks. He arrived in Kirksville a couple of days before jury selection and went over his notes.

The key to winning the case and gaining the conviction of James Scott hinged on two main points: Jimmy's confession, albeit a weak one, and motive. Motive isn't an element of the offense, but courts allow motive to be introduced to show the accused person's reason for allegedly committing the crime. Additionally, motive is substantial when a potential life sentence hangs in the balance and when you're trying to convict someone on circumstantial evidence. An infuriating motive like causing a natural disaster in order to party would be especially substantial because no one died from James Scott's actions. There was still no precedent on the books. Timothy Steinmann in West Alton wasn't scheduled to go to trial for his charge of Intentionally Causing a Catastrophe until a year-and-a-half from then. The docket moved slower in that part of the state thanks to its proximity to St. Louis and the larger caseload. Even though Steinmann's arrest preceded Jimmy's arrest, Marion County Prosecutor John Jackson would become the first attorney in Missouri to try a case on the basis of the obscure 1979 criminal statute.

This case percolated with irony. Was Jimmy in West Quincy to help or harm? Did he truly want to strand his wife? If so, how come he went the next day to pick her up? And why had neither of them filed for divorce? Yet the most ironic element of the case was that James Scott, an Illinois resident, was about to go on trial for violating a Missouri law that carried with it up to a life sentence in the state penitentiary. If he had committed the same crime in Illinois, the most he could have been charged with was criminal damage to property, a crime that carried a maximum sentence of seven years in prison.

◄○►

Kirksville, Missouri, the county seat of Adair County, was a quaint college town in the north-central section of the state. Like many small Midwestern settlements, commerce still thrived in the town square, just as it did at the turn of the century. Residents often held car shows there, as well as the weekend farmer's market. Foreclosed property was sold at auction every few months. It was also where the mammoth 100-year-old courthouse stood; a three-story yellow limestone edifice, with a gracefully-sloping mansard roof and more than three dozen dormer windows. A block and a half away stood the Adair County Jail, cattycorner to the sheriff's office. Jimmy was driven in an Illinois Department of Corrections van to this burg two days before his trial.

Jeff Estes, his lawyer, brought him a pressed white oxford shirt and a pair of pleated black trousers, which was a nice change from his prison boiler suit. He checked into the jail and waited until Halloween morning for a jury of his peers to be selected from the local population.

Jimmy's skin crawled on the morning of October 31, 1994. Courthouses always did that to him. He prayed for the best and was cautiously optimistic because Estes portrayed a confident air.

Ten years to life was nothing to sneeze at: That was hard-core murder-type time. Jimmy wanted to have a chance to take the witness stand in his own defense, to look the judge and jury in the eye and level with them like a man. He felt he could convince all those present of his innocence, but Estes had other plans. He advised his client not to testify. John Jackson, he said, was no fool. He was a hell of a trial lawyer and would pick Jimmy apart if he had a chance to question him. Additionally, questioning Jimmy under cross examination would give Jackson the chance to introduce the ex-con's past as a juvenile delinquent and former arsonist. Missouri law states that unless a defendant testifies, his prior convictions are not admissible. By keeping his client seated, Estes was protecting him from self-incrimination.

Voir dire commenced at nine o'clock sharp. Jimmy was marched into court handcuffed, accompanied by his attorney. He reluctantly took his seat in the defendant's chair. Jimmy carried a thick black book under his arm and placed it atop the wooden table. Then a bailiff approached him and removed the manacles.

Jimmy peered around the antiquated courtroom. Wooden seats and benches were made of rich, dark mahogany and smelled of furniture polish. It reminded him of being back at Calvary Baptist Church.

Across the isle to his right sat John Jackson. They briefly sized each other up and then quickly averted their eyes. Jimmy did not want to get into a staring contest with a man who was trying to strip him of his freedom. Jackson didn't want to look too closely at a man he was preparing to send to prison for the rest of his life.

Moments later, Judge Normile was seated and the bailiff led in prospective jurors, all of whom took their assigned seats. Jimmy was too ashamed to look at these people. It's a hard pill to swallow when total strangers are charged with determining your fate. Twelve totally unfamiliar men and women were about to sit in judgment over James Scott. They were no longer his equals; they were no longer mortal. To Jimmy, these people were super-human. And like with all divine deities, Jimmy felt compelled to pray before them. He took the book he brought into the courtroom—the King James Bible—and opened to page one. Then he started reading. He paused every now and again to see what one of the newly-paneled jurors looked like, and then he started back up with the Good Book. Cautiously optimistic indeed, but Jimmy was hedging his bet. In the event that the ruling was not in his favor, he would use his court time to make peace with God. For should he be forced to spend the rest of his life in a Missouri prison—especially one of the notoriously violent maximum security units— James Scott might very well be forced to meet his maker several decades prematurely.

—◄○►—

John Jackson's parade of witnesses made convincing arguments. Heavy, torrential rains on July 13—three days before the levee broke—posed the greatest risk. The Mississippi River reached its highest stage at that time, and if the levee were going to break, it would have happened right then and there.

The jury, mostly working class and elderly, appeared to be listening intently. Because there had been so much pretrial coverage, a majority of the people summoned for jury duty were excused for cause. Both the prosecution and the defense used up all their preemptory challenges as well. The group that was left were individuals who didn't follow the news, for whatever that was worth. They didn't read newspapers avidly, and they didn't watch local or national news coverage. By in large, they represented the populace that Jimmy belonged to: the uninformed.

They did their job though, taking notes throughout the prosecution's testimony and studying James Scott's expressions each time a witness inferred that he was the cause of mass destruction.

Jackson questioned the various officials with an engaging tone and steady directness. Similarly, Jeff Estes raised the question of whether the levee would have failed regardless of Jimmy's presence. Some people answered that they couldn't say for sure. Norman Haerr drew an analogy of a basketball game in the final moments. The home team was behind by one point and they were going up for the easy lay-up when the referee stops the game with about 10 seconds left. They couldn't prove they were going to win, but they felt they could have. Some of the jurors actually nodded their heads as he spoke.

Midway through the state's evidence—and on just the second day of the trial—John Jackson grew edgy. He feared his lack of physical evidence might negatively influence the jury. Detective Neal Baker did an excellent job with his testimony. He painted the picture of a career criminal who confessed to making the situation worse. But Jackson didn't see the nodding heads that he had when Haerr was on the stand. He made a 12th-hour decision to go to his star witnesses, Joe Flachs and Cory Anderson.

Estes objected. He hadn't been notified about these witnesses prior to trial, as was the defendant's right, and now the trial was half over. The state, he maintained, was committing a procedural error. But the judge overruled the objection and allowed the boys' testimonies.

Joe was abruptly pulled out of prison in Illinois and hauled to Kirksville. Cory's mother had to take off work and drive her son over the state line to testify in quite an intimidating setting.

Under direct questioning Joe told a similar version of what he told Officer Dennis Boden the day he walked into the QPD looking for Detective Baker. Jimmy had admitted to him that he broke the levee, that he'd done it with malice, and that he'd used a shovel. The jury looked stunned. This was the first they'd heard of Jimmy's motive, and they couldn't see beyond such a senseless act. Then Joe said something that stunned the prosecutor. He announced to the court that Jimmy had told him he was going to break the levee prior to July 16. This new evidence was introduced without preparation or warning. Jackson immediately did an about-face and wrapped up his questions.

The damage had been done. Estes seized on the opportunity to blow holes in Joe's earlier statement, and he used Joe's current predicament—that of being an inmate in Illinois—to destroy his credibility.

Cory Anderson wasn't as easy to discredit. He had no prior convictions and he also made the wife-stranding comment. Estes pointed out to the jury that Cory heard these statements at a party. The party, he asserted, had been attended by a bunch of other underage youths, all of whom were consuming alcohol. Furthermore, Jimmy wasn't the only person who had made a comment about how it'd be neat if the levee broke and the fishing in West Quincy all of a sudden became world class.

Yet in a shy manor, Cory simply replied that he heard what he heard. His testimony was uncomplicated and effective.

After the state rested, Estes called the defense's first witness: Missouri Air National Guardsman Sgt. Duke Kelly. Kelly testified that a man did approach him on July 16 and mentioned a trouble spot. He said that he walked north for a ways with this unidentified individual and seeing that there was no one where they were walking, decided to turn around and head back to the Bayview Bridge, where his men were assembled. Estes developed an enthusiastic catch in his voice. He believed that Duke was confirming Jimmy's story—the true story. But as soon as Jackson cross-examined the sergeant, he testified that he couldn't say definitively that James Scott, the man sitting before him and reading the King James Bible, was the man with whom he spoke. He was, after all, the NCOIC, or the noncommissioned officer in charge. Everybody that day was talking to him, including reporters. It wasn't said aloud, but Kelly inferred that someone could have seen him on television and inserted his name into an investigation. The jury looked unimpressed.

On November 4, the defense called its last witness: Dr. Charles Morris, professor of civil engineering at the University of Missouri-Rolla. He was the only person who could offer an exculpatory reason for the levee failure, and he was the one wild card that made State's Attorney Jackson edgy. Morris would give scientific reasons for the Great Midwestern Floods. Not only could he explain the breaking of West Quincy's levee, but also he could tell the jury just why the Midwest suffered from the 500-year flood.

Estes began with some introductory questions. Morris listed his credentials and admitted that he was no stranger to testifying on scientific matters. The jury responded with body language. They sat on the edges of their seats as Morris described his theory of piping. He used a large blown-up aerial photo of the section of levee in question, taken several hours before it broke. They couldn't see overtopping, but Morris demonstrated his theory by drawing attention to the contrasting shadows. Those, he said, illustrated that the levee was undulating—that parts of it were caving in on itself.

He spoke intelligibly and with an air of sophistication that the Kirksville jury hadn't heard before. State's Attorney Jackson looked on and scribbled furiously on his steno pad. Jimmy continued reading the Bible. He was already at Acts.

The direct examination of Dr. Charles Morris continued for a little over an hour when a juror's action made the court turn on its ear. An elderly panelist in his mid-60s looked around the box and observed his fellow jurors. They were looking at Morris but several of them were fidgeting with their hands. Although the man wasn't the foreman, he took it upon himself to speak for the group.

As Morris was in mid-sentence, the juror raised his hand. The professor stammered at the gesture and continued speaking. Estes turned to look at the man, and then he turned to look at his rival at the prosecutor's table. John Jackson stopped scribbling and shot the judge a puzzled glance. It was the most preposterous action that either of the officers of the court had ever seen. The same went for Morris. In all the trials he'd been involved in, a juror had never interrupted testimony with a question. Indeed, a juror would send a note to the judge through the bailiff from time to time, but to actually engage the court as though it was a fourth grade classroom was certainly a new one.

Even more incredible was the judge's response. Judge Bruce Normile stopped the esteemed professor's testimony and called on the juror.

"What's the problem?" Judge Normile asked.

"Well, judge, I don't understand," the elderly man sheepishly answered.

"What exactly don't you understand?"

"I don't understand what Dr. Morris is talking about."

The sparring attorneys locked eyes, as if to prompt the other to object. Estes didn't want to piss the jury off during his witness' testimony, so he kept quiet. Jackson, on the other hand, didn't want to give the crafty engineer a chance to explain himself. If the jury didn't understand it, that was their problem. Jackson had a Perry Mason moment: There was no correct way to broach this oddity, and he, too, didn't want the jury to think he was afraid of the PhD. He kept mum.

"Who else in the jury is confused?" Normile solicited, addressing the entire jury. Three more hands went up. The judge turned to face Morris. "Would you mind taking your photo and walking over to the jury box?"

Morris smiled. "No judge, I don't mind."

The professor propped the photo against the wooden railing and pointed to the questionable areas in the photo as he explained piping in layman's terms. Some of the jurors nodded their heads in agreement, while others continued to stare blankly. Another juror, this one a woman, raised her hand. Morris called on her as he would a sophomore student during an 8:40 a.m. lecture.

"Yes," Morris said to her.

"Can you explain what the straw is for?"

He did. Morris detailed—again—how straw protects the outer surface of the levee from eroding, but does nothing to stop the internal erosion—known as piping. Then another hand went up. And another. Morris was engaged in a full-fledged college course. John Jackson became so angry and turned so red that it looked as though he might explode.

He sprung from his seat when it was his turn to cross-examine Morris. The professor's testimony was potentially harmful to the state, as everything he said made sense. Jackson couldn't attack the man's credentials: Morris was very well regarded in scientific circles. What was more, Jackson couldn't maintain that the PhD was saying anything he could to earn Jimmy's freedom: Morris told the jury that he'd never even met James Scott, and he was seeing the suspect in person for the first time on that day. Jackson decided to discredit the professor the only way he could. He asked Morris where he was on July 16.

"I was in Rolla."

"So you weren't in West Quincy?"

"No."

"And you weren't even within 100 miles of the Mississippi River?"

"That's correct."

"So you're speaking about a theory, is that right?"

"Yes."

"A theory based on pictures?"

"A theory based on my professional opinion of the pictures."

"But a theory nonetheless?"

"Correct."

"Thank you, your honor. I have no further questions."

◄○►

The jury began deliberations on the afternoon of November 4, 1994. Neither party knew how long they would caucus. Because the trial was one giant oddity, Jackson and Estes wouldn't be surprised if they deliberated for four minutes or four weeks.

As it happened, they deliberated for four hours. Estes and Jimmy sat impatiently as the jury foreman handed the bailiff the verdict.

Jimmy held the Bible tightly with both hands. He squeezed it so hard that the tips of his fingers ached. It was as if he were calling on God to somehow make that piece of paper in the bailiff's hand read "not guilty." He felt like it was possible if he prayed hard enough.

Judge Bruce Normile read the scrawl and then addressed the court for the record.

"Will the defendant please rise. Has the jury reached a verdict?"

"We have, your honor," the 20-something-year-old foreman said.

"What say you?"

Jimmy looked down at the Good Book as the foreman stood and prepared to speak. This was the moment of truth. It'd either be the end of a horrible nightmare or the beginning of a new one. Estes placed his hand on Jimmy's shoulder. He wanted to evoke a sympathetic gesture. The defense attorney had done his best, and he—like Jimmy—hoped that his best was good enough. He studied the faces of the jurors, looking for a sign. Usually, when a jury convicts a man, they can't stand to look at him as the decision is rendered. This jury, true to form, was an impossible read. Half of them looked directly at Jimmy and the other half looked around the court, as if they were antique dealers assessing the worth of 100-year-old mahogany benches. "Man, this is the weirdest case," Estes thought, and gave his client one last moment to pray.

"In the matter of the State of Missouri versus James Scott, we the jury find the defendant guilty of Intentionally Causing a Catastrophe."

Jimmy let out a sorrowful sigh and lowered his chin. Then he gently shook his head. Estes tried to console him. "Don't worry, Jimmy. I'll appeal the sentence. This isn't over yet."

James Scott found no comfort in his court-appointed attorney's words. All he wanted to do was to speak to the judge and plead his case to the jury. He regretted taking his attorney's advice and sitting quietly the whole time.

The judge set a sentencing date for Monday, December 5. Jimmy would spend the next 31 days in the Adair County Jail.

During that time, he did little but reflect on the trial. He replayed everyone's testimony over in his head and tried to dissect each statement. He tried to get into the minds of his jurors to see what they could possibly be thinking. How could they find him guilty after Dr. Charles Morris made such a convincing argument, and with no physical evidence at all? The only reason he could think of was a statement John Jackson made during closing arguments: "He said he was going to break the levee so he could strand his wife in Missouri so he could have parties, so he could have affairs." That was Joe Flachs speaking through a proxy. The kid was a snitch, a turncoat—and according to James Scott, a liar. At that very instant, Jimmy stopped feeling sorry for himself, and he even stopped feeling sorry for the farmers and residents who lost everything, a sentiment he'd expressed earlier in the newspapers. At that very instant, Jimmy turned his fury toward Joe Flachs, a miserable convict who had an ax to grind.

That anger remained in his belly on December 5, when he went in front of Judge Normile again to receive his sentence. The judge cited the convict's past crimes, specifically the fires from 1988. Then he dwelled on Webster Elementary, implying that Jimmy was a born loser.

"The court hereby sentences you to life in the Missouri State Penitentiary."

Jimmy stood straight and tall. His face turned beet red, but he didn't move a muscle. As he involuntarily posed for the packed courtroom, while a throng of onlookers and reporters gauged his reaction, James Scott became the first person in Missouri history to be arrested, charged, tried, convicted, and sentenced of Intentionally Causing a Catastrophe. And even though nobody died; even though nobody was even injured, Judge Normile felt that 14,000 acres of property damage, more than a million squandered volunteer man hours, and the ensuing pain and suffering caused by the flood was surely worth the life of one career criminal.

Jimmy exited the courthouse in handcuffs. A barrage of reporters hounded him with questions, rudely sticking microphones and tape recorders in his face. They asked if he was sorry for what he did and what he thought the sentence should have been. One tenacious amateur reporter asked if he thought the sentence was fair. Jimmy stopped walking for a moment and looked the reporter square in the eye. "Lies came before truth," was all that he said. And with that, he was loaded into the back of a squad car and driven back to his Illinois penitentiary. The Illinois and Missouri sentences would run concurrently, not that it mattered anymore. No sooner would the prison gates swing wide at the end of the sentence for his Illinois crimes then the state of Missouri would snatch him up and imprison him, possibly for life.

Shock set in as the police car drove east over the Mississippi River. "How am I going to make it on the inside?" he asked himself. "How can I possibly make this work?" The answers didn't come to him in a flash, and it didn't matter. He'd have the next 30-plus years to think about it. A life sentence means you're eligible for parole in what would be considered half your life. Maybe by 2023, when his first parole hearing came up, he'd have answers to those questions.

◄○►

Earl Basswood, like most Quincy residents, received the news of Jimmy Scott's life sentence through the media. He read with sheer amazement how a Kirksville jury ignored all signs of stress along the levee and placed the blame squarely on the shoulders of the Webster Elementary School fire starter.

Basswood had been pleased to learn of the venue change. There was simply no way Jimmy could have gotten a fair shake in Marion County. People 100 miles removed from the damage and destruction would be significantly more impartial and sympathetic to the disaster. Or so he thought.

Newspapers interviewed Quincy residents on their reaction to Normile's sentence. Everyone who spoke expressed great relief that Jimmy was not only found guilty, but that he would no longer be a bother in their town—at least until 2023. The rest of the country received the same news as the locals, but they didn't truly understand what a scourge James Scott has been on Quincy for his entire life.

"I doubt it would be safe for him to come walking down through that area if he was to get out tomorrow," Ralph Martin told the press. He owned a service station in West Quincy, which was subsequently leveled by the Mississippi River. He'd since rebuilt and went on with his life, and although he was made whole again, he maintained that a life sentence was appropriate. "I can't think of a whole lot of things you could do to the guy that would bring back things."

"There's something wrong with him," said Cheryl Stratton, whose husband's chiropractic practice was destroyed. "He's sick to get such pleasure out of causing disaster for people." She thought that Jimmy was exactly where he belonged.

In all the media coverage immediately following the trial, only one source recognized the sentence as excessive. The *Associated Press* had to go all the way to Colorado to find that dissenting voice. "I'm not trying to second-guess the judge," said Denver criminal defense attorney Larry Pozner. "But it is extraordinary to get a life sentence for a property crime, even when the damage is extraordinary."

And still, there were those residents that felt a life sentence was too generous for their local scoundrel.

"If you ask me, they should have had the trial here locally," said Jack Freiburg, an insurance agent in Quincy. "Know what we would have done? We'd have hung him from the Bayview Bridge and let the birds get at him. The birds should get a crack at Jimmy Scott, too."

Bob Hoffmeister, a farmer who was instrumental in bulldozing and building runoff chutes on the West Quincy levee—and who testified against James Scott—thought Jimmy was a sick man who could do no right. Asked what sealed his decision as to Scott's guilt, Hoffmeister said just knowing the guy over the years was enough knowledge.

"We knew he was the man; it was only a matter of proving it," he said. "I knew in my mind he'd have to brag about it in a bar, and so we convicted him on circumstantial evidence. He's a menace to society and too dangerous to be free."

While the Denver defense attorney thought Jimmy's punishment was too harsh, Hoffmeister thought it wasn't harsh enough. "This individual is too dangerous to be in society," he said. What would he suggest? "Maybe hang him from a tree and everybody go home for lunch."

Earl Basswood read the town reaction and grew nauseous. Guilty or not, Jimmy never had a chance. Basswood knew personally some of the people commenting about James Scott and wasn't surprised. To Basswood, Jimmy was never innocent until proven guilty. He was guilty until proven guilty, and then sentenced accordingly.

The River Ranger contemplated the irony in the case, much as Jeff Estes had; as John Jackson had; as James Scott had. Water puts out fire. Jimmy Scott had now been convicted for crimes concerning two natural elements on the polar opposite ends of the spectrum. And the court damned him for the breaking of a dam.

Earl Basswood couldn't help but feel sorry for the man, especially because he could have offered evidence that would have helped. But it was too late. Earl Basswood mused that the dam had, in effect, damned James Scott to eternity.

CHAPTER EIGHTEEN

Jimmy spent every minute he could playing sports. The Illinois Department of Corrections provided inmates with adequate yard time and offered a variety of activities. Jimmy joined the softball team and assumed the role of star second baseman. He also frequently engaged in pickup basketball games and was a marksman at throwing horseshoes.

He often asked after his younger brother, who was serving out the rest of his sentence 100 miles away. Despite losing an eye, the kid was making it through okay. While that gave the convicted levee breaker some relief, the relief didn't last long.

In February 1994, Suzie Scott filed for divorce. Apparently, the wife-stranding motive for causing the flood resonated with her after all. She'd stood by her man during his trial and even indicated to friends that she didn't believe the state's case. Still, he was convicted for the disaster, and she couldn't in good conscience stand by a man who caused so much community anguish. That and she saw no reason to stay married to a man who would be locked up until they were at least 55 years old, assuming he made parole his first time in front of the board.

Then in July 1995, the case of Timothy O. Steinmann came to a lackluster conclusion. The West Alton man who had been charged with Intentionally Causing a Catastrophe—even before Jimmy—pled his case down to a reduced charge of first-degree property damage. Assistant prosecutor Philip Groenweghe decided that it'd be next to impossible to prove that Steinmann deliberately rammed his johnboat through the levee. Steinmann received a five-year prison sentence and was ordered to pay a

$5,000 fine—the maximum penalty under the law. James Scott remains the only man in Missouri history to be convicted under the 1979 Intentionally Causing a Catastrophe law.

Come February 1997, three years after Jimmy's first trial, he received the first whiff of good news, even though he was careful not to put too much stock into it. Public defender Jeff Estes was as good as his word. He'd filed an appeal, citing John Jackson's failure to notify the defense about two witnesses whose testimony had implicated James Scott. The court of appeals ordered a new trial for the convict, but the state wasn't prepared to give up so easily.

Marion County's new prosecuting attorney, Tom Redington, appealed the appellate court's ruling. The case worked its way all the way up to the Missouri Supreme Court. While they argued the tenets of Estes' motion and Redington's counter-motion for dismissal, Jimmy continued going about his daily prison routine. Indeed he was given new hope, but hope can be the most dangerous emotion in prison. Should Jimmy bank on a new trial and it not go forward then he'd have the next 30 years to ask himself "what if?" or more accurately, "why not?" He chose, instead to hope for the best while assuming the worst.

In July, while Jimmy was sitting in his cell watching television, Redington and new Marion County Public Defender Raymond Legg received the long-awaited news from the Missouri Supreme Court. In a 23-page report, the Court held that prosecutorial misconduct marred James Scott's chances of receiving a fair trial.

Redington wasn't thrilled with the idea of prosecuting a case that had been prosecuted already, especially because he had quite the caseload. Nevertheless, he filed a motion to have the trial held locally in Marion County. The judge assigned to the case, Robert M. Clayton II, approved the motion. He recognized, however, that an impartial jury would be extremely hard to come by in those parts. After all, Marion County is the county immediately across the river from Quincy, Illinois, and the place where the crime took place. All the media coverage leading up to and then after the first trial helped the local folks make up their minds about Jimmy Scott's guilt. In order to avoid another potential technicality for the Missouri Supreme Court to latch onto, Judge Clayton ordered that although the trial would be held in Marion County, the jury would be pulled from Pettis County, 160 miles away.

Tom Redington met with former state's attorney Jackson to discuss the particulars of the case. Redington decided that he would proceed in much the same manner as his predecessor. The state's evidence hadn't changed. Neither did the witness list. Redington just needed to be sure to have Joe Flachs and Cory Anderson deposed and ready for trial prior to the judge slamming the gavel and getting things under way.

For his part, defense attorney Raymond Legg needed a new strategy going forward. Jeff Estes did a fine job he thought, but the end result was a life sentence, so something had to change.

He met with Jimmy several times in prison and tried to gather more exculpatory evidence. The convict didn't know what else to say. As far as he was concerned, his admission to moving sandbags was taken completely out of context. He told Legg several times that he never *intended* to cause the West Quincy flood. Focus on the defendant's lack of intent, he suggested.

Legg scrambled to shore up his own witness list. Judge Clayton scheduled the jury selection to begin on April 27, 1998, nine months after the supreme court's ruling. It was ample enough time, he figured, and he wanted to make sure he could get the best people possible. The problem Legg would have was budgeting time for an adequate investigation while still upholding his role as the Marion County public defender.

First, he contacted Dr. Charles Morris at the University of Missouri-Rolla, who once again agreed to testify. Legg then tracked down a Marion County Jail guard who worked the questionable section of the West Quincy levee in the days preceding the break. He and Jimmy became acquaintances while the suspect was locked up. During that time, the guard made some rather ominous statements that Legg would raise at trial.

He tracked Duke Kelly down. Because his previous testimony was pretty skimpy, Legg just subpoenaed him. Duke couldn't say definitively that Jimmy Scott talked to him about a trouble spot, but he'd testified in the first trial about a man coming and telling him about a trouble spot on July 16. He'd come in handy.

Finally, the public defender decided he needed one more expert witness. Instead of putting a call into the Mississippi River Rangers—where he might have spoken with Earl Basswood—Legg called the University of Missouri's flagship campus in Columbia. In the same manner by which Jeff Estes found Dr. Charles Morris, that's how Legg found Dr. R. David Hammer.

Hammer was a professor of soil and atmospheric sciences at the University of Missouri for the last 12 years. He'd also been directly involved with the Great Midwestern Floods of 1993. Hammer had two graduate students who were doing their thesis on levees and their response to flood waters at that time, so he had not only stayed up to date with all the news coming off the floodplain, but he'd familiarized himself with the Army Corps of Engineers handbook on levee maintenance.

Legg called Columbia and spoke with Hammer in November 1998. Much like Morris, Hammer said he'd consider testifying once he knew all the particulars surrounding the case. He requested a topographic map of the area drawn to scale showing the 10 miles of West Quincy levee, as well as an overhead photo taken right before the levee broke.

Hammer studied the map first. He looked at the bends in the Mississippi River, at the proximity of the railroad bridge, and at the vegetation. Then he looked at the aerial photograph of that same section and observed the levee conditions, including the bulldozed section of the West Quincy levee, the plastic tarp sans a sandbag wall on the area in question, and the height of the water.

Before the professor asked Legg to tell him exactly where the levee broke, he made an educated guess. Then he took the topographic map to six colleagues who knew nothing of the upcoming trial of James Scott, but who knew river systems. Four of the men were fellow professors at the University of Missouri and two were scientists high-up in the U.S. Geological Survey department. Hammer gave them the scenario: "This levee broke. Show me where you think it occurred."

He polled each man individually and didn't reveal his predecessor's answers. And each man picked a spot within a quarter-mile area of the spot Hammer picked—three of the men picked the exact same spot.

When Hammer responded to Raymond Legg and told him where he believed the break to have occurred, the defense attorney said he nailed it. The spot he indicated was *exactly* where the break occurred.

Hammer agreed to testify, and he spent the better part of the winter months synchronizing his own knowledge of levees with the Army Corps of Engineers levee maintenance manual as well as the Corps post-flood report. He studied the effects pre-existing high-water conditions have on dikes, and he poured over dozens of photos taken pre- and post-flood.

Dr. R. David Hammer didn't have a soft stomach. He'd been around the block a few times, not only as a soil scientist but also as a combat pilot. After he earned his engineering degree from the United States Naval Academy in 1968, he took a commission in the U.S. Marine Corps. Hammer went through infantry officer's basic training at Quantico, and then flight training at Pensacola, Meridian, and Corpus Christi. When he was all trained, Hammer flew A-4 Skyhawks for six years. He went to Vietnam and served in an A-4 squadron with the 1st Marine Air Wing. Hammer's missions were to seek and destroy surface targets in support of the ground forces, to escort helicopters, and to serve as bait for NVA surface-to-air missiles and anti-aircraft gunfire—as a way to flush out enemy posts and see just where Charlie had dug in. Suffice to say, most of the friends he made in flight school and many with the 1st Marine Air Wing didn't make it back.

Hammer did, though, and pursued advanced study of soil science and engineering. He received his master's degree from the University of Illinois and his PhD from the University of Tennessee.

With such a résumé and with so much life experience at a young age, not much shocked Hammer in 1997. As the trial date neared and as he continued his research into the West Quincy levee break, however, the professor was genuinely stunned by what he discovered.

There are six parameters that if met are likely to cause a levee to fail under flood conditions, according to the soil sciences and engineering communities. If any one of these six parameters is met then the levee in question will most likely become a victim of the river it buttresses.

First, long, straight stretches of the river—where the river is straight and there aren't any meanders to de-energize the flow—there's a higher probability of levee failure downstream. Especially when the river is moving at a faster-than-normal speed. The Mississippi River was flowing at 35-miles per hour on July 16. When the river bends, that's akin to driving your car at 35 miles per hour into an earthen wall.

Second, if the river is constricted in a channel, then the offshoot has a tremendous amount of velocity. Across from the West Quincy levee sat the town of Quincy on its hard, limestone bluff. The bluff juts out and narrows the river, pushing the current into the earthen West Quincy levee. The effect is the same as if a man was standing in a garden with his garden hose and put his finger over the nozzle. When you compress the stream from the hose, the flow accelerates through the constricted nozzle and heightens the pressure, giving that man a water pick that can be used to blow debris off of, say, a porch. On a river system, the current starts to act as a water pick as it moves through the narrow channel, thereby increasing its erosive capability.

Third, the presence of wing dams. Wing dams are jetties of rock constructed by the Corps of Engineers at perpendicular angles along river banks. They are intended to stabilize channels and keep river levels high in the middle for barge traffic. When the river velocity or the volume of the river is high and the water is flowing over the wing dams, this creates turbulent flow. On the Mississippi River, as well as the connecting Missouri River, Hammer and other scientists noted a number of levee failures just downstream from these large wing dams.

The fourth parameter concerned the Burlington Northern railroad bridge, located just upriver from the levee break. The footings of the railroad bridge—or any bridge on a river—cause turbulent flow, which exacerbates levee failure. Hammer had seen it a hundred times, especially after the Great Midwestern Floods of '93. In fact, more than 90 percent of the flooded areas he studied that summer were directly downstream from bridge footings.

The abruptly thinning tree line was the fifth determinate. University of Missouri soil scientists and engineers wrote several reports over time claiming that there's a very strong correlation between the width of a vegetative buffer that grows on the river side of a levee and the levee's success rate. In lay terms, when there are large trees, like a mini-forest of oak, maple, or beech trees, in between the levee and the river, the mini-forest acts as a buffer. It slows down the current before it slams into the levee. In this particular spot of the West Quincy levee, there was a thin row of cottonwood trees—a very minimal buffer, at best.

Finally, there was the exact location of the break. The pressure on the walls of the levee was consistent with a "perfect storm" scenario, especially because the Illinois side of the Mississippi River was all limestone. There's no way it was going anywhere, so the limestone countered all the affected force generated by the river and diverted it to the other side: To the West Quincy side.

"Well I'll be damned," Hammer said to himself. If just one of these parameters was met, a levee could fail. The levee in West Quincy, he noted, met all six parameters.

If that wasn't enough, Hammer noticed what he considered to be a seventh variable. His eyes kept coming back to one aerial photo taken the morning of July 17, the morning after the break, as the Mississippi River furiously emptied into the surrounding farmland. The professor noticed a huge brown blotch where it broke, shaped like a "V." He'd seen it before—20 years earlier along rivers flowing through a canopy jungle. It was the imprint of seepage and internal piping. When the decision was made to bulldoze the levee a week before it broke (the Fabius River Drainage District's last-ditch effort to raise the walls high enough so that the levee wouldn't be overtopped) they pushed so much sand away from the backside of the levee that they exposed the original levee: The one built by people like Reverend Grimm's grandfather back in the 1920s. That was a gumbo levee, or a levee made from clay-like sediments. It was more impervious to piping or seepage than a sand levee. The levee atop the original was built by the Army Corps of Engineers in the 1960s. It was a sand levee. Water moves much more easily through sand particles than it does through clay. By bulldozing, Hammer observed, the structural integrity of the old and newer levees were weakened, and the bulldozing exposed a seam in the two. Mississippi River waters exploited that seam and seeped right through the middle of the levee. After all, the plastic tarp laid over the top to prevent erosion wasn't pulled 18 or so feet into the water. The middle of the levee—weakened by bulldozers—was continually being battered by the river, caused by all six parameters. Heavy rains and mounting water pressure was more than the West Quincy levee could handle. When a levee fails, it leaves behind telltale signs of why it failed. Hammer saw a sign staring him in the face as he repeatedly looked over that one aerial photo.

Next, he decided to meet Raymond Legg in the defense attorney's Hannibal office and drive out to the exact spot. Even though it'd been more than four years since the Great Midwestern Floods, Hammer wanted to personally examine the area in question. Once again, he was shocked by what he saw.

Thousands of softball-sized stones, commonly known as riprap in scientific parlance, had been strewn all along the section of levee that broke on July 16, 1993. It was done as a repairing measure. However, riprap is extremely expensive and it's hard to truck in. The question, to Hammer, was if a single person had sabotaged the levee, why go through all the trouble and expense of bringing all that rock in? To Hammer, the answer was simple. He figured that the Fabius River Drainage District and the Corps of Engineers realized after the floods of '93 why, where, and how levees break. The presence of the riprap indicated that this particular location was a spot where the levee *wants* to break. To Hammer, the presence of the riprap was an admission that this section of the levee was weak.

◄○►

Jury selection commenced in the town of Sedalia, Missouri, in Pettis County on Thursday, April 23, 1998. The pool of candidates were informed that if selected, they'd be loaded onto a school bus and driven three hours away to Hannibal, where the trial would be held. On that day, 27 jurors out of a pool of 97 were dismissed out of hand.

"Anyone chosen is going to have an inconvenience, I understand that," Judge Clayton told perspective jurors. "That is not enough to warrant release."

Many of the excused were quite aware of the West Quincy break from the news and of James Scott in particular. Prosecuting attorney Tom Redington and defense attorney Raymond Legg had a much harder time in paneling a jury than either initially thought. Some people had family in the flooded area of Marion County and some had made the trek north and volunteered their help. One prospect was dismissed because he was a retired agent with the Missouri Department of Conservation who knew a thing or two about what makes levees fail. But what really diminished the jury pool was the hometown newspaper.

The *Sedalia Democrat* had newspaper stands all over town, and several stationed on the street corners adjacent to the courthouse, as well as one right at the courthouse's threshold. Beginning on April 23 and for the following two days of jury selection, the *Democrat* ran front page stories—above the fold—of the impending trial of James Scott. The articles spoke in detail of the flood, of what he stood accused of, and it even said that this would be his second trial. Given the proximity of the newspaper boxes to the courthouse, it was almost impossible for jurors not to see news coverage of the trial. There were even used, already-read copies of the newspaper scattered around the inside of the courthouse. Somehow, not all of the 97 pairs of eyes who would be questioned as potential jurors managed to see or get wind of the coverage—or so they claimed, anyway. And a couple of prospective jurors, by their own admission, couldn't read.

Like in the first trial of Jimmy Scott, the jury was primarily elderly, some admittedly illiterate, as well as some stay-at-home moms who were too busy raising their children to follow the news. People like Rebecca Brockway, a mother of three from Sedalia. All of her children were under the age of 10, so she had her hands full at home. In fact, right when she got her summons to appear at the Pettis County Courthouse, she was in the midst of planning her 9-year-old daughter's birthday party.

Redington and Legg agreed upon Rebecca Brockway, who felt it was her civic duty to be a part of the process. She did voice her hesitation, however, at being driven three hours away from her family and sequestered in a foreign city, and she really didn't want to miss her daughter's 10th birthday. Nevertheless, the need outweighed her hardship, much as it did some of the other jurors chosen.

Eight women, four men, and three alternates were finally paneled on Friday afternoon. They were given an hour and a half to go home, pack (enough clothes for up to two weeks), and say goodbye to their spouses and/or children. At five o'clock sharp, they were instructed to report back to the Pettis County Courthouse. Anyone not on the courthouse steps would be pulled out of their homes by officers and driven in a police car to Hannibal. That instruction made Rebecca Brockway very apprehensive. She already recognized the importance of this case, but the thought of a cop pulling her away from her family was enough to make her want to cry.

Luckily, the authorities didn't need to conduct any extractions. Everyone reported on time. An officer of the court accompanied the jurors during the bus ride to Marion County on that late Friday afternoon. They were allowed to speak amongst themselves but they weren't allowed to discuss the upcoming trial in any way, shape, or form. As such, the total strangers made small talk for the first hour and then turned their attention to the rolling Missouri countryside for the remainder of the drive.

The closer they came to Hannibal, the further away from home they felt. The topography changed in front of their eyes. These people, who lived at the foot of the Ozarks, now observed flat farmland as far as the eye could see. They drove through spits of rain, which grew incrementally heavier the closer they came to Hannibal. As if Mother Nature was purposefully sticking her thumb in the eye of the Marion County locals—or maybe of James Scott—the county and surrounding areas were under a flood watch. River towns were once again at the mercy of a rising Mississippi River. The rains weren't nearly as bad as those in 1993, but the threat of flooding roused all those old painful memories from five years earlier.

The busload of 12 Pettis County jurors and three alternates checked into their Hannibal motel just after eight o'clock on Friday evening. Trial was set to begin at 10 o'clock the next morning. Not only were they disoriented, but the jury wouldn't have time to sleep off their road weariness, and they had to sit in court on a Saturday to boot.

Come Saturday morning, the jurors had to cross what amounted to a media picket line to get into the courthouse. Hordes of print and broadcast journalists milled about the 97-year-old structure, thereby creating a foreign site not usually seen around the picturesque Classical-style building, with its four Corinthian columns and its huge charcoal-gray rotunda. It was an intimidating site for the jurors indeed, but not nearly as intimidating as the makeshift television studio set up in Judge Robert Clayton's courtroom.

New York City came to sleepy Hannibal, Missouri, in the form of Court TV. The cable network requested and received permission from the judge to broadcast gavel-to-gavel coverage of the levee breaker's second trial.

Rebecca Brockway felt daunted by the scene. "This is just like the circus when it rolls through Sedalia," she thought. "Only there aren't as many clowns and freaks at the circus."

◄◉►

"In 1993, war came to Marion County. All up and down the Mississippi River, there was a war against the river," prosecuting attorney Tom Redington said in his opening statement. "Right across the river from Quincy, Illinois, people were winning that war. Thousands of people had pitched in to fight this war. Children, grandparents, brothers, and sisters, whole families had worked. The West Quincy levee had to be saved, and the river was losing, until the evening of July 16, 1993, when this man, James Scott, sabotaged that levee."

Redington stood in the middle of Judge Clayton's courtroom and pointed the finger at Jimmy. The ex-con sat in his defendant's chair with an angry expression on his face. He wore a buttoned-down blue and white striped shirt with a pen affixed to the shirt's front pocket. His khaki pants were pressed and clung tightly to his legs. However, his black high-tops and mullet haircut portrayed the appearance of a tough. Not even the wire-rimmed glasses and trimmed mustache could offset his rough exterior.

Jimmy sat biting his tongue as Redington told the jury about a biblical struggle between nature and man. Even though man had fought a futile battle throughout the state, the people of Quincy and West Quincy had fought the good fight—and they were winning. Jimmy wanted so badly to stand up and speak. Here he was in a second trial for his life, and his attorney decided he would keep him seated and quiet. Again.

Jimmy didn't bring a Bible to court this time. He brought a yellow notepad and a blue pen. He would take notes and aid in his own defense, albeit with locked lips. There was no way he was going to sit idly by this time. He'd tell Raymond Legg exactly what the inaccuracies were each time one arose.

Legg didn't look as lawyerly as his contemporary for the state. Redington wore a lint-less black suit, accessorized with black suspenders and a black and white tie. He stood straight and tall, and he didn't fidget when he spoke. His oversized gold-rimmed glasses didn't swallow his face, but rather, when coupled with his perfectly kempt black and red beard, made him look like the most professional, well-groomed, and intelligent man in the court. Legg, on the other hand, looked more of-the-people. His black suit was also well-pressed, but it was large on his already-stocky body. He wore a blue dress shirt and a green polka-dot tie. His gold-rimmed glasses, mustache, and buzz cut made him look simple. His diction was coarser than the prosecutor's, and he slumped his shoulders and bulled his neck. He didn't have much of a poker face and was becoming noticeably steamed as the diminutive prosecutor spoke.

When it was time for the defense to mount its opening statement, Raymond Legg improvised. He seized upon Tom Redington's war analogy, though he spun it in his client's favor by incorporating an environmental twist.

"Ladies and gentlemen," Legg began, "in July 1993, up and down the Mississippi River and the Missouri River, mankind was waging a war against nature. Mankind was waging a war that it could not win. That it did not win. It was a desperate effort. It was a heroic effort. It was a last-ditch effort, but an effort that was doomed to fail."

With that, the second trial of James R. Scott, the only man in Missouri history to be convicted of Intentionally Causing a Catastrophe, was underway. Again.

Redington paraded witness after witness in front of the court. Fabius River Drainage District Commissioner Norman Haerr announced that they would have won the war but for Jimmy Scott. Don Bawmann from the Corps of Engineers said that the Corps stood by their work and the levee— especially in that section—was "rock solid." Juror Rebecca Brockway listened to direct testimony and the subsequent cross examination and tried mentally to rank each witness. The score, she thought, was even until Redington called the state's next three witnesses.

Eric Epping and Cory Anderson testified to hearing Jimmy plot to break the levee prior to the flood. They were small and young. Taken together, they were very convincing. Then Redington wheeled out a television for Joe Flachs' testimony. He had been paroled from prison and was currently under house arrest, which is why he couldn't be present in the courtroom. The state's attorney played Joe's videotaped testimony, and as the troubled teen spoke, Rebecca Brockway and company became incensed.

"Did Mr. Scott say anything at this party [at Dan Leake's house] on July 13 about the flooding problems?" Redington asked the boy in the videotape.

"He just said that he wished that the levee would break so his wife wouldn't come home," the boy on the television screen answered.

"[On July 16], did he tell you why he wanted the levee to break so his wife couldn't come home?"

"He said he just hated her and he wanted to party."

"Did he describe to you how he [broke the levee]?"

"He said he had a shovel and stuck it in the side and would take his hand and put it in a circular rotation."

Rebecca Brockway's anger was palpable. She furrowed her brow and shifted her gaze between James Scott, the television screen, and her fellow jurors. When Redington entered Reverend Roy Grimm's homemade video into evidence and played the boat tour of the flooded area for the jury, Rebecca became consumed with rage and disgust, but that still wasn't the worse of it.

A few witnesses later, Redington pulled out his trump card. Dan Leake, Jimmy's half brother and his confidant throughout adolescence, was sworn in as a witness for the state.

Dan walked up the step and took his seat before the court. Jimmy lowered his head and refused to make eye contact. His own half brother, his own flesh and blood, was about to implicate him.

Robert and Sharon Scott sat in the front row of seats reserved for spectators. The color drained from Dan's mother's face and she, too, refused to make eye contact with her son. Robert Scott, Dan's stepfather, did in fact look at the witness. Squarely in the eye. His mouth was agape and he squinted at the sight in front of him, as if it were a mirage. Surly Dan Leake wasn't going to testify against his brother, especially when Jimmy was on trial for his life. That's not how Robert and Sharon raised their boys. And yet, there he was.

"Did the defendant ever tell you that he wanted to break the West Quincy levee?" Redington asked in a tranquil tone.

"He mentioned it, yes," Dan said in a sorrowful voice. Because he'd had previous run-ins with the law, he knew better than to lie under oath. He told the jury what he knew and hoped for the best.

"Did he tell you why he wanted to do that?"

"To keep his wife over there."

"He told you, in fact, that he was going to break the levee?"

Dan looked around the courtroom for a moment. He thought back to the conversations he had with Jimmy around the time of the flood, especially when he suspected that his half brother knew something and wasn't telling. Dan Leake could blow this case wide open, and he knew it, so he tempered his response.

"I wasn't thinking he was serious at the time. I mean, I really . . . I . . ."

"Did you ever ask him if he broke the levee on that night [July 16]?"

"Yes, I did."

"How did he respond?"

"He wouldn't answer me. He just acted like he had something to do and he walked away and he said he was going to leave."

Rebecca Brockway was livid. She kept thinking of the video Reverend Grimm made. All that water. So much destruction. As Jimmy's half brother spoke, she grew confident that the man in front of her with the mustache, the glasses, and the blond mullet was in fact to blame. Rebecca looked around the jury box to gauge her colleagues' reactions to this latest bizarre information. Some shared her anger, some looked unfazed, and one elderly juror was actually asleep. Rebecca looked at the judge to see whether he noticed the snoozing woman. The judge did not look back.

Apparently the elderly juror wasn't the only sleepy person in the courtroom. Detective Neal Baker testified to the events that led to Jimmy's confession. When Redington played the tape of the confession, Baker let out a barbaric yawn. Rebecca noticed, and Court TV caught it, but no one else flinched.

The defense didn't call its first witness until April 29, 1998, six days into the trial. By now, Rebecca Brockway was downright edgy, as was the rest of the jury. They'd been holed-up in Hannibal—away from their families—and were only permitted five minutes of phone time per day to call home and check on things. The call was placed in front of a police officer in order to ensure that the trial wasn't discussed. Rebecca wanted to go home, but she had sworn to do her level best as a juror. She'd listen to what the defense had to say and she'd deliberate with the rest of her associates. Then she'd return home to Sedalia and celebrate her 9-year-old's birthday.

◄○►

Public defender Raymond Legg called Duke Kelly to the stand, and Jimmy breathed a sigh of relief. Although the Missouri Air National Guardsman didn't do all that much for the suspect in his first trial, he did confirm that a man approached him with information about a trouble spot. And although he didn't say definitively at the first trial that the man who approached him was Jimmy, at the very least, Duke's testimony would lend credence to the accused liar's alibi.

Legg began his questioning much like his predecessor, Jeff Estes, had begun four years earlier in Jimmy's 1994 trial. He asked Duke questions that confirmed his position as the NCOIC and he asked him about his whereabouts on July 16, 1993. Duke answered as he had four years earlier, but then the questioning took a bizarre turn.

At the first trial, Duke testified that a man informed him of a problem area in between the Bayview Bridge and the railroad bridge. He said he walked north for a little bit with this man and then decided that it was a waste of his time going all the way up there. Others would be patrolling that section of the levee, and his concern was with his men over at the Bayview Bridge. As such, he walked north along the levee with a man, and then he walked back by himself.

But that's not what he told Raymond Legg. Duke said under oath that he had no recollection of walking north of the Bayview Bridge on the afternoon of July 16. Thus, because he had no recollection of walking north, he duly had no recollection of walking back south. Duke Kelly's answers threw a wrench in the defense's case. The public defender asked Judge Clayton if he could approach the bench for a sidebar.

"Judge, I'm surprised by this witness's testimony. He previously testified that he walked up there with somebody. I'm surprised by the witness's testimony because he had previously testified in this matter that he had walked up the levee with somebody who tried to point out trouble spots to him.

"My intent is to try to ask a couple more questions to see if that would refresh his memory; if not, to use his prior testimony for that purpose. I at some point need to start treating the witness as hostile."

Judge Clayton didn't know what to do. The defense was saying that it might have to treat its own witness as hostile. Legg had cause for concern, as Duke Kelly just did an about-face on the stand. But the rule of law stated that neither attorney could prejudice the jury by tipping them off to a past trial for the same case. The jury was not supposed to know that James Scott's previous conviction had been overturned. Judge Clayton allowed Legg a little bit of latitude, but cautioned him.

"[Mr. Kelly], do you recall testifying previously in this case?" Legg asked the witness when proceedings recommenced.

"Yes, I do," the Missouri Air National Guardsman answered.

"And do you recall being asked about walking north of the levee?"

"Yes."

"And you recall being asked if anybody was with you?"

"Yes."

"And do you recall answering, 'Not on the way down; I went by myself.'"

"I believe so."

"And do you recall being asked, 'Was anybody else with you on the way back?'"

"Yes."

"And do you recall saying, 'Yes?'"

"I believe I do recall saying that, yes."

"Okay. Do you recall being asked, 'Did the individual you walked with try to warn you of any trouble spots?'"

"You're asking me if I was asked that, or if I recall being asked that?"

"Yes," Legg said cryptically.

"I recall that," Duke answered in kind.

"And do you recall saying, 'I would say yes'?"

"At that time."

"And you don't remember that now?"

"That is correct."

"Because it's been, what, five years?"

"From '93 to '98, yes, sir."

"Do you recall anybody telling you about any trouble spots on the levee, or trying to tell you about any trouble spots on the levee?"

This strange question-and-answer period continued for the next five minutes, and not one single juror followed the dialogue. Rebecca Brockway sat in her seat looking irked. Duke Kelly was telling the defense attorney that he recalled all this information, but that now he didn't recall any of this information. "Well which is it?" Rebecca asked herself. Moreover, Legg asked Duke about testifying before in the matter. Rebecca was paying more attention than anyone on that jury, and she didn't remember Duke Kelly testifying on any of the last six days. She had the sneaking suspicion that this wasn't the first time James Scott had stood trial for breaking the West Quincy levee, and she got the sneaking suspicion that defense attorney Raymond Legg was losing control of his case.

Later in the day, after the surprising exchange with Duke Kelly, Legg called John C. Martin to the stand. Martin didn't testify at the first trial, and it was by sheer luck that Legg found him in Maywood, Missouri, 10 minutes inland from West Quincy and just over the Marion County line in Lewis County. The only reason he'd found Martin was because of Jimmy. Yet another statement Jimmy made checked out.

Martin was a guard in the Marion County Jail while Jimmy was locked up awaiting arraignment in 1994. Guards always got along with Jimmy. He was a likeable, affable guy who spoke in a simple Midwestern monotone and who seemed like an honest crook—a rarity in the poke. Back then, Jimmy told Martin what he was in for, and Martin told him that he actually worked as a volunteer on that exact stretch of levee two days before and also the day before the break. Throughout the course of their jailhouse conversations,

John C. Martin got the feeling that Jimmy was indeed telling the truth—that he had nothing to do with the failure of the West Quincy levee.

"What was, when you were on it, the condition of the levee that you observed?" Legg asked his witness.

"Wet mostly all the time," Martin replied.

"How wet would you say it was?"

"Saturated. Saturated wet."

"Why would you say that it was saturated wet?"

"Because of the job that we were given to do. It was a continual process of stamping in the straw in the riblets and in the—the runnels where the water was coming through."

"Did you notice any erosion on the levee?"

"There was places of erosion, yes, sir."

"Where did you notice that erosion?"

"It was mostly at the lower half or lower side of the levee itself."

"Did you notice any bulldozer tracks?"

"There was some, yes, sir."

"Do you remember a plastic that was covering the top of the levee?"

"Yes, sir. The top of the levee was covered with a black plastic."

"Do you remember anything unusual concerning that plastic?"

"It was—it was weighted down with sandbags at different lengths."

"Did you ever notice any water coming out from underneath the plastic?"

"Yes, sir."

"How much water did you observe coming out from underneath the plastic?"

John C. Martin thought for a moment. He looked off to the side and tried to replay the events leading up to the West Quincy levee break. "In certain areas if we noticed some water coming out from underneath the plastic, we would then put some sand back underneath the plastic and weight it down with a sandbag."

The jailhouse guard essentially said that he and other volunteers did the exact same thing that Jimmy Scott reportedly did when he noticed trouble spots on the levee. They moved sandbags around to stem the flow of water.

Legg hoped that his point wasn't lost on the jury, many of whom were now squirming in their seats. The trial was dragging on. He thought some of the jurors looked tired, and they couldn't have been comfortable in the courtroom. Not only because of the subject matter, but also because the Court TV cameras added an unnecessary surreal element to the entire atmosphere.

Legg used Martin to not only drive the point home that others had conducted themselves in the same manner as James Scott prior to the flood, but he was setting the jury up to hear from his last two witnesses—his two star witnesses.

Rebecca Brockway anxiously awaited the testimony of Dr. Charles Morris from the University of Missouri-Rolla when he was sworn in. She knew UM-Rolla was a preeminent engineering school in the state, and the science component of this case intrigued her. It also meant that the case was nearing its conclusion; she'd be heading home to her family before too long.

The rest of the jury, however, didn't share her enthusiasm for Dr. Morris' appearance. That elderly juror was studying the back of her eyelids again. Out cold, Rebecca observed. And no one else seemed to notice.

Morris launched into his piping theory of the West Quincy levee. He told the courtroom that this levee was in a process of eminent failure. Morris made it very clear that he wasn't applying a label of "guilty" or "innocent" to James Scott. He couldn't say definitively whether the suspect broke the levee or not, although he did say that if someone intentionally dug into that levee with the aim of breaking it, then that man would have died in the process. The river would have swept him away, and the undercurrent would have drowned him.

Morris said he was there to tell the jury—because it was important that they understand from an engineering perspective—that nothing had to be *done* to the levee. It was too wet, the pressure on its walls too high, the Mississippi River waters too strong, and too many pipes formed in the levee's interior as a result of the bulldozing. If anything, Morris said, the volunteers, the Corps of Engineers, and the Fabius River Drainage District should be patted on the back and commended for a job well done. They staved off the inevitable: They kept the river at bay long enough to evacuate all the residents to higher ground. Lives were saved thanks to those heroes, because if it weren't for their efforts, the levee would have given way a week or so earlier.

The professor's testimony went significantly smoother under direct examination than it had in the first trial. No one raised his or her hand and everyone seemed to "get it." All except for this one juror whom he noticed nodding off while he testified. Still, it was much easier than in 1994. Easier, that is, until Redington got a crack at him.

The state's attorney wasn't nearly as courteous toward the esteemed professor as John Jackson had been. In fact, he was downright contentious. Redington questioned Morris' expertise, asking how a man who wasn't anywhere near the incident could make such a cocksure statement as to eminent failure. He also asked Morris about his testimony on November 3, 1994. Redington thought Morris had changed his story—back then, he said the statements James Scott made were inconsistent. Today, he said they were consistent. After 15 minutes of cryptic back-and-forth dialogue, Morris clarified that the statements James Scott made about the levee being lower in one portion—where he moved sandbags to stem overtopping water—was consistent with this mode of piping. Redington then abandoned that line of questioning, but it did affect the jury—or the members of the jury who were awake, anyway.

Rebecca Brockway was extremely confused by what she heard. Redington was seemingly badgering Dr. Morris. He kept asking the scientist about levee structure and maintenance, and when the scientist answered, Redington changed his tone and prefaced his questions with lines like, "as you sit here today, you can't tell me the size of the sand in the West Quincy levee, can you?"

The size of the sand!

She knew the state's attorney was on to something, even though the points seemed to be ridiculously minute. She knew because Dr. Charles Morris from the highly-regarded University of Missouri-Rolla College of Engineering grew noticeably rattled. Redington calculated his inflections and was precise in his hectoring cross-examination. The professor was flustered.

"As you sit here today, you really can't tell us specifically why the levee failed in West Quincy on July 16, 1993, because you weren't there, is that right?" Redington summed up.

"I was not there, that's correct," Morris replied.

"You could not rule out sabotage, could you?"

"I don't believe sabotage was necessary for the levee to fail."

"My question, sir, was you can't rule out sabotage, can you?"

"That's true," the professor said. What he didn't say was that he never meant to rule out sabotage. All he wanted to do was to demonstrate that the levee was going to fail with or without James Scott's interference. But by then, he just wanted out of there.

"Nothing further, Judge," Redington said, and he quickly turned his back on Dr. Charles Morris.

"You're finally excused," Judge Clayton said. Morris didn't stick around Hannibal to hear the outcome of the trial. He was way too angry with how he was treated. He was equally angry that the public defender didn't raise objections to the prosecutor's browbeating. Morris looked over the faces of those jurors and didn't see any allies.

He walked off the stand, exited the courtroom, and washed his hands of Hannibal and of James Scott. It would be more than a year before Dr. Charles Morris learned what the verdict was.

◄○►

Dr. R. David Hammer from the University of Missouri was the last witness for the defense. Hammer had studied-up on this particular levee prior to the trial, and he read numerous reports from his colleagues who had worked that exact stretch of land regarding its condition. Coupled with his own extensive knowledge of river systems, Hammer believed he could introduce to the jury elements of reasonable doubt from the perspective of science. Nothing about the West Quincy levee made it any more special than other levees, which had failed at the rate of one a day upriver from them, nor of the sister levee right there in Hannibal, which failed after the West Quincy levee.

Under direct testimony, Legg queried Hammer about his experience as an engineer and a PhD in soil sciences. When the doctor established his credentials, Legg asked specific questions about the West Quincy levee. Hammer cited reports he read in the U.S. Geological Survey. That's when the state's attorney began his long line of objections.

"Judge, it's hearsay," Redington said. "He didn't perform the study. It's hearsay."

Despite Hammer citing findings by the U.S. Geological Survey, which was published in the Journal of Science—one of the most prestigious scientific journals in the world—Judge Clayton sustained the objection. Nothing that the professor learned secondhand would be admissible.

Legg had one of his legs cut out from underneath him within the first 15 minutes of his witness's testimony. He shifted gears.

Next he questioned Dr. Hammer about the six parameters that could deem a levee fallible. Hammer wasn't even halfway through his explanation when Redington raised more objections.

Hammer was discussing the parameter of a vegetative buffer between the river and the earthen dam. "Two really good reports that were done by myself and colleagues at the University of Missouri show that there's a very strong correlation between the width of the vegetative buffer between the levee and the normal river channel."

Redington renewed his previous objection. "Judge," he began, "I object to him testifying about very good works by somebody else. It's hearsay."

"He said he participated," the judge said. "Overruled."

But Redington had another ace up his sleeve: He wouldn't be outgunned by some academic. "I object to him calling his own work very good."

Hammer looked at the jurors, much like Morris had before him. He'd been in plenty of trials, and in the past, he tried to convince the jury that he was a nice guy, that he was credible, and that he knew his stuff. By all accounts, Dr. Hammer was likeable and honest. That's how his classes became some of the most popular in the university's soil science department. So in the time it took Redington to object, Hammer studied the jury and gauged their reaction. They looked tired and they looked bored. One woman, he could have sworn, was asleep. But for the face of Rebecca Brockway, this jury seemed to be quite apathetic. They looked disinterested, and they made Hammer's job nearly impossible. Since he wasn't making any friends with this jury, he'd be damned if he'd let a lawyer push him around.

"My very average work shows . . ." Hammer began before the judge could rule on Redington's objection.

"No objection to that," the state's attorney said rather glibly.

"My very average work, in which we looked at and investigated 22 levee breaks along one stretch of river, showed a very strong correlation."

Some of the jury laughed at the pissing match between the prosecutor and the defense's star witness. It was the first sign of life they'd showed all afternoon, and that's what Hammer thought of their reaction: laughable.

He thought he could win them back. Hammer somehow connected with a jury who had been bored stiff with technical jargon. He made it through the six parameters and was in relatively good form going into cross examination.

"Did I hear you right, sir?" Redington began. "You said it would have failed?" The prosecutor wasted no time whatsoever launching a counteroffensive.

"I believe the probability was overwhelming that the levee would have failed," the professor replied.

"But you didn't offer an opinion, did you sir, as to what caused it to fail on July 16, 1993?"

"It would be very difficult to say the exact cause because when you ask me that question you're asking me do I know exactly how. I think it failed by piping."

"But you don't know, do you?"

"No one knows."

They sparred for almost 20 minutes. Redington asked the witness if his opinion would change if he knew, hypothetically, that Cory Anderson, Eric Epping, and Joe Flachs all testified that James Scott admitted to sabotaging the levee. Hammer responded each time that he didn't know these people, just as he didn't know James Scott. He wasn't making a presumption of guilt or innocence, he maintained.

"What if Eric Epping said James Scott told him he was going to break the levee? Does that change your opinion about whether or not it was sabotaged?"

Hammer considered his answer. Redington spent all day refuting the professor as an expert in science, objecting when he cited industry studies, objecting when he cited his own studies, but now he wanted the scientist to comment on the statements of people he never met or heard of. "I don't know Eric, so it wouldn't change . . ." he began, but was abruptly cut off.

"Doesn't change your opinion at all?" Redington asked in a surprised tone.

"No, it doesn't," Hammer said.

"If Joseph Flachs says that James Scott told him he broke the levee, does that change your opinion about whether or not it was sabotage?"

"No."

"If Cory Anderson says that James Scott said, 'I told you I was going to do it and now it's done,' does that change your opinion about whether it was sabotage?"

"No."

By the time Hammer was excused, Rebecca Brockway was utterly bewildered. Hammer was indeed a star witness, a man who knew levees. He didn't seem to crack the way the other professor had. This professor from the University of Missouri was unflappable. If he could be so undoubting about the levee's failure because of natural causes, couldn't it be that the professor was right? After all, in addition to levees and river systems being his specialty, Dr. R. David Hammer was a Marine. And Missourians don't take military service for granted; they are fiercely proud of their fighting men and women.

Rebecca Brockway had a lot to consider as Judge Clayton excused them for the day and informed them that they'd meet the following morning for instructions and deliberation. She wasn't the foreman, but she paid the closest attention to the testimony—all the testimony. Brockway and her compatriots were excused at 5:51 p.m. They'd reconvene at eight o'clock in the morning on April 30, 1998.

They'd only been out of the courtroom for a matter of minutes when Raymond Legg made a motion before the court for a directed verdict of acquittal. "The state failed to prove the defendant's criminal agency in this matter beyond a reasonable doubt. I don't believe at this point that there's sufficient evidence to take this case to a jury."

The judge asked Tom Redington if he had any comment on the motion before the court.

"Judge, my argument isn't any different than at the conclusion of the state's case," he said quite matter-of-factly. "We have proven sufficiently to submit this matter to a jury; that a catastrophe was created, and based upon the reasonable inferences from the evidence presented that this defendant knowingly caused that catastrophe."

Judge Clayton didn't need to recess on the matter. He was confident in his role as the court's officer and overseer. As he had for most of the trial, he sided with the prosecution.

"The defendant's motion for judgment of acquittal is denied," Clayton said.

◄O►

James Scott appeared confident as he marched into the Marion County Courthouse on April 30. He spent the night in jail replaying the trial in his head, the same way he had after his first trial. The case in Judge Clayton's court wasn't without its flare-ups and tiffs, but it wasn't a circus sideshow like in 1994, except for Court TV, which had cameras galore. Jimmy was on television for more than a week. This time, he hated every minute of it.

He hunkered down in the defendant's chair the next day, preparing to be there for a while. Given all the evidence presented, his attorney assured him that this case wouldn't be decided in a matter of hours. But like he was with so many elements of the trial, public defender Raymond Legg was wrong.

The jury deliberated for two hours and 55 minutes. They came in with their heads lowered. Nobody made eye contact with the defendant.

The clerk handed Judge Clayton the verdict. He verified it, returned it to the clerk, and asked the defendant and his attorney to rise.

James Scott stood before the court in his blue and white striped shirt, oversized glasses, mustache, and mullet and stared at the clerk as he read the verdict.

"We, the jury, find the defendant, James R. Scott, guilty of causing a catastrophe as submitted in Instruction Number 5."

Jimmy's bottom lip began to tremble and his face seized up. He squinted hard and tried not to cry, but an audible sob escaped his mouth. Sharon and Robert Scott lowered their heads as the clerk read the jury's decision. Sharon sat calmly with her head bowed in shame. Robert, the stoic one, choked back some tears.

Judge Clayton thanked the jury for their time and scheduled a sentencing date for July 6, 1998, six weeks hence. Court officers took James R. Scott into custody. He'd spend the next six weeks in the Marion County Jail before being remanded to the custody of the Missouri Department of Corrections after sentencing.

Before he exited the courtroom, Jimmy turned and hugged his mother. No words were spoken, which was for the best. Just hearing his mother's voice would have touched a deep chord and unhinged him. Her hands—soft and familiar—almost managed to do what words most certainly would have, but Jimmy wouldn't break down as he held steady. Two officers flanked him as they exited the court, right past a barrage of reporters shouting questions, and the glaring lights of Court TV's cameras. He didn't make a statement to the media as he had after the first trial. He was more emotional this time. Jimmy tried to push all thoughts of a lengthy prison sentence out of his mind. He tried to live in the moment—the last moment he'd walk around the outside world without handcuffs and manacles, albeit for only 50 paces. The last time he'd breathe free air for at least 10 years; the last time he'd ever see some family members alive. Jimmy sang softly to himself as the officers walked him down the courthouse steps to an awaiting squad car. He looked around frightfully for the moonlight ladies. He squinted through the exploding flashbulbs, searching for shades of deep greens and blues, though he saw nothing but angry faces and hollow stares. Jimmy tried to clear his head and mumbled James Taylor's words. He knew that where he was going, hundreds of edgy TV-watching men were anxiously awaiting the arrival of Sweet Baby James.

◄○►

Jimmy met his attorney in Judge Clayton's courtroom on July 6, 1998. He'd shaved his mustache during the wait in jail, but the mullet was still there.

The convicted levee breaker looked thin. He wasn't taking too well to the state-issued grub and he was too depressed to eat anyway. Jimmy's mind had been on his July 6 sentencing date. The prospect of receiving a life sentence once again made him lose his appetite.

Raymond Legg appeared to be in a chipper mood, much too chipper a mood for Jimmy's liking. After all, his client was about to get shipped to the Big House. The public defender told Jimmy he had a surprise for him, one that the court would surely honor. They had to, Legg assured his client. It's the law.

Judge Clayton called the court to order, and Legg immediately made a motion for a new trial.

"It has come to my attention that on May 8 [eight days after James Scott was found guilty], in the U.S. Court of Federal Claims in Washington, D.C., that the Fabius Drainage District, along with other drainage districts along the Mississippi River, filed a lawsuit against the U.S. Army Corps of Engineers alleging that their conduct and their actions from the 1930s to the 1940s created substantial erosion of the banks of the Mississippi River and substantial seepage within the flood plains of the Mississippi River.

"As the court will recall, a large part of our defense at trial in this matter was that the failure of the West Quincy Levee was due to natural causes.

"The existence of this lawsuit, and what I believe to be the facts of the lawsuit, would have supported that defense. . . . I find it inconceivable that prior to the trial in this matter that a government agency located in the State of Missouri, mainly the drainage district at issue here, was not aware of this lawsuit. They joined in this lawsuit, they knew of the lawsuit prior to the trial, they surely discussed its merits prior to trial. That information should have been disclosed to me under *Brady v. Maryland*[1] and was not. And for that reason, we should be afforded a new trial."

Tom Redington was given a chance to respond. As was his cool demeanor, he made the mere mention of this lawsuit seem obscure and rudimentary. "Mr. Legg presented his defense through his expert witnesses," the prosecutor said to the judge. "There is certainly no prejudice to this defendant at all. And again, it's a lawsuit that was filed after this trial was

---

[1] After the petitioner had been convicted in a Maryland state court on a charge of murder in the first degree (committed in the course of a robbery) and had been sentenced to death, he learned of an extrajudicial confession of his accomplice, tried separately, admitting the actual homicide. (226 Md 422, 174 A2d 167.)

conducted. It is at this point merely allegations against the Corps of Engineers, which raises issues which Mr. Legg already presented to the jury; and the jury in this courtroom wholly rejected that theory, convicting the defendant."

Judge Clayton briefly considered the defendant's motion. "I think you raised 46 or 49 points," he said to Legg. "I studied those and I believe that in consideration of the knowledge I have of the case that they are not well taken. And the Court overrules and denies the motion for judgment or acquittal and for new trial."

What Judge Clayton didn't know—and what Raymond Legg didn't know either for that matter—was that official documents existed written by the Corps themselves that essentially cleared James Scott of any wrongdoing.

Documents from the Corps of Engineers showed that six other levee systems upriver from West Quincy were overtopped in the week preceding this one's failure. Interestingly, the Corps classified the Fabius River Drainage District (a.k.a. West Quincy levee) as having been overtopped and not sabotaged as of August 1993, two months before Scott was arrested and charged, but during the time all the speculation was circulating throughout town.

According to the Corps' internal document, "On July 1 (1993), drainage districts and towns started raising their main stem sand levees by using bulldozers and pushing sand from the landside slopes. . . . In addition, during this period underseepage and through seepage became major problems. Many boils were located, and the ones that were moving material were ringed with sandbags. Of particular concern was the through seepage in the area where the sand levees were pushed up and the flood waters were over the elevation of the clay cores of the main stem levee." The Corps recognized problems with the West Quincy area before the flood; they singled out the bulldozed area. According to the Corps of Engineers, Dr. R. David Hammer's theory was right on the money.

Jimmy began to tremble. He'd spent the last six weeks preparing for the worst, only to have his hopes built back up minutes before Judge Clayton was to sentence him. The convicted levee breaker didn't think he could handle any more surprises. He couldn't stand to look at another lawyer or journalist. As the judge prepared to read him his fate—of which the state's attorney recommended the maximum life sentence—James R. Scott thought he was going to have a nervous breakdown. The depression and circumstance was too much for him. He hoped—nay, he prayed that he'd have a heart-attack and die right there in the middle of the court. Ten years or life, either way that was too much time for him to handle, especially because to be found innocent would have meant going home. In the time it took for Jimmy to be tried, convicted, and sentenced in Missouri for a second time, he had been paroled in Illinois for the truck vandalism/burglary and bad checks.

Jimmy had been through a lot in his life, but this was absolutely unbearable. The 27-year-old was done with living. Now he just needed to hear from the judge. Perhaps then Jimmy could go to sleep, could wish goodnight to the moonlight ladies, and hopefully, never wake up.

Judge Clayton cleared his throat as he began his sentence. Jimmy sat with his hands clasped, his fingers interlocked, and his head bowed. He never looked at the judge.

"The Court, in light of the seriousness of the crime, has taken a new look at the reasons for punishment. All of you know that I've not been on the bench too long; and I won't call this my trophy case, Mr. Scott, but it is certainly a large and serious and important case.

"I disagree with your lawyer regarding the strength of the state's case. I thought the evidence was substantial and convincing. Even though much of it was circumstantial, those circumstances seemed to link very nicely together at each step of your plan here.

"I think there's a certain irony that you have spent your life in arson and, what I hope will be your final criminal act, ends up with water. So maybe the water will put the fire in you out.

"I think you have a problem with unbridled assaultive behavior. I'm not sure where your anger comes from, but I cannot and will not run the risk that you may or may not be able to curtail your aggressive impulse and anger. You are a threat to society.

"You are in touch with reality, but you are out of touch with empathy. It seems that you have no ability or will to understand things from someone else's point of view, or even to imagine how these people feel, particularly after you have victimized them.

"I can't take your property as you took theirs, but I can take your liberty, which I hope that as you have time to contemplate, you will find is more precious.

"You are a career criminal. There is a perversion about this because you obviously get a sense of excitement, or power, or sexual arousal, or all of the above when you commit these acts.

"So in consideration of all of these matters, and no legal cause or reason having been shown why sentence and judgment of the court should not now be pronounced against you, and upon the verdict of the jury finding that you were guilty of the charge of Causing a Catastrophe under Section 569.170 of the Revised Statutes of Missouri, it is now the order, sentence, and judgment of the court that you be sentenced as a prior and persistent offender to the Department of Corrections of the State of Missouri on the charge of Causing a Catastrophe to a term of life imprisonment in the Department of Corrections, with such enhancements to that punishment as are authorized by law."

EPILOGUE

◄○►

The Jefferson City Correctional Center, formerly known as the Missouri State Prison, was an unsettling place. Yellowish limestone walls, colored that way because of too many years and too little care, towered as high as those of any other building in the state capital. Picture the prison from *Natural Born Killers*, complete with four stories of cells stacked on top of each other and wrought-iron bars clanging around the clock. Then factor out sound dampening devices like carpeting, drapes, or even wallpaper. The joint was an echo chamber from dusk 'til dawn, even in the middle of the night, when the cons were supposed to be sleeping.

The windows were small and filmy, obstructing any and all views. They also dimmed the sun's brightness and made nightfall seem that much darker.

Originally constructed in 1836, with buildings built as early as 1868 still in use, the prison was an aging hulk, yet sturdy enough to hold more than 2,000 men, most of whom would spend the majority of their adult lives within its walls. Inmates lived in cells no larger than the average residential bathroom. In fact, they *were* bathrooms—with beds squeezed in as well. Inmates from all four corners of the state always referred to the place by an insider's moniker: The Walls.

The penitentiary initially opened the same week as the battle of the Alamo in Texas, 1836. By the 1930s, the Missouri State Prison was the largest in the United States, and it had remained the largest and oldest operating prison west of the Mississippi River.

On September 22, 1954, convicts feigning sick overpowered several guards and stoked a 15-hour riot in which four prisoners died. Scores of guards and prisoners were injured, and the prison sustained $3 million in property damage. A fifth prisoner later died of fatal wounds inflicted during the fray. The Missouri State Prison was thereafter called: "The bloodiest 47 acres in America."

Some high-profile inmates graced The Walls. Pretty Boy Floyd did Missouri time for the 1925 robbery of Pevely Dairy in St. Louis. James Earl Ray, who assassinated Martin Luther King Jr. on April 4, 1968, in Memphis, Tennessee, broke out of the Missouri State Prison a year earlier by hiding in an outgoing bread box.

Perhaps The Walls most famous prisoner was a St. Louis tough named Charles Liston. Nicknamed "Sonny," the 200-plus pound behemoth robbed the Unique Café on Market Street of $37 in 1954. At 22, Sonny marched into the Missouri State Prison, where he began serving a five-year stretch. He was a fairly well-behaved inmate, save for a couple of yard fights. His soft-spoken, simple manner caught the attention of Rev. Edward Schlattmann, the prison chaplain who also doubled as the prison athletic director. He and Father Alois Stevens took the brute under their wings, teaching him how to read and how to be a productive member of society. They also introduced Sonny to boxing. He was a raw talent, knocking inmates out cold with the awesome strength of his left hook. He refined his technique while inside the Missouri State Prison, becoming the joint's undisputed heavyweight champion, and upon parole, later ascended the professional boxing ranks, culminating with the heavyweight championship of the world.

Jimmy was himself a high-profile name when he was marched into the Jefferson City Correctional Center in July 1998. He'd been a fixture on Court TV, and his name had appeared on newspapers' front pages on and off for almost a decade. He'd also been on the NBC, ABC, and CBS nightly newscasts as well as CNN, the Cable News Network. Those involuntary appearances were what had Jimmy concerned the most as he began his life sentence in Jefferson City. Convicts watch television, too. They knew all about the West Quincy levee—some JCCC prisoners had friends and family who were directly affected by the Marion County levee break. And inmates love to "initiate" their new brethren. Jimmy had a big red target painted on his back as he rode the Missouri Department of Corrections bus from Hannibal to Jefferson City. Before he even set foot inside the 162-year-old structure, he knew that some of the joint's long-timers were anxiously awaiting his arrival, and couldn't wait to make his acquaintance.

Jimmy reverted back to his jail personality. No longer did he strive to be the life of the party, nor did he seek the local or national spotlight. Immediately after being processed at the Jefferson City Correctional Center, Jimmy was no longer Jimmy. Jimmy was no longer James Scott, either. The convicted levee breaker underwent a metamorphosis the second he was issued prison blues. He became #1001364. He needn't tell the other inmates what he was in for; they already knew.

Inmate #1001364 went to great lengths to stay clear of other cons. The most violent offenders of both races—the ones who essentially ran the day-to-day operations—took notice of #1001364's casual demeanor. He kept his head lowered and his nose clean. He aligned himself with the Aryans, as had been his custom when in prison before, but he also interacted with the blacks on the prison basketball court and the baseball diamond without incident. That and he was one heck of an athlete. Number 1001364 was always one of the first guys picked when teams were chosen during yard time, and he rarely boasted of victory the way many other inmates were wont to do.

He procured a job in the prison panel factory earning $.10/hour and spent his days shaping wood into cabinet doors. Jefferson City Correction Center was a self-sustaining facility. Its various industries taught men a skill and brought in income for the state. Inmate #1001364 was a hardworking, diligent employee, waking at 5 a.m. and punching out at 5 p.m. He never complained about the dusty, dirty working conditions, and he never called in sick, even when Midwestern winters turned the factory into a refrigerator and the cold, coupled with sawdust, gnawed away at his lungs. Because of his work ethic, #1001364 was promoted to factory foreman. He was also moved to the honors cellblock, where inmates enjoyed spacious eight-by-twelve-foot pods versus the seven-by-eleven-foot ones in general population.

When the Jefferson City Correctional Center relocated in 2004 from its storied downtown site to 8200 No More Victims Road, some 10 miles outside of town, #1001364's job title and honors status relocated with it. He's been, by all institutional accounts, a model prisoner ever since landing in the maximum security penitentiary. In fact, because of his exemplary standing with prison brass and his ability to work well with others,

#1001364 was given his choice of a second job. He mulled it over and decided that he wanted to contribute to his community—to help those in need, the same way he maintains he tried to on July 16, 1993.

Inmate #1001364 also works in the prison hospice, where he attends to the terminally ill convicts, like his mother did for so many years on the outside. The work is rewarding for him. He is afforded the opportunity of sending a condemned man to the afterlife with a semblance of comfort on his face. It also helps to take his mind off his lonely predicament.

Work and sports keep him occupied, but prison is structured in such a way that men are forced to spend prolonged periods of time contemplating what landed them there. Inmate #1001364 does nothing other than think about July 16, 1993, and all the other criminal activities that taken together earned him a life sentence at The Walls—old and new.

He sometimes endures severe bouts of depression when he thinks about how much life he's lost and about those he loves. He regretfully thinks of Suzie and wonders where she's landed. He thinks about the time they spent together at parties and at Villa Kathrine Castle on Front Street, when they were alone in thought with only the brilliant orange glow of a setting Midwestern sun to keep them warm. He wonders where his daughter is: what she looks like and whether the 18-year-old is college-bound or if she's slipped into the depths of the party culture. He prays for the former. He thinks about Mike, worries about Jeff, and wonders why Dan turned states evidence. He'll never get the chance to ask his half brother that question: Dan Leake died in his sleep in March 2006. He was 47.

Mostly, though, inmate #1001364 thinks about the future, 20-plus years into the future, when he may one day be permitted to return to the free world. Not Quincy: he's vowed never to so much as stick his big toe back in that town, and he'll never say another word to Joe Flachs.[1]

Probably for the best. The townspeople have moved on, much like their contemporaries across the creek in West Quincy. Everything's been rebuilt over the years, and the remnants of the Great Midwestern Floods of 1993 have been washed away like so much murky Mississippi River water. The

---

[1] At press time, Joe Flachs was awaiting trial in Adams County for felony possession of more than five grams of methamphetamine.

only reminder of that bygone time—from a passerby's perspective—is a giant barge marooned at a farm along U.S. Route 24.

The mental scars are still there, though. Those will never go away, not in his lifetime, which is what inmate #1001364 is destined to give up if he is never paroled. To this day, he remains the only person ever convicted under Missouri's law of Intentionally Causing a Catastrophe.

INTERVIEWS AND BIBLIOGRAPHY

◄○►

PROLOGUE

City of Quincy, Department of Economic Development

"Heavy Rain Threatens to Swamp Peninsula," *Memphis Commercial Appeal*, July 16, 1993.

Husar, Edward. "Witnesses Stunned as Levee Breaks, Explosion Erupts," *Quincy Herald-Whig*, July 17, 1993.

"Indian Grave Levee Breaks," *Quincy Herald-Whig*, July 12, 1993.

Dr. Charles Morris, in discussions with the author, May 26, 2006.

National Railway Historical Society

James Scott, in discussions with the author, December 12, 1999, May 27, 2006.

Saul, Tom. "Gas Station Ignites Night," *Quincy Herald-Whig*, July 17, 1993.

Webber, John. "Runaway Barge May Have Triggered Ayerco Fire," *Quincy Herald-Whig*, July 17, 1993.

CHAPTER ONE

Freemantle, Tony and Cragg Hines. "Fighting a Flowing Foe," *Houston Chronicle*, July 9, 1993.

Hampel, Peter. "The Great Flood," *St. Louis Post-Dispatch*, August 24, 1998.

Michigan Technical University

Mike Parks, in discussions with the author, July 11, 2006.

James Scott, in discussions with the author, December 12, 1999, May 27, 2006, July 6, 2006.

www.en.wikipedia.org/wiki/Cilice#Usage

www.jimmyakin.org/film_and_tv/index.html

www.knapheide.com

CHAPTER TWO

O'Neil, Tom. "Levee Break Suspect Drew Attention Early," *St. Louis Post-Dispatch*, October 8, 1993.

James Scott, in discussions with the author, December 12, 1999.

State v. Scott trial transcript, April 23–25, 1998.

www.geocities.com/shoeless1920/Quincy.html

CHAPTER THREE

Justine Barati, Rock Island (Illinois) U.S. Army Corps of Engineers, in discussions with the author, July 19, 2006.

Mark Clark, engineer, Rock Island (Illinois) U.S. Army Corps of Engineers, in discussions with the author, July 20, 2006.

Editors, "Great Flood of '93," *Quincy Herald-Whig*, July 11, 1993.

Ron Fournier, Rock Island (Illinois) U.S. Army Corps of Engineers, in discussions with the author, July 19, 2006.

Norman Haerr, in discussions with the author, July 20, 2006.

Miklasz, Bernie. "Sandbags Are Pags' Order of Day," *St. Louis Post-Dispatch*, July 14, 1993.

Mussetter, William. "Armory Transformed into Wartime Command Center," *Quincy Herald-Whig*, July 13, 1993.

Ozley, Emily. "Fabius Crew Fights Seepage," *Quincy Herald-Whig*, July 13, 1993.

Petterson, Roger. "Flooding Spreads through Failed Levees," *Associated Press*, July 10, 1993.

Saul, Tom. "Volunteers Vow to Keep Bayview Bridge Open," *Quincy Herald-Whig*, July 11, 1993.

Shaw, Bernard. "Quincy, Illinois, Fights to Protect Bridge from Flood," *CNN*, July 15, 1993.

State v. Scott trial transcript, April 23–25, 1998.

U.S. Army Corps of Engineers

Wilson, Kelly. "Guardsmen Stepping in to Join Levee Fight," *Quincy Herald-Whig*, July 12, 1993.

CHAPTER FOUR

CBS This Morning, transcript, July 14–16, 1993.

Mark Clark, engineer, Rock Island (Illinois) U.S. Army Corps of Engineers, in discussions with the author, July 20, 2006.

Eardley, Linda. "Flood Widens Reach, Stretches South," *St. Louis Post-Dispatch*, July 3, 1993.

Gertz, Deborah. "Crews Armed with Sandbags, Straw for Battle against High Water, Seepage," *Quincy Herald-Whig*, July 14, 1993.

Norman Haerr, in discussions with the author, July 20, 2006.

Hummel, Rick. "AL Makes It 6 in Row," *St. Louis Post-Dispatch*, July 14, 1993.

Mussetter, William. "Area's Heroism Touches Those on National Scene," *Quincy Herald-Whig*, July 14, 1993.

Rimer, Sara. "The Midwest Flooding," *New York Times*, July 15, 1993.

State v. Scott trial transcript, April 23–25, 1998.

U.S. Army Corps of Engineers

CHAPTER FIVE

Norman Haerr, in discussions with the author, July 20, 2006.

Husar, Edward. "We Heard a Pop and Somebody Saw the Trees Moving," *Quincy Herald-Whig*, July 17, 1993.

Pitluk, Adam. "Levee Case to Be Revisited," *Columbia Missourian*, October 12, 1998.

James Scott, in discussions with the author, December 12, 1999, May 27, 2006.

State v. Scott trial transcript, April 23–25, 1998.

U.S. Army Corps of Engineers

Yates, Ronald E. "Quincy Stares Down 'Beast' at Its Door," *Chicago Tribune*, July 16, 1993.

CHAPTER SIX

Adams County (IL) Courthouse Records

"Cards Take Their 12th in Row," *Associated Press*, April 25, 1982.

Cullumber, Jim. "Webster School Fire Intentional," *Quincy Herald-Whig*, April 28, 1982.

———. "Three Juveniles Charges with Arson," *Quincy Herald-Whig*, April 29, 1982.

Jim Doellman, Chief, Quincy Fire Department (retired), in discussions with the author, September 15, 2006.

Hampel, Paul. "The Great Flood," *St. Louis Post-Dispatch*, August 24, 1998.

James Scott, in discussions with the author, December 12, 1999, May 27, 2006.

Staff, "Fire Destroys Webster School," *Quincy Herald-Whig*, April 25, 1982.

State v. Scott trial transcript, April 23–25, 1998.

"Webster School: 1904–1982," *Quincy Herald-Whig*, April 25, 1982.

www.city-data.com

www.maine.gov/dps/fmo/fireinv.htm

CHAPTER SEVEN

Adams County (IL) Courthouse Records

Cullumber, Jim. "Webster School Fire Intentional," *Quincy Herald-Whig*, April 28, 1982.

———. "Three Juveniles Charges with Arson," *Quincy Herald-Whig*, April 29, 1982.

Jim Doellman, Chief, Quincy Fire Department (retired), in discussions with the author, September 15, 2006.

Hampel, Paul. "The Great Flood," *St. Louis Post-Dispatch*, August 24, 1998.

Staff. "Fire Destroys Webster School," *Quincy Herald-Whig*, April 25, 1982.

"Webster School: 1904–1982," *Quincy Herald-Whig*, April 25, 1982.

www.maine.gov/dps/fmo/fireinv.htm

CHAPTER EIGHT

Adams County (IL) Courthouse Records

Cullumber, Jim. "Webster School Fire Intentional," *Quincy Herald-Whig*, April 28, 1982.

———. "Three Juveniles Charges with Arson," *Quincy Herald-Whig*, April 29, 1982.

Jim Doellman, Chief, Quincy Fire Department (retired), in discussions with the author, September 15, 2006.

Hampel, Paul. "The Great Flood," *St. Louis Post-Dispatch*, August 24, 1998.

Staff. "Fire Destroys Webster School," *Quincy Herald-Whig*, April 25, 1982.

"Webster School: 1904–1982," *Quincy Herald-Whig*, April 25, 1982.

www.maine.gov/dps/fmo/fireinv.htm

CHAPTER NINE

Adams County (IL) Courthouse Records

Cullumber, Jim."Webster School Fire Intentional," *Quincy Herald-Whig*, April 28, 1982.

———. "Three Juveniles Charges with Arson," *Quincy Herald-Whig*, April 29, 1982.

———. "Webster Trio May Be Tied to Other Fires," *Quincy Herald-Whig*, April 30, 1982.

Jim Doellman, Chief, Quincy Fire Department (retired), in discussions with the author, September 15, 2006.

Hampel, Paul. "The Great Flood," *St. Louis Post-Dispatch*, August 24, 1998.

James Scott letters

Sharon Scott, in discussions with the author, September 23, 2006.

Staff. "Fire Destroys Webster School," *Quincy Herald-Whig*, April 25, 1982.

"Webster School: 1904–1982," *Quincy Herald-Whig*, April 25, 1982.

www.maine.gov/dps/fmo/fireinv.htm

CHAPTER TEN

Det. Neal Baker, in discussions with the author, May 27, 2006, November 2, 2006.

Guns N' Roses, *Appetite for Destruction,* Geffen Records, July 21, 1987.

Metallica, *Master of Puppets,* Elektra Records, February 21, 1986.

Poison, *Look What the Cat Dragged In,* Capitol Records, August 2, 1986.

Derek Schnapp, Spokesman for the Illinois Department of Corrections, in discussions with the author, October 23, 2006.

James Scott letters

Sharon Scott, in discussions with the author, September 23, 2006.

James Taylor, *Greatest Hits,* Warner Brothers, November 1, 1976.

"Quincy Man Sentenced for Arson," *Quincy Herald-Whig*, May 10, 1988.

CHAPTER ELEVEN

Det. Neal Baker, in discussions with the author, May 27, 2006, November 2, 2006, November 7, 2006.

Poison, *Look What the Cat Dragged In,* Capitol Records, August 2, 1986.

James Scott letters

Sharon Scott, in discussions with the author, September 23, 2006.

"Quincy Man Sentenced for Arson," *Quincy Herald-Whig*, May 10, 1988.

CHAPTER TWELVE

Det. Neal Baker, in discussions with the author, May 27, 2006, November 2, 2006, November 7, 2006.

Hemming, Marianne. "Scott Gets 14-Year Term; Court Told Help Please Ignored," *Quincy Herald-Whig*, June 23, 1989.

James Scott letters

Sharon Scott, in discussions with the author, November 23, 2006.

www.idoc.state.il.us

"Quincy Man Sentenced for Arson," *Quincy Herald-Whig*, May 10, 1988.

CHAPTER THIRTEEN

Det. Neal Baker, in discussions with the author, May 27, 2006, November 2, 2006, November 7, 2006.

Earl Basswood, in discussions with the author, October 29, 2006.

Cox, Robert. "Surviving Under Fire," *The American Banker*, December 2, 1992.

Ducat, Vivian. "Act of God or Sabotage," *Court TV*, October 16, 1998.

Carrie Flachs, in discussions with the author, November 9, 2006.

Bob Nall, in discussions with the author, November 3, 2006.

Leavitt, Paula. "Physical Abuse Down at Military Academies," *USA Today*, November 24, 1992.

James Scott letters

Sharon Scott, in discussions with the author, November 23, 2006.

State vs. Scott trial transcript, April 23–25, 1998.

WGEM-TV 6 p.m. and 10 p.m. newscasts, Quincy, Illinois.

CHAPTER FOURTEEN

Det. Neal Baker, in discussions with the author, May 27, 2006, November 2, 2006, November 7, 2006.

Earl Basswood, in discussions with the author, October 29, 2006.

Ducat, Vivian. "Act of God or Sabotage," *Court TV*, October 16, 1998.

Johnson, Eric. "Two Missing after Barge Capsizes," *St. Louis Post-Dispatch*, December 6, 1992.

Bob Nall, in discussions with the author, November 3, 2006.

James Scott letters

Sharon Scott, in discussions with the author, September 23, 2006.

Staff. "Flood Waters Claim More Land," *Quincy Herald-Whig*, July 14, 1993.

State v. Scott trial transcript, April 23–25, 1998.

Tackett, Michael. "Rivers, Danger on the Rise in Des Moines," *Chicago Tribune*, July 14, 1993.

Twain, Mark. *Life on the Mississippi*, 1883 (courtesy of the University of North Carolina library system).

WGEM-TV 6 p.m. and 10 p.m. newscasts, Quincy, Illinois.

Wigginton, Bob. "Levee Break 'Suspicious'," *Quincy Herald-Whig*, July 22, 1993.

www.science.nasa.gov/headlines/y2000/ast06oct_1.htm

CHAPTER FIFTEEN

Det. Neal Baker, in discussions with the author, May 27, 2006, November 2, 2006, November 7, 2006.

Earl Basswood, in discussions with the author, October 29, 2006.

Hummel, Rick. "Cards Win 13–11, End Skid," *St. Louis Post-Dispatch*, July 24, 1993.

John Jackson, in discussions with the author, November 7, 2006.

Duke Kelly, in discussions with the author, December 3, 2006.

Thomas Lindsey, research librarian, University of Texas at Arlington.

"Marlins Topple Giants," *Chicago Sun-Times*, August 28, 1993.

Bob Nall, in discussions with the author, November 3, 2006.

James Scott letters

State v. Scott trial transcript, April 23–25, 1998

Wigginton, Bob. "Levee Break 'Suspicious'," *Quincy Herald-Whig*, July 22, 1993.

www.enchantedlearning.com/geology/soil

www.quincyparkdistrict.com

CHAPTER SIXTEEN

Det. Neal Baker, in discussions with the author, May 27, 2006, November 2, 2006, November 7, 2006.

Earl Basswood, in discussions with the author, October 29, 2006.

Dan Campbell, in discussions with the author, November 3, 2006.

Hummel, Rick. "Cards Win 13–11, End Skid," *St. Louis Post-Dispatch*, July 24, 1993.

John Jackson, in discussions with the author, November 7, 2006.

"Jim's Dandiest," *Chicago Sun-Times*, September 27, 1993.

Duke Kelly, in discussions with the author, December 3, 2006.

Thomas Lindsey, research librarian, University of Texas at Arlington.

"Marlins Topple Giants," *Chicago Sun-Times*, August 28, 1993.

Bob Nall, in discussions with the author, November 3, 2006.

Potash, Mark. "Test of Best Rarely Super," *Chicago Sun-Times*, January 21, 1992.

James Scott letters

State v. Scott trial transcript, April 23–25, 1998

Swanson, James L. "Manhunt: The 12-Day Chase for Lincoln's Killer." William Marrow, February 2006.

James Taylor, *Greatest Hits,* Warner Brothers, November 1, 1976.

Wigginton, Bob. "Levee Break 'Suspicious'," *Quincy Herald-Whig*, July 22, 1993.

www.enchantedlearning.com/geology/soil

www.quincyparkdistrict.com

CHAPTER SEVENTEEN

Det. Neal Baker, in discussions with the author, May 27, 2006, November 2, 2006, November 7, 2006.

Earl Basswood, in discussions with the author, October 29, 2006.

Dan Campbell, in discussions with the author, November 3, 2006.

Cohen, Sharon. "Sabotage or Nature's Rage?" *Associated Press*, October 29, 1994.

Ducat, Vivian. "Act of God or Sabotage," *Court TV*, October 16, 1998.

"Man Is Charged with Causing Levee Break," *Associated Press*, October 2, 1993.

English, Nordeka. "Trial Is Set over Break in Levee," *St. Charles Post*, March 16, 1994.

———. "Levee Break Suspect Admits to Lesser Act," *St. Louis Post-Dispatch*, July 22, 1995.

———. "Man Accused of Using Boat to Ram Levee," *St. Charles Post*, October 1, 1993.

Glass, Doug. "Guilty Verdict Brings Relief to Victims of '93 Levee Break," *Chicago Sun-Times*, November 6, 1994.

Hoversten, Paul. "Would-Be 'Hero' Charged in Levee Break," *USA Today*, October 4, 1993.

John Jackson, in discussions with the author, November 7, 2006.

McCullough, David. *Johnstown Flood.* Gloucester, MA: Peter Smith Publisher, 1987.

Missouri Revised Statutes Chapter 569, "Robbery, Arson, Burglary and Related Offenses," Section 569.070.

Charles Morris, in discussions with the author, May 25, 2006.

Bob Nall, in discussions with the author, November 3, 2006.

Pitluk, Adam. "Dammed to Eternity," *The Riverfront* (St. Louis) *Times*, January 26, 2000.

"Second Trial Begins for Man Accused of Causing Flood," *Associated Press*, April 24, 1998.

James Scott letters

State v. Scott trial transcript, April 23–25, 1998.

Stone, Richard D. *The Interstate Commerce Commission and the Railroad Industry: A History of Regulatory Policy.* New York: Praeger, 1991.

Wigginton, Bob. "Levee Break 'Suspicious'," *Quincy Herald-Whig*, July 22, 1993.

www.wes.army.mil/REMR/pdf/ei/m-1-4.pdf

CHAPTER EIGHTEEN

Det. Neal Baker, in discussions with the author, May 27, 2006, November 2, 2006, November 7, 2006.

Earl Basswood, in discussions with the author, October 29, 2006.

Brady v. Maryland, 373 U.S. 83, 226 Md 422, 174 A2d 167.

Rebecca Brockway, in discussions with the author, November 3, 2006.

Dan Campbell, in discussions with the author, November 3, 2006.

Ducat, Vivian. "Act of God or Sabotage," *Court TV*, October 16, 1998.

R. David Hammer, in discussions with the author, November 4, 2006.

John Jackson, in discussions with the author, November 7, 2006.

Lessmeister, Susan. "_____," *Sedalia Democrat*, April 23, 1998.

————. "_____," *Sedalia Democrat*, April 24, 1998.

————. "_____," *Sedalia Democrat*, April 25, 1998.

Missouri Revised Statutes Chapter 569, "Robbery, Arson, Burglary and Related Offenses," Section 569.070.

Bob Nall, in discussions with the author, November 3, 2006.

"New Trial Ordered for Man Convicted of Breaking Levee," *State Journal-Register*, July 23, 1997.

English, Nordeka. "Levee Break Suspect Admits to Lesser Act," *St. Louis Post-Dispatch*, July 22, 1995.

Pitluk, Adam. "Dammed to Eternity," *The Riverfront* (St. Louis) *Times*, January 26, 2000.

James Scott letters

State v. Scott trial transcript, April 23–25, 1998.

United States Navel Academy Library

EPILOGUE

Bell, Kim. "'The Walls' of Time," *St. Louis Post-Dispatch*, February 8, 1998.

"Minnesota Has Lower Recidivism Rate," *Corrections Professional*, September 6, 2002.

"Missouri State Prison Unlocks Stories of Past," *Associated Press*, September 10, 2006.

Pitluk, Adam. "Dammed to Eternity," *The Riverfront* (St. Louis) *Times*, January 26, 2000.

Remnick, David. *King of the World.* New York: Random House, 1998.

James Scott letters

www.crimelibrary.com

ACKNOWLEDGMENTS

◄o►

In 1998, when I was a student-reporter for the *Columbia Missourian*, Editor Sharon Harl put the story of James Scott on my desk. *Court TV* had recently broadcasted coverage of Jimmy's second trial, and I was assigned a write-up. I interviewed Jimmy over the phone from his home at The Walls in Jefferson City, Missouri, and I was immediately hooked by this story. Not just because of its precedence-setting legal ramifications, but the scientific and social significance of this case were unlike any true crime book or article I'd ever read: A man who allegedly broke a levee to strand is wife on the other side. And if a man had committed the same crime right across the Mississippi River in Illinois, the most time he could have served was seven years.

Throughout the course of interviewing the players, I made initial contact with Dr. R. David Hammer at the University of Missouri and Detective Neal Baker of the Quincy Police Department. I'd speak with these men countless times over the years, again in 2000 when I wrote an article for the *Riverfront Times*. Hammer and Baker have always been dedicated to their respective opinions of this case, and I thank you both for your candor and honesty. Thank you to Safir Ahmed and Roland Klose, my editors at the *Riverfront Times* who let met do a 5,000 word feature on James Scott. I've never meant to assign guilt or innocence to inmate #1001364, but rather, to answer the question that Copy Editor Kerry Bailey posed in my story's subhead: Was he simply an easy scapegoat for a town raging at its devastation? It is my intention that the reader forms his/her own opinion.

Thank you to Kevin Hanover at Da Capo Press for realizing the potential of this story, and for being a tremendous editor for this book and for *Standing Eight*. To my agent, Robert Guinsler, and the first-rate team at Sterling Lord Literistic.

Scott Wintrow stepped up and accompanied me into the Jefferson City Correctional Center (old and new) and took fantastic photos. Photographer Jennifer Silverberg shot the cover, also stepping way up and coming with me to a maximum security prison. Thank you to the Missouri Department of Corrections for granting us access.

Virtually everybody associated with this case spoke to me during the course of my investigation (with the exception of Joe Flachs, who only offered to talk if I paid him). In Illinois, thank you to Baker, Bob Nall, Carrie Flachs, Sharon and Robert Scott, Raymond Legg, Earl Basswood, and a very special thanks to Gerri Berendzen and the rest of the staff at the *Quincy Herald-Whig*, who did the best job covering the Great Flood of all the dailies anywhere in the country.

In Missouri, thank you to Hammer, Dr. Charles Morris, Dan Campbell, John Jackson, Tom Redington, David Dormire, and Duke Kelly.

As a reporter for *Time*, I witnessed two catastrophic floods while writing this book. This book is dedicated to the brave men and women of the U.S. Army's 4th Infantry Division, whom I was embedded with during Hurricane Katrina (and who fought so gallantly in Iraq), and the brave men and women of Task Force Bowie from the Texas National Guard, whom I was embedded with during Hurricane Rita. Thank you to Howard Chua-Eoan at *Time,* as well as Cathy Booth Thomas and Greg Fulton.

I wrote this book during the days I wasn't teaching journalism at the University of Texas at Arlington. A debt of gratitude to the Department of Communications for working with my schedule, and to Tom Lindsey at the UTA Library.

As with *Standing Eight*, Rocky Loessin and Jared Hamilton proved excellent research assistants and travel partners when we drove the whole length of the Mississippi River. Your input was invaluable.

Finally, thank you for the moral support of my wife, Kimberly, my daughter, Madeline, my mother, Sharon, and my sister, Jessica.

INDEX

◄○►

Head Start program, 67
Heetco Jet Center, Quincy, Illinois, 23
Hoffmeister, Bob, 29, 256

ICA. *See* Interstate Commerce Act (1887)
IDOC. *See* Illinois Department of Corrections
Illinois, 1, 2, 7, 10, 22, 37
Illinois, University of, 2, 263
Illinois Department of Corrections (IDOC), 158, 160, 167, 240, 241, 246, 259
Illinois National Guard, 1, 23, 24, 36
Indian Grave Drainage District, Illinois, 184
Indian Grave levee, Illinois, 2
Intentionally Causing a Catastrophe law (1979), 245, 254, 259, 260, 270, 283, 288, 293
Interstate Commerce Act (1887) (ICA), 230–231
Iowa, 2, 7, 29, 37
"I Won't Forget You" (Poison), 131

Jackson, John, 194, 203, 226, 229–234, 237, 241, 244, 245, 246–248, 250–254, 257, 260, 278
Jacksonville Correctional Center, Illinois, 159
JCCC. *See* Jefferson City Correctional Center, Missouri

Jefferies, George, 39
Jefferson City, Missouri, 242
Jefferson City Correctional Center, Missouri (JCCC), 289–293
Johnstown, Pennsylvania, 230–231
Johnstown Flood, 230–231, 237
Journal of Science, 280

Kelly, Duke, 36, 47, 49–50, 202, 222, 244, 249–250, 261, 273–275
Ken, Thomas, 10
Kentucky, 2
Keokuk, Iowa, 7, 37, 178
King, Martin Luther, Jr., 290
Kirksville, Missouri, 240, 245, 246, 249
Knapheide, Harold, III, 39–40, 188, 244
Knapheide Manufacturing Company, 11, 26, 29, 30, 35, 39–40, 46, 52, 53, 188, 190
Kroger's Grocery Store, 125, 136, 142

La Grange, Missouri, 37
Lake Conemaugh, Pennsylvania, 231
Lambert Field, St. Louis, Missouri, 36
Leake, Dan, 15, 16, 18, 27–28, 32, 40–41, 45, 61, 62, 98, 115, 117, 118, 121, 125–126, 131, 136, 139, 146, 170, 172, 173, 177, 184, 197–200, 207, 213, 271